RELIGION AND BELIEF LITERACY
Reconnecting a Chain of Learning

Adam Dinham

With Alp Arat and Martha Shaw

First published in Great Britain in 2021 by

Policy Press, an imprint of
Bristol University Press
University of Bristol
1-9 Old Park Hill
Bristol
BS2 8BB
UK
t: +44 (0)117 954 5940
e: bup-info@bristol.ac.uk

Details of international sales and distribution partners are available at
policy.bristoluniversitypress.co.uk

© Bristol University Press 2021

British Library Cataloguing in Publication Data
A catalogue record for this book is available from the British Library

ISBN 978-1-4473-4465-0 paperback
ISBN 978-1-4473-4463-6 hardcover
ISBN 978-1-4473-4466-7 ePub
ISBN 978-1-4473-4464-3 ePdf

The right of Adam Dinham to be identified as author of this work has been asserted by him in accordance with the Copyright, Designs and Patents Act 1988.

All rights reserved: no part of this publication may be reproduced, stored in a retrieval system, or transmitted in any form or by any means, electronic, mechanical, photocopying, recording, or otherwise without the prior permission of Bristol University Press.

Every reasonable effort has been made to obtain permission to reproduce copyrighted material. If, however, anyone knows of an oversight, please contact the publisher.

The statements and opinions contained within this publication are solely those of the author and not of the University of Bristol or Bristol University Press. The University of Bristol and Bristol University Press disclaim responsibility for any injury to persons or property resulting from any material published in this publication.

Bristol University Press and Policy Press work to counter discrimination on grounds of gender, race, disability, age and sexuality.

Cover design by Robin Hawes
Front cover image: Istock: MATJAZ SLANIC

For Zachariah and Joshua

Contents

List of figures and tables		vi
Foreword and acknowledgements		vii
Introduction		1
1	The broken chain of learning: the crisis of religion and belief literacy and its origins	9
2	Policy framings of religion and belief: consolidating the muddle	27
3	Religion and belief in Religious Education	43
4	Religion and belief across schools	61
5	Religion and belief in university practices	85
6	Religion and belief in university teaching and learning	103
7	Religion and belief in professional education and workplaces	113
8	Religion and belief in community education and learning	135
9	The future of religion and belief literacy: reconnecting a chain of learning	153
Notes		167
References		171
Index		189

List of figures and tables

Figures

1	A broken chain of learning about religion and belief	3
2	A reconnected chain of learning about religion and belief	165

Table

1	Summary of current and potential key messages in learning spaces	157

Foreword and acknowledgements

This book brings together research and thinking over ten years about the relationship between religion and belief and the public sphere. It reflects my journey through three distinct phases. In the first, I wanted to open up the connections between religion and belief and public policy at a time when many were noticing how much policymakers were suddenly saying on a topic that had previously been marginal to the point of invisibility. In this, I had the experience of repeatedly coming up against a widespread lack of ability among policymakers to talk about religion and belief in the first place, despite much appetite to do so.

This necessitated a second phase – which was a sideways step in many ways – designed to address this deficit. In this stage, the notion of 'religious literacy' became central. This was a period of working out an approach through which actors and organisations could recover the ability to talk well about religion and belief, whatever their own particular stance. In this book, this has evolved into 'religion and belief literacy', as explained in the introduction.

After five years working to open up this idea, and to make it available to a policymaking audience, I have more recently returned to the bread and butter of exploring connections between religion and belief and public policy. This has included work on religion and belief in media, civil society and law but the main focus has been on the policies and practices framing schools, universities and professional training, especially in the area of health and social care. The book is an exploration of religion and belief in these learning spaces, examined through the lens of religion and belief literacy.

I have had the good fortune to work with many excellent colleagues in this area over the years, and I am especially grateful to Chris Baker, Beth Crisp, Grace Davie, Abby Day, Matthew Francis, Panagiotis Pentaris and Tim Stacey for their collegiality and hard work as we unpicked the issues together in various projects and fields. In this book, particular thanks are due to Martha Shaw and Alp Arat, who worked with me on reviews of the policy and literature, especially around religion and belief in workplaces (Alp) and schools (Martha). The book owes much to their professionalism and friendship, and I am very grateful to them both.

Introduction

A chain of learning about religion and belief

Many have observed a return of religion and belief to the public sphere (see, for example, Dinham et al, 2009; Micklethwaite and Wooldridge, 2009). As a key voice in this debate, Habermas (2005: 26) notes 'a postsecular self-understanding of society as a whole in which the vigorous continuation of religion in a continually secularizing environment must be reckoned with'. His assertion relies on several elements: the continued expansion of religion globally and its power to shape culture and politics, as well as individual behaviour; the inherent discrimination of a one-size-fits-all secular vision of the public sphere that requires religious citizens to modify their religious identity; and the struggle of liberal democracies to challenge the materialism of global capitalism (Habermas, 2005). Liberal democracies, says Habermas, need to rediscover the wisdom, discernment and discipline that are linked with 'pre-political' religious sources because they are independent and self-generating, beyond the influence of both state and market.

With or without an interest in such wisdoms, migration and globalisation ensure the increasing diversity of religion and belief everywhere anyway, and the challenges of such encounters are unavoidable. While critics have argued that the ubiquitous nature of the term 'post-secular' risks its devaluation (Beckford, 2012), it nevertheless captures the persisting, pervasive, fluid and uncertain nature of religion and belief in public space. The renewed visibility of a religiously plural public sphere, characterised by more blurred and fluid encounters, is one of the hallmarks of the current policymaking and practice context.

At the same time, Hervieu-Leger argues that for religion to be understood in the modern world, there must be a connection to its deep roots in traditions and times in which it was not defined as irrelevant. This leads her to the concept of a 'chain of memory' by which individual believers become members of a community linking past, present and future (Hervieu-Leger, 2000). She also argues that modern secular societies in the West have neither fully outgrown nor found secular substitutes for religious traditions. Modern societies have become 'amnesiacs', she thinks, forgetting the chain of memory that binds them to their religious pasts and brings them to their presents. The irony, she suggests, is that at the very moment when that memory is most lost, a growing appetite for some sort of 'spiritual' life is emerging, and what is opening up is a space that religion and belief might distinctively fill.

This book picks up on Hervieu-Leger's 'chain of memory' to consider a different sort of chain in relation to religion and belief – a chain of learning – which might also be needed as the secular or post-secular wrestle with the reality of a religiously pervaded world. This addresses horizontal connections in the here and now, as well as vertical ones to the past and future. What we know about religion and belief is based on what we learn about them, and we do that learning in a variety of spaces and settings, which are contested and compete with each other. In formal educational spaces, like schools, colleges and universities, this takes place in 'subjects' or disciplines, like religious studies, theology, philosophy and citizenship. These present a muddled mix of Christian socialisation, personal and spiritual formation, the empirical study of religion and belief phenomena, and a preoccupation with public policy anxieties about cohesion and extremism. The content, structure and purposes are unclear. More recently, we might add subjects with little sense of a direct or past connection to religion or belief, like geography and law (see Baker and Dinham, 2017), which focus on how diverse publics mix, and how this plays out in debates or disputes.

Outside of them are semi-formal learning spaces, especially professions and workplaces, which emphasise religion and belief in relation to service provision and employment practices. Likewise, learning takes place in informal spaces, which we often call 'communities'. These emphasise faith-based volunteering and cohesive citizenship. They each reflect varying perspectives on religion and belief from which we learn to think about what, if anything, to do about them.

Each learning space is itself shaped by what policy is seeking: welfare might frame religion and belief in terms of their contributions to care (Putnam, 2000; Dinham, 2015a); security and foreign affairs might emphasise religion in terms of extremism and sectarianism (Francis and van Eck Duymaer, 2015); education might think of the importance of socialising young people in schools for a Christian and multi-faith society (Clarke and Woodhead, 2015; Dinham and Shaw, 2017); while university and employment policy might emphasise workplace readiness for religion and belief diversity and inclusion (Crisp, 2016; Aune et al, 2019). Each of these framings has its own inner logic, including normativities, which variously broadly construct religion and belief as both positive (contributing to society) and negative (a threat to it). However, do these 'logics' line up? Are they sufficiently in touch with each other to, at least, be capable of coherent disagreement?

Introduction

Figure 1: A broken chain of learning about religion and belief

Schools	Workplaces
Educational, confessional and formational with the right to withdraw	Avoiding litigation; the whole person at work

Religious Education	Universities	Communities
The Christian citizen in a plural Britain	Secular but diverse; religion and belief as an operational matter but outside the curricula	Religion and belief as heroes and villains

As individuals pass through these spaces of learning, what messages are they taking in at different times and places, and are they cogent?

At the core of this book is the suggestion that publics struggle with religion and belief, and that this is, at least in part, because of the competing, and sometimes conflicting, messages that we get about them. Why should we know about religion and belief, and where? How should we think about them, and who are the religious and believers anyway? Is there a chain of learning about religion and belief that could give an overall sense of the religion and belief landscape and how to think about it, that is, a series of links, each of which makes sense in relation to the others, even where they contest? Can this be bought into focus, or are the messages inherent in each destined to remain a muddle, at odds with the others, breaking the chain and leaving us bewildered and confused?

A broken chain and the problem of religion and belief literacy

These questions are at the core of what I have previously called a 'religious literacy' deficit (see Dinham, 2011). This key concept is put forward as an issue for everyone, regardless of their own religion, belief or none, and the chapters that follow argue that religious literacy is best addressed through a chain of learning that is connected up across the spheres in which publics converge and learn: schools, universities, the professions, workplaces and communities. The book explores how this chain is currently broken, reflecting the emergence of a muddle of ideas about religion and belief without internal or overall coherence. This is not to say that a diversity of perspectives is invalid; indeed, it is welcomed. However, the relationships and boundaries between them need clarity and critique if they are not to present as simply contradictory, muddled and bewildering. In the absence of such clarity, this book reveals varying combinations of loose conceptions of society as secular, not sacred, of religion and belief as private, not public, and of religious people and believers as either heroes or villains. The book explores how these binary assumptions are reflected in and reproduced by the policies that frame each sphere of learning, and then how they play out in practice. The reframing of these policies is explored as the basis for challenging their own underlying assumptions, and making sense of each other's perspectives in a newly reconnected chain of learning.

This brings together a body of research on religious literacy since around 2010 and responds to a growing number of calls for more religious literacy from a wide range of spheres. In the UK, these include the Commission on Religion and Belief in British Public Life (2015), *A New Settlement in Religious Education* (2015), the Equalities and Human Rights Commission (Dinham and Shaw, 2013), a number of national government departments, and the heart of government and policy in 10 Downing Street. These calls are echoed in the US, Australia and Europe, where migration and globalisation increase the visibility of, but not necessarily the ability to engage well with, religion and belief.

This is also a time at which new courses in the study of religion as a contemporary challenge are emerging in university departments across the developed world. These are often called 'religion and society', or similar, and include a wide range of perspectives, mostly from theology, religious studies and sociology, but also from politics, professional studies, education studies and media studies. Many are preoccupied with Islam, betraying an anxiety that risks adding to the 'othering' of Muslims.

Religion and belief literacy

At the same time, the language of religious literacy implies religion, in the singular, and does not refer to belief at all. It is challenged by the elasticity of lived religion and belief. The nomenclature has been debated in many conversations before. When the Religious Literacy Leadership Programme was established in 2010, the programme board wrestled with the label repeatedly, concluding in the end that no title would fully capture what was meant and therefore that 'religious literacy' would do the job. I argued then that it operates adequately as a metaphor with language learning, which requires vocabulary but also grammar and narrative. Thus, just as language learning adds up to more than a mechanical process, the same might apply to how we approach religion and belief. I also argued that it operates, at the same time, as a practice, that is, as a way of engaging with the challenge of religion and belief diversity in a context that has lost its language on these issues. Those points remain but the 'religious' in 'religious literacy' has sometimes proved a barrier to precisely the opening up that the concept aims to enable. Too often, it is heard as an agenda for more religiousness, with a religious starting point and protagonists. It is also capable of a misconceived narrowing of the canvas of concerns to refer only to the established world of religious traditions. For me, this logic culminates in a shift in language from 'religious literacy' to 'religion and belief literacy'. This book uses this wider term as an evolution of religious literacy. The addition of 'belief' is intended to make explicit the inclusion of the broadest range possible, which means the nine world religions, new and revived forms of religion and belief (such as Wicca and Druidism), spirituality, non-religious beliefs (like humanism and existentialism), non-religion, world views, and values. It also firmly places the endeavour in the context of a pluralist and constructivist conception of religions and beliefs that welcomes them all but commits to none. In this, the term more fully reveals the non-confessional – but not secular – starting foundation of the concept. Religion and belief literacy is not about more religion and belief, but about a better quality of conversation about the religions and beliefs that are everywhere anyway.

Modelling learning

A key observation in the chapters that follow is that religion and belief literacy is both socialised and learnt – that how and where we learn what both models and informs how we think about religion and belief. While treated in schools as a discrete and marginalised subject for children, at the same time, it overlaps with citizenship and sex education, and is colonised in communities with anxious policy instrumentalisations about migration and extremism. Thus, it will be *experienced* primarily in those ways rather than engaged with more openly as an ordinary part of billions of identities and lived experiences around the world.

Likewise, the book will show that learning about religion and belief is a lifelong process, to be engaged in by publics in schools, universities, professional training, workplaces and communities, where everyone is a learner. Crucially, learning happens in different combinations, in different orders, with different modes, for different purposes and at different paces for each individual. Some sort of sharedness across the learning spheres, wherever one goes next, would help, even where that sharedness highlights the disagreements. This sets up religion and beliefs themselves as open modes of learning and exploration, to be approached and explored from all sorts of angles and experiences. In this perception, they are not flat, unmoving, doctrinal and fixed. This reflects the importance of connecting the chain of learning across all the spaces through which people pass in everyday life so that the fullest range of thinking and contestations about religion and belief landscapes are more or less consistently revealed in their complexity and by recognising the boundaries and competitions between ideas. Instead of muddle, we might find clarity, though certainly also complexity.

The chapters

In Chapter 1 the book considers the problem of religion and belief literacy and its origins, locating it as a 20th-century challenge arising out of a willing transfer of care and education from churches to the state after the Second World War. Now well in to the 21st century, how can a new visibility of religion and belief meet a public sphere that had thought itself secular, and how does what we learn about religion and belief help and hinder?

Chapter 2 turns to the overarching themes framing religion and belief in 21st-century public policy. This reveals a long gap from around 1945 to about 2000 when religion and belief were barely noticed in the public sphere, underpinned by vaguely secular assumptions. At the same time, the religion and belief landscape was changing dramatically, just as few people were watching. What seemed to subsequently burst back into public prominence was a preoccupation with religion and belief as deeply problematic. This has landed in policy approaches focused predominantly on extremism, cohesion and equality, each designed to manage the risk.

The next six chapters explore how these overarching policy themes are reflected in key spaces of learning: two in schools (Chapter 3 on religious education [RE] and Chapter 4 on religion and belief in the wider life of schools); two on universities (Chapter 5 on operations and Chapter 6 on teaching and learning); one on workplaces and the professions (Chapter 7, focusing on health and social care settings in particular); and one on community learning (Chapter 8, focused on cohesion and extremism initiatives and out-of-school settings).

The final chapter brings together the themes in an attempt to summarise what each learning sphere suggests to us about religion and belief, drawing attention to the inconsistencies and confusions, as well as how they might helpfully be ironed out. A religion and belief literacy analysis is applied to explore how the chain of learning might be reconnected.

1

The broken chain of learning: the crisis of religion and belief literacy and its origins

Introduction

A number of events press for a strong and informed public conversation about religion and belief, such as: 9/11; the rolling back of welfare states and the turn to faith groups to plug the gaps; and new law on equality that includes non-religious beliefs, like atheism and humanism, alongside traditional religion, like the world religions, as well as non-religion, like environmentalism and veganism. However, as Davie (2015: xiii) observes, we find that we have largely lost our ability to talk about them: 'At precisely the moment that British people need them most, they are losing the vocabulary, concepts and narratives that are necessary to take part in serious conversation about religion.'

This chapter focuses on the origins of this loss of religion and belief literacy, which it locates in two public spheres: welfare and education. After all, almost everybody goes to school, and most of us use welfare and care services of some sort at one time or another. Coupled with the fact that both have their roots in organised religion, this gives these spaces enormous public traction in relation to religion and belief, despite so much of it having been forgotten. The saintly names of so many schools and hospitals are one echo of this memory; the wimpled headwear of nurses, though now (just) gone, is another.

What this especially denotes is that the period *before* the loss of religion and belief literacy in Britain and the West was, by its very nature, almost entirely Christian. Although there was a degree of plurality, and an awareness of some other religions, these were largely treated as essentially exotic. Yet, at the very moment that we stopped paying (much) attention to religion and belief, they entered a period of dramatic change. This has meant massive declines in Christianity, increases in other world religions, a huge growth in atheism and non-religion, and a shift towards informal and revival forms of religion and belief, especially associated with varying ideas of spirituality. All of this has been happening while the public sphere has been largely looking away. Where it has been thought about at all, change in religion and belief has frequently been mistaken for some sort of simple decline in Christianity, often explained in terms of secularisation, which has itself gone largely undefined and undebated outside the academy. Occasional controversies popped up in this period, notably around Sikh police officers' headwear in the 1970s and Salman Rushdie's book *The Satanic Verses* in 1988. However, these were viewed as occasional and exceptional, not part of a consistent public presence of religion and belief. In this period, plurality and diversity were framed as issues of ethnicity, not religion and belief.

The resulting challenges of religion and belief literacy are rooted here in the post-war period, in which the *deliberate* dilution of religious socialisation post-1945 has been followed by the *accidental* invisibility of religious social action and its disconcerting re-emergence after 1980, and then a striking renewal of religion and belief as a public sphere issue around the turn of the century, and especially after 9/11. What emerges is a tension between a loss of public religion and belief and its subsequent re-emergence after a prolonged period in which it was not really talked about. How can the conversation be recovered?

Religion and belief literacy

The term 'religious literacy' can be traced back to Ward's (1953) article titled 'The Right to Religious Literacy' in the American journal *Religious Education*. There it is used to mean that 'the child ... has a right ... to know God, to know nature, to know the mind and its possibilities, and to know that the knowledge-life as well as the love-life of man has a kind of infinity' (Ward, 1953: 380). This highly confessional, and un-self-questioning, coinage was followed by sociologist Vladimir de Lissovoy's (1954) article 'A Sociological Approach to Religious Literacy'. Taking a far more critical stance, in reflections on what ought to be included in an undergraduate introduction to sociology in his university in New York, he observes: 'it is important for the prospective teacher to understand, not only the structure and function of religious institutions found in most communities, but to have knowledge and understanding of the basic religious principles which are inherent in the major denominations' (De Lissovoy, 1954: 419). This reflects a view of religion as a series of traditions, the key features of which can be learnt. Of course, this has been superseded by a focus on religion *and belief* (implying non-religious beliefs too), which are thought of as 'lived' and fluid, not fixed and traditional.

A prolonged period of quiet followed before Wright's (1993) *Religious Education in the Secondary School: Prospects for Religious Literacy* linked literacy with religion in the context of schools. At this time, sociology and politics were imbuing 'literacy' with a richer set of meanings than the learning of systems of grammar and vocabulary. Literacy was coming to be seen in terms of narrative experiences and sets of social practices, at least partially constructed in the frame of the language(s) being used. The new literacy studies fostered the idea of multi-literacies, and related these to cultural competence: the ability to reach across languages into whole other frames of reference and being. In these contexts, Wright framed his arguments for a new RE in schools, aimed at improving the prospects for better religious literacy. According to him, religious literacy is located in RE in schools and should be about a critical dialogue between the horizon of the child and the horizons of his or her own religion or non-religion, as well as those of others.

More recently, Stephen Prothero has taken things further back towards Ward's approach, though with a more political than confessional purpose. For him, religious literacy is about the recovery of a loss of knowledge about traditions, *not of religion itself* (Prothero, 2008). He traces this in the US to the minimising of Christian denominational differences in the 19th century for the sake of Christianising the nation in a sort of coalition of the Christian willing. This produced a drive towards common denominators that continued into the 20th century. He argues that this has translated into a 'spiritual marketplace' in which doctrine is ignored in favour of a shared commitment to a shared conservative brand of morality. He sees this blurring of Protestant beliefs as so embedded in the public square that Americans must know something about Protestant beliefs and the Bible if they are going to be able to participate in that public sphere intelligently. In Prothero's analysis, religious literacy can be broken down into further subdivisions, which include ritual literacy, confessional literacy and denominational literacy. In order to remedy widespread religious illiteracy, he thinks that dedicated courses should be introduced in schools and universities.

Others, like Diane Moore (2006), go outside of schools, blending aspects of cultural studies as a way of overcoming religious illiteracy. Moore wants religious literacy to provide us with resources for how to recognise, understand and analyse religious influences in contemporary life as a basis for peace-building. She draws attention to: ignorance as regards the distinction between devotional expression and the non-sectarian study of religion; the controversy about women and Islam; the multiplicity, as opposed to homogeneity, of traditions and beliefs; change over time; and the cultural specificity of religions that make the same traditions differ from place to place. She emphasises an ability to perceive the connections between a complexly religious world and the social, political and cultural.

Another approach takes this further, seeing religious literacy as 'harmony'. Michael Barnes and Jonathan Smith (2016) insist on a broadly multi-faith perspective. They say that it is the very specificity of faith commitments that gives them life, and that the task is not to elide, but to value, difference. For them, religious literacy resides in reflection not only on the cultural and historical roots of difference, but also on the processes internal to the community. This is about a deep engagement with lived religion. At the same time, they point to a dialogue between contemporary realities and the wisdoms residing in religious traditions, which they see as potential resources for society to draw on, with or without doctrinal commitment to them.

Ford and Higton (2016) develop this, exploring the role of theology and religious studies. For them, theology and religious studies are not the same as religious literacy, though may be used as tools to achieve it. This has been criticised for being an intellectual and therefore somewhat elite endeavour, likely to appeal to and work only for a limited number of participants. They also focus on Christianity, though they are firm that their approach can apply to other traditions too. Notably, they do not address its efficacy for non-religious and non-traditional beliefs. The process that they outline is one of serious dialogue between a prevalent and ancient world phenomenon – in their case, Christianity – and a public realm that simply cannot do it, or itself, justice while ignoring it. For them, talk within and about a public realm is simply not possible without taking seriously the pervasive religion within it, regardless of one's own religion, beliefs or none. To stop short of theology is to assume that there are conversation-stopping beliefs – what they call 'erratic boulders' – that cannot be engaged with, whereas they perceive 'argumentative structures' in all the traditions that precisely enable this kind of dialogue, and that theology can actively assist in uncovering. Engagement in what they call this 'conversational mode' will lead to religious literacy, they argue.

Across the field, there is a shared concern about the need to tackle the decline in religion and belief literacy for the good of society, and this is the argument that is picked up by the notion of the chain of learning. In this conception, religion and belief literacy is important because it would appear that too many have lost the ability to talk about religion and belief in the public sphere, putting everybody, religious and non-religious, at a disadvantage because religion and belief are so central an aspect of many human lives. This takes us well beyond schools, however. As has been argued elsewhere, 'there is an urgent need to re-skill public professionals and citizens for the daily encounter with the full range of religious plurality' (Dinham, 2016: 110) across the widest of settings and sectors. One response is the religious literacy framework that has emerged from a decade or so of work in this field (Crisp and Dinham, 2019), culminating in the evolution of the label in this book to 'religion and belief literacy'.

The religion and belief literacy framework

The framework consists of a journey through four phases. The first phase is called 'categorisation' and is concerned with the need to understand the conceptual landscape in which religion and belief are framed and what people think is meant by these terms. In particular, it is concerned with how individuals and communities themselves categorise or define religion and belief. In the 21st century, this arguably incorporates potential for stretchy definitions of religion and beliefs to include consumerised, deformalised, revival and non-religious beliefs, values and world views. The critical thing is that each person or organisation knows what *they* mean and can articulate this clearly. It is intended to encourage understandings of religion and belief as lived experiences that manifestly affect the way in which people live their lives (Schilbrack, 2010), rather than as historic perspectives or cultural artefacts (Boisvert, 2015).

The second phase of this framework is 'disposition'. This involves an exploration of the often unconscious emotional and atavistic assumptions that people bring to discussions about religion and belief (Kanitz, 2005), and making these explicit. There may be significant gaps between what people feel, what they think and what they know in relation to religion and belief, and these can readily be conflated. Being able to identify these assumptions and emotions is seen as a critical precursor for a thoughtful engagement with diverse religions and beliefs. It often translates into an institutional 'stance' (Dinham and Jones, 2012), which adds a further layer to the context in which professionals and workplaces respond to religion and belief diversity when they encounter it.

'Knowledge' is the third phase of the religion and belief literacy framework. While some general knowledge of the religions and beliefs that are likely to be encountered may be important, equally significant is having the capacity and openness to acquire further knowledge from credible, well-evidenced and transparent sources when required. This entails developing the confidence and experience to ask appropriate questions appropriately. It recognises that the lived experiences of any religion or belief are fluid and permeable, and can vary considerably, so that religiously literate people are those who are able to understand religion and belief as changing and heterogeneous – as identity rather than tradition.

The final phase in the framework is 'skills'. Having developed clarity about how religion and belief are understood in the social and conceptual landscape, being aware of one's assumptions and having some knowledge of some religious practices and beliefs all inform the skills required. There is a dearth of research underpinning the sorts of skills that are needed given that the skills required should be related to the challenges and needs at hand in any given sector or setting. The religion and belief literacy framework concludes that this requires new research to plug the gaps – whether large-scale and formal, or swift and informal. The scope and scale will depend on the needs, timescales and resources available. Important work has already been undertaken around death and dying, for example, in hospices (Pentaris, 2019), and on working with indigenous communities in Canada (Coates et al, 2007) and Australia (Bessarab and Ng'andu, 2010), though the extent to which this has entered their respective target fields of social work education and practice is debatable. The opportunities for identifying the religion and belief challenges in every setting are extensive, as are the possibilities for translating findings into skills through training and practice.

Overall, the framework is intended for thinking through the implications and challenges of religions, beliefs and world views in different situations and real-life contexts, starting with the understanding that religion and belief literacy resides in an improved quality of conversation about the category of religion and belief itself, which first of all irons out all of the muddled binaries and assumptions. Such a framework, then, requires an exploration of disposition – the atavistic and emotional feelings that we each carry about religion and belief – and only then leads to a discovery of the knowledge and skills that are needed. This sees religion and belief literacy as contingent and setting-specific. It is a stretchy, fluid concept that is variously configured and applied, and should be adapted as appropriate to the specific environment.

The loss of religion and belief literacy: welfare and the willing transfer of care

How has religion and belief literacy been lost? In Britain and much of Europe, a key part of the explanation lies in a 'willing transfer of care' (Dinham, 2015a) from churches to states. This encapsulates the central problem posed by moving from a Christian public sphere to a hugely religiously diverse one while paying almost no attention to the change while it was happening. In correspondence and discussion between two of the leading protagonists at the beginning of this process in the UK – Temple and Beveridge – the idea of welfare took shape in ways that have fundamentally altered the public role of religion and that began the loosening of the chain of learning.

William Temple, Bishop of Manchester, Archbishop of York (1929–42) and Archbishop of Canterbury (1942–44), had set out a manifesto for welfare in *Christianity and the State* (Temple, 1928), in which he first coined the term 'welfare state'. He subsequently elaborated on this in *Citizen and Churchman* (Temple, 1941) in 1941, and then in *Christianity and the Social Order* (Temple, 1942), which was published in 1942 by the famous popular British publisher Penguin. This 'sold out, running for several reprints' (Timmins, 2001: 23). In it, Temple (1942) asks: 'What right has the church to interfere?'; 'How should the church interfere?'; 'What are Christian social principles?'; and 'What is the task before us?' It is notable that these questions were familiar and recognisable to the general public of the time. These were regarded as acceptable interventions to be made by a churchperson in the public sphere – a fact that contrasts with 21st-century attempts, for example, Archbishop Rowan Williams's (2006) comments on sharia law in 2006, which were met with widespread incredulity in the popular press. These were expressions of outrage that a religious figure should be intervening in public life. Yet, in the context of the Second World War, Temple (1942: 84) is welcomed in commenting that 'the national debt will be a heavy burden ... and there will be the need to reconstruct the devastated areas of many towns with all the adjustments of rights, vested interests and social welfare which any planning must involve'. For him, 'The structure of life as we knew it ... has already been profoundly modified' and the question was 'How far do we want to restore it if we can?' (Temple, 1942: 84). His goal was to explore what Christian thought might have to say on these fundamental matters of the shape of future society. He concluded that what must be rebuilt is: 'the family as the primary social unit' (Temple, 1942: 85), for which he identified housing as a key issue; the 'sanctity of personality' (Temple, 1942: 87), for which he prescribed good health and education; and 'the principle of fellowship' (Temple, 1942: 90), for which he wanted the end of educational division and the maintenance of a 'Christian character' in state-provided education for all.

Temple's book goes on to draw on Christian theology to argue for employment for all – 'every citizen should be in secure possession of such an income as will enable him to maintain a home' (Temple, 1942: 99) – as well as liberty and leisure. He concluded that 'the aim of a Christian social order is the fullest possible development of individual personality in the widest and deepest possible fellowship' (Temple, 1942: 100). These ambitions reflect what seem to the 21st-century ear like long-past conceptions of religion and belief in the public sphere. The boundaries between secular and sacred, between private and public, are notably differently drawn. Indeed, these very binaries had relatively little public meaning at that time. In this context, Temple's vision of a Christian-based social order gained easy traction in his relationship with William Beveridge. Beveridge was a civil servant with whom Temple had worked in the 1920s at the Settlement Movement's Toynbee Hall in the East End of London. The goal of the Settlement Movement was to 'find friends among the poor, as well as finding out what poverty is and what can be done about it' (Timmins, 2001: 17). Beveridge's role was critical. He was considered an authority on unemployment insurance from early in his career, serving under Winston Churchill on the Board of Trade as director of the new 'labour exchanges' (later 'job centres') and then as permanent secretary at the Ministry of Food. He was also director of the London School of Economics and Political Science from 1919 until 1937, when he was elected Master of University College, Oxford. In May 1941, the Minister of Health, Ernest Brown, announced the formation of a committee of officials to survey and make recommendations on existing social insurance and allied services. Beveridge was asked to chair this committee, and it has been suggested that this was regarded as a quiet and harmless parking place for Beveridge, whom many regarded as a bore. Far from it, however, the committee published the report *Social Insurance and Allied Services* in 1942 (Beveridge, 1942). This revolved around a number of principles that echo Templeton's vision: 'The first principle is that ... when the war is abolishing landmarks of every kind, [this] is the opportunity for using experience in a clear field. A revolutionary moment in the world's history is a time for revolutions, not for patching' (Beveridge, 1942). The second principle presented what became the foundational pillars of the welfare state in Britain:

> [that] organisation of social insurance should be treated as one part only of a comprehensive policy of social progress. Social insurance fully developed may provide income security; it is an attack upon Want. But Want is one only

of five giants on the road of reconstruction and in some ways the easiest to attack. The others are Disease, Ignorance, Squalor and Idleness. (Beveridge, 1942)

These 'giants' translated into the National Health Service (NHS) (disease), state schools (ignorance), council housing (squalor) and employment policy and job centres (idleness).

The third principle was that 'social security must be achieved by cooperation between the State and the individual' (Beveridge, 1942). A key aspect was that this 'should not stifle incentive, opportunity, responsibility; in establishing a national minimum, it should leave room and encouragement for voluntary action by each individual to provide more than that minimum for himself and his family' (Beveridge, 1942). The proposal that emerged was that all people of working age should pay a weekly national insurance contribution (Beveridge, 1942). In return, universal benefits would be paid as entitlements to people who were sick, unemployed, retired or widowed. Beveridge argued that this system would provide a minimum standard of living below which no one should be allowed to fall.

Beveridge's arguments were widely accepted and when Attlee won the 1945 British general election for the Labour Party, he announced that he would introduce the welfare state first described by Temple (1942) in *Christianity and the Social Order*, and fleshed out in the 1942 Beveridge Report. Temple said of this that it was 'the first time anyone had set out to embody the whole spirit of the Christian ethic in an Act of Parliament' (Barnett, 1996: 29).

Paradoxically, this was at once both a high-water mark of religion and belief in the public sphere, and a critical moment for the loss of religion and belief literacy. Before 1948, welfare especially but education too had been largely the provenance of the churches, and huge amounts of schooling, social work, community work and charity were done in Christian parishes and congregations. After the war, it was largely done – or at least seen to be done – by the state. At that time, church and state were widely regarded as sufficiently close that little distinction was drawn in the public imagination; likewise, it was of no concern to the church that one might be taking over the functions of the other. At the same time, it was of little concern to the public that services were constructed as embodiments of Christian theology, as Temple had put it. Yet, over the coming years, it resulted in a growing separation of the public language of the church and the public language of care, with profound effects on the religion and belief literacy of publics.

On the upside, this transfer of care from church to state reflected the undoing of centuries of paternalism, sexism and top-down philanthropy that the war had done so much to undermine. It also challenged the random nature of welfare provision that emerged when it was left to the 'well-meaning amateurs' (Prochaska, 2006). Until then, welfare had been something of a postcode lottery, whereby the parish in which you found yourself would largely determine the quality and availability of care. On the downside, it has been argued that the welfare transfer loosened the connection between people and parish that had so effectively engaged people, not just in individual concerns, but, through the family, to communities and to notions of the common good.

While nobody should romanticise the idea of pre-1940s' church-focused communities, there have nevertheless been regular waves of anxiety in public policy about a crisis of community ever since, and countless government initiatives have sought to address it in the UK – from the community development projects of the 1970s, to the New Deal for Communities in the 2000s. All have depended heavily on a rhetoric of 'restoring community' and all have relied on the participation of churches and other faiths, which they see as being somehow good at community. They have all tended to dictate the goals in political terms, such as increased employment, reduced crime and a better built environment. They have also all seemed incapable of encapsulating those alternative preoccupations with which faiths are also concerned, such as love, hospitality, generosity and the good (see Dinham, 2012b). In these ways, policy could be said to overburden faith groups with an inchoate hope that they will somehow restore community but little or no sense of what that really means. Those aspects that might have some chance of doing so – relationality, hope, love and so on – remain largely outside the public discourse as secular welfare services continue to disconnect users from it, despite some valiant attempts via 'social prescribing' and a renewed, if limited, focus in parts of the public sphere on mindfulness and well-being.

Yet, the reality of the welfare state has always been more mixed than this. Despite the appearance of a nationalisation and therefore secularisation of care and education, faith groups have maintained a constant and consistent presence, often working in the most disadvantaged areas from which other agencies have withdrawn.

Invisible presence

The 'willing transfer' from church to state has frequently been equated with a resultant secularisation too. Public professionals, such as the new NHS doctors, social workers and state-employed teachers, had apparently taken on the public functions of the churches, using a new language of the professions, displacing the language of religion and belief. Yet, despite a certain shift away from the religious articulation of welfare and education as an expression of the Christian gospel, as Temple had seen it, faith groups continued to play a crucially important role, albeit less visible. This was not only possible, but necessary, because politicians immediately knew that the welfare state on its own would not result in the eradication of society's 'five great evils'. There was neither sufficient money nor political agreement to establish the welfare state in its entirety. Choices and priorities were made right from the beginning, and even before the NHS was established in 1948, it was realised that the balance of contributions and the benefits they yielded would always be unstable. Even though the welfare state was able to ensure a certain minimum level of inclusion for the first time, it was nevertheless piecemeal, not total.

In the welfare sphere, this meant a continuation of significant amounts of community-based work that was largely under the radar by comparison to state provision. In the early part of this period, this remained largely Christian. As changes in religion and belief gathered pace in wider society, this became reflected in a growing plurality of multi-faith community initiatives too. However, from the start, during the 1950s in particular, there was renewed enthusiasm for community-based policies rooted in neighbourhood and self-help – precisely the sorts of work that faith-based providers had always been good at. By then, it was apparent that architectural renewal was insufficient for the successful building of communities after the destruction of houses and public spaces during the war. The Gulbenkian Report (Younghusband, 1968: 22) took this crisis of community up in the 1960s, envisaging new kinds of work in communities that would be 'concerned with affecting the course of social change through the two processes of analysing social situations and forming relationships with different groups to bring about desirable change'. It identified a set of values that should underpin community, which reflected those of many faith-based endeavours, though it did so in avowedly non-religious language. First, it said, people matter and policies and public administration should be judged by their effects on people. Second, participation in every aspect of life is of fundamental importance. Third, work in communities should be concerned with the distribution of resources towards people who are socially disadvantaged. Churches at the time widely noted the similarities with the social gospel. Much of this community work was conducted in neighbourhood-level projects and many of those were initiated by faith groups. In part, this was catalysed by the Church of England's parish system, which ensured that there were staff, buildings and resources in every area of the country (Dinham et al, 2009: 124). Bodies like the Churches Community Workers' Alliance emerged to support this work. These were new ways of being present. However, actors from across the religious traditions were active in this period, and continue to be so. Although prolific, Christian and non-Christian faith-based initiatives were far less visible and recognisable than the old parish-based welfare. Welfare would not all be done by the state, after all. Yet, state – secular – forms and language were now in the ascendant when people thought and talked about care. Nevertheless, it was a context that religion and belief groups could identify with in terms of the insistence on human worth and value, and on critiques of the shape of politics and society. They were prolific in providing interventions in communities at this time, and they were able to thrive in a context that was friendly to them. Although secular welfare had quietened faith-based care, it had not silenced it entirely.

Religion and education

In education, the persistence of religion and belief has been even more marked. A friendship between William Temple, and another politician, the Education Secretary, Rab Butler, was an important factor in this sphere too. Right from the outset of the national welfare state in the 1940s, it was immediately obvious that the state could not provide education for all without the existing church schools. Of course, this makes the education story a predominantly Christian one at the outset too, though plurality has led to complex debates and turns more recently. A settlement was reached that incorporated the church schools, which continues today. In practice, this meant offering one of two statuses to church schools: voluntary aided, where the state provides 10 per cent of funding and the church provides the rest in return for retaining overall control of admissions and governance, and the school can teach denominational RE; or voluntary controlled, where state funding is complete, all staff are employed by the state, governance is majority secular and RE follows the local authority-agreed syllabus, though with some delegated powers. They would choose their status within an overall policy framework set out in the Education Act 1944. As Chapter 3 explores, this set an educational framework of a broadly Christian character, making religious instruction (later RE) compulsory and mandating a daily act of Christian collective worship, arrangements that continue into the 21st century.

Bringing these schools in as part of a significantly expanded state provision means that approximately a third of all state schools in the UK have been provided by churches ever since. Of a total of 20,117 state schools in England in 2014 (the date of the government's first data release), 6,211 primary schools (37 per cent) and 633 secondary schools (19 per cent) are described as faith schools. Of these, 99.1 per cent of secondary and 96.1 per cent of primary schools are Christian (4601 Church of England and 1986 Catholic). In recent years, other faiths have joined the mix, though in very small numbers (48 Jewish schools, 18 Muslim and eight Sikh), totalling 0.9 per cent of primary and 3.9 per cent of secondary schools. Three things are apparent in relation to this provision: first, there is a persistence of religion and belief in the public sphere that is understated and poorly understood; second, it is almost entirely Christian, which has resulted in a widespread acceptance of Christian schools as a normal part of the system of state education; and, third, publics are nevertheless unsettled by the more recent emergence of schools of other faiths, which has resulted in a number of often heated and challenging debates. This reveals a tension between private faith and public education that is yet to be resolved, as well as a broader tension about the place of religion and belief in public life, and our ability to discuss it.

Anxious re-visibility

This emergence of non-Christian faith schools, and the controversies that have resulted, alongside a renewed visibility of faith-based services in the welfare sphere, have together reacquainted publics with religion and belief after a prolonged period in which they had barely been noticed. What is more, the plurality of the religion and belief landscape is largely unfamiliar to a public that remembers it as something much more like the 1950s. It is rooted in a wider rolling back of the state and a renewed and more visible involvement of other providers, including a plurality of faith groups, in the provision of all sorts of services. This began with Thatcher and her governments after 1979, which had come to regard the state as part of the problem, not a solution. As Milowski and Plehwe (2009) observe, the aim of the state in this period was to minimise its own role and to maximise markets, work, competition and self-help. This had the effect of handing back larger portions of service provision to non-government providers. Although there has been much debate about the extent to which this succeeded (see Clarke, 2004), the mixed economy of welfare that followed has since been joined by an increasingly mixed economy of education too. This has had the unintended effect of readmitting faith providers into spaces where publics had become used to secular state actors. It has allowed religion and belief actors to practise visibly once again in at least five spheres of activity.

First, they continue to provide services through community projects. These are usually very local and respond to locally identified need, often with locally resident staff and volunteers. Second, they provide services on a larger scale through tendering for hitherto public sector services, especially in housing and social care. Third, they have increasingly provided strategic services as partners and networks. For example, infrastructure bodies like the Interfaith Network and the Faith Based Regeneration Network (FbRN) received government funding during the 2000s to connect religion and belief groups with both each other and secular bodies, and to communicate with national and regional government in order to enable their practical contributions to be made. Fourth, they have increasingly provided services as social enterprises. Fifth, the continuing provision of education by churches has been joined by new educational provision in schools of other religions, giving rise to a surge in anxiety, as reflected in controversies such as 'Trojan Horse' in Birmingham, where a number of schools with majority-Muslim student bodies were reported to have suffered 'entryism' via school governor bodies by Muslims apparently intent on radicalising the schools. It is notable that this was reported as a 'faith schools' issue despite the fact that none of the schools was, in fact, a faith school; rather, they were state schools with a majority of Muslim pupils.

These spaces represent and reflect a variety of approaches, goals, practices and values with which faith groups are engaging, and that variety almost certainly reflects the variety within the wider landscape of religion and belief. This is complex and is taking place after decades in which religion and belief were widely regarded as outside of the public sphere. As a consequence, questions have arisen about the legitimacy of faith in the public sphere, as well as about the activities themselves, with suspicions of the possible agendas associated with them. Debates have abounded, in particular, in the UK and US, about perceptions of services with inappropriate or unpleasant strings attached, ranging from enforced prayer to imposed cures for homosexuality (see Dinham et al, 2009). All this takes place in the context of several generations used to secular services using secular language. In this context, welfare and its faith-based providers confront a political sphere that both valorises religion and belief as resources, and yet gives practically no account of what they mean to those who live them out. Thus, faith-based provision turns out to be widely present at the margins of visible welfare and at the core of state education – a sort of buttress for the state, which has no language with which to understand it or hold it to account.

Religion and belief literacy and public anxiety

The loss of religion and belief literacy inherent in the story of the welfare state is complex, and is accompanied by two other significant social changes. Together, they generate an element of anxiety that deeply inflects the recovery of religion and belief literacy. First is the extent of religion and belief change since Temple had felt able to describe the welfare state as the 'fullest expression of Christianity in an Act of Parliament' (Barnett, 1996: 30). The evidence suggests that religion and belief are both much less formal and significantly less creedal than they were 50 years ago. There is also much more religious diversity in general, alongside pockets of religious and non-religious intensity. For example, in the 2011 Census in England and Wales, Knowsley was the local authority with the highest proportion of people reporting to be Christian (at 80.9 per cent) and Tower Hamlets had the highest proportion of Muslims at 34.5 per cent (over seven times the average figure in England and Wales). At the same time, 38 per cent of responders to the 2019 British Social Attitudes Survey reported identifying as Christian, down from 66 per cent in 1983 when the series began. The proportion of the population identifying as Anglican (belonging to the Church of England or sister churches in Scotland and Wales) has fallen from 40 per cent in 1983 to just 12 per cent in 2018. Likewise, in England and Wales, while Church of England attendance has fallen to 1.5 per cent of the population,[1] the breakdown of attendees has also changed: less than one third are now Anglican; less than one third are now Catholic; and over a third (44 per cent) are now charismatic and independent. Muslims and nondenominational Christians have increased. Muslims now make up 5 per cent of the population. According to other sources and other questions, *what* we believe has changed too. Belief in 'a personal God' roughly halved between 1961 and 2000: from 57 per cent of the population to 26 per cent. However, over exactly the same period, belief in a 'spirit or life force' doubled: from 22 per cent in 1961 to 44 per cent in 2000. On the other hand, between 1998 and 2018, belief has declined in life after death (from 50 per cent to 42 per cent), in heaven (from 45 per cent to 37 per cent) and in miracles (from 32 per cent to 26 per cent) (British Social Attitudes Survey, 2019). Others note evidence of consumerist behaviours in religion and belief as people pick religions and ideas within religions to build their own frameworks of belief, often separate of creed and organisation (see Davie, 2015). Critically, the number of people in England and Wales reporting 'no religion' is at 25 per cent according to the 2011 Census and 52 per cent according to the 2019 British Social Attitudes Survey (2019).

In the context of so much change, there are a number of helpful contributions to understand what is going on. One account is found in Grace Davie's (1994) idea that there is more believing without belonging. This has been inverted by Hervieu-Leger (2000), who suggests the phenomenon alongside of belonging without believing. On the other hand, Abby Day and David Voas (2007) say that what we are seeing is a corruption of 'proper' religious forms into a sort of 'fuzzy fidelity'. However, Woodhead (2013) says that it is a wrongly fundamentalising interpretation to say that *real* dogmatic religion is declining, leaving people with a muddled and fuzzy residue. She thinks that the exact opposite is true: 'Turn it on its head and you see it the right way round: real religion – which is to say everyday, lived religion – is thriving and evolving, whilst hierarchical, dogmatic forms of religion are marginalised'.[2] Davie (2006) also brings our attention to what she calls 'vicarious religion': the phenomenon by which large numbers of non-religious people are grateful to the minority who hold the space open for them to turn to at times of stress, need or celebration.

This all points to how religious forms, as well as the religious mix and the mix of religion and non-religion, have been changing in this period. It is important to grasp this because there appears to be both a *real* religion and belief landscape and one imagined by policymakers and publics, and there is a growing gap between them (see Dinham, 2012a). This is likely to affect both how policymakers seek to shape services and practice and how providers provide them, as well as how publics perceive their willingness and ability to use them. There is a serious risk that they will shoot wide of the mark, targeting provision, or depending on volunteers, in the wrong places. This is one important implication of the broken chain of learning.

The second significant change is associated with 9/11 and the growth in violent extremism, and its subsequent visibility. This has tended to broadly distort perceptions of religion and belief, and is widely criticised for having especially done so in relation to Islam. Stereotypes of religion and belief based on anxiety about extremism and violence are not conducive to the better quality of conversation that religion and belief literacy seeks. Yet, in relation to religion and belief, it is violence, alongside homophobia, sexism and abuse, about which most is heard.

The relationship between religion and belief and the public sphere has proved persistent and complex, and religion and belief have changed dramatically precisely in the period when we were thinking about them least. However, the period in which we did not talk well – or much – about religion, that is, the period of state welfare in the second half of the 20th century, leaves us precarious on the subject now in practically every walk of life. The welfare state first accidentally quietened religion and belief as the primary language of care. Then, the increasingly mixed economy deliberately and visibly readmitted religiously based actors at the heart of the public sphere in a context of far greater diversity and plurality, alongside far less capacity for addressing it. This is the conundrum of religion and belief literacy as it presents through the lens of the welfare state, including education. It confronts the public sphere with the urgent need to reskill its public professionals and citizens for the everyday encounter with the full range of religion and belief plurality. Yet, we prepare those very professions and publics for the encounter within the mid-20th-century mode, as if religion and belief do not matter.

Conclusion

So, where are we now? We find a sort of 'fuzzy secularity' alongside a general muddle, often tinged with indifference and sometimes with hostility. Many people have a vague sense that religion and belief ought *not* to matter while, at the same time, grasping that it somehow does. However, the majority are largely unable to articulate the debate because it has been left out, or behind, in educational interventions at every level. Liberalism's solution – to confine religious debate to Habermas's public reasons, that is, to somehow rise above the fray in some sort of public neutrality – has predominated but does not seem adequate. Even if it were conceptually appropriate, since 2010, the law prohibits discrimination in employment and services on the grounds of religion or belief, and would no longer permit it.

Policy perceives this to the extent that it has been making efforts to respond to the more visible religion and belief that it has noticed. In policy terms, the responses are attempts to answer what boils down to three difficult questions. One asks: how do we prevent atrocities in the name of religions? This is the security agenda. A second asks: how do we respond when atrocities happen? This is the cohesion agenda. A third asks: how do we engage with the religion and belief that is there in ordinary everyday life, regardless of its role in cohesion and security, and their opposites? This is the equality, diversity and inclusion agenda. The challenge is that different educational interventions – formal and informal – fragment these issues across varying combinations of perspectives and preoccupations. They find themselves underpinned by a range of starting points about both what the problem is and how to solve it. Is the task security, cohesion or equality? Is there anything intrinsically important about religion and belief that might add a distinct dimension, apart from a policy goal, for example, connecting with the wisdoms within religions and beliefs, or drawing on them as sources of relationship and community? Spaces of learning are frequently unclear about their own starting points regarding: which religions and beliefs count; how to be inclusive in practice, rather than merely stating a commitment to 'inclusion'; whether they should be regarded as public or private; and whether the public space in question is secular, and what being secular means if so. Policy spheres, which frame and reflect these spaces, are just as confused. We are presented with the challenge of how to enable spheres of learning to engage with ideas of religion and belief that can help: how do we reconnect the broken chain of learning?

2

Policy framings of religion and belief: consolidating the muddle

Introduction

When it comes to religion and belief, a confused public sphere is reflected in a confused policy sphere. Many have noted a widespread and growing diversity of religion and belief as a result of continuing traditional forms, evolving informal ones and the globalisation and migration that has characterised Western development over recent decades, especially since the turn of the 21st century (Davie, 2015; Woodhead and Catto, 2012). In response, a number of policy approaches have emerged that aim to address this, dominated by varying combinations of preoccupation with extremism, cohesion and equality. While each of these overlaps with the others, at the same time, they are distinct. They also sometimes accidentally compete, as in the challenge of demystifying Islam at the same time as 'othering' it, and in handling sometimes competing protections, notably, religious opposition to same-sex marriage and marriage equality. As responses, the dominant policy spaces imply a degree of anxiety about religion and belief as risky and problematic, and in need of a solution. These broad responses to the 'problem' of public religion and belief form an important part of the context for what happens about religion and belief in spaces of learning. They shape how we imagine religion and belief, as well as how we respond. They will be the focus of this chapter.

Cohesion

A key focus of policymakers' interest in religion and belief is anxiety about relationships between and beyond religious traditions, and solutions have been sought that reflect this. In Britain, multiculturalism has been an important lens and governments have valorised the notion of 'community cohesion' between multiple identities as a basis for managing plurality. The resulting policies have tended to take two directions at once. On the one hand, cohesion is aligned with good citizenship in efforts to engage people of all faiths and none in public activities that would get people working together and therefore living well together. On the other hand, a bundle of 'Prevent' policies seeks to tackle religious radicalisation and violent extremism, understood as a particular problem of Islam – though efforts have also been made to balance and rebalance policy to challenge the 'othering' of Islam that is often thought to have resulted, as well as to take account of Far Right political extremism and nationalism.

Weller (2007: 44) locates the cohesion focus in interfaith initiatives, which he traces back to the World Parliament of Religions held in Chicago in 1893, translating to Britain in the Religions of the Empire Conference in 1924. The World Congress of Faiths followed in 1936. It is Weller's (2007: 44) view that 'the colonial and imperial projects of the nineteenth century turned out, in many ways, to have been a significant catalyst for a growth in consciousness about religious diversity and plurality'. He identifies a period when interfaith activity was really only for its 'enthusiasts' (Weller, 2007: 44) but that it subsequently gained much greater and broader purchase in more formal and political organisations, especially in reaction to the Jewish Holocaust. Immigration and later globalisation have driven the interfaith and multi-faith agenda further.

It has also been noted that 'community cohesion' is a narrative that, on the one hand, 'denies the conceptual complexities' of community (Robinson, 2005: 1412) and, on the other, overstates the case that communities are fragmenting. It has also been criticised on the grounds that it 'is unwarranted in maintaining that the problem is with minority ethnic communities' (Robinson, 2005: 1412). Yet, Cantle (2005: 3) locates the drivers of the community cohesion agenda precisely in immigration, which results, he says, from persecution and war, from the search by many nations for labour forces beyond their borders, from tourism, and from what he calls 'tourism into residency'. Cantle (2005: 6) is clear that this reflects and has resulted in communities fracturing, and that 'the immigration problem was now, more evidently than ever before, a matter of "race"'. Yet, he also notes that 'ethnic and faith divisions have now begun to replace those based upon ideas about "race"' (Cantle, 2005: 12). Thus, under the impetus of growing concerns about Islam following the events of 9/11 in the US, the angry young Asians of that summer in some English northern cities were already popularly cast as 'Islamic militants' and the disturbances as faith riots, not race riots (see Amin, 2002: 964). Yet, as Robinson (2005: 1415) also observes, 'community cohesion has no place in the lexicon of urban theory or public policy prior to the street confrontations of summer 2001'.

In the 2000s in Britain, cohesion policy coalesced around a significant government report called *Face to Face, Side by Side: A Framework for Partnership in Our Multifaith Society* (DCLG, 2008). This document promoted faith-based social action and dialogue as key strands in public policy for achieving community cohesion, with the added benefit of the participation of faith groups in the mixed economy of welfare. The policy regarded faith communities as well positioned to:

> add to social capital ... through offering local networks with links to those who might otherwise be left out; knowledge of local needs and ideas for how these might best be met; management capacity, such as the capacity to host and run community meetings about local issues; a major source of volunteers; leadership in organizing their communities to be active, linking the development of citizenship to the beliefs and teachings of faith traditions; focal points for engaging the wider local community in projects to improve the neighbourhood and the quality of life for those living in it; and inter-generational activities, so young and older people can be brought together to learn from each other. (DCLG, 2008: 28)

These developments were accompanied by national funding streams, notably, the Faith Communities Capacity Building Fund (FCCBF). Many faith communities responded by obtaining funding to devise new projects to support interfaith dialogue and multi-faith social action. In 2005/06 and 2006/07, it supported 338 faith-based capacity-building initiatives and 238 interfaith initiatives. Funded projects gave an indication of which faiths they would be working with. Of 139 projects in receipt of large grants, 609 faith groups were identified as the end beneficiaries.

A new national body, the Faith-Based Regeneration Network (FbRN), was also founded and funded to broker relationships between the organisational leaderships of faith traditions, network their faith-based social action and engage them with non-faith bodies, especially local and national government. Other bodies that already existed turned to the funding to continue and extend their work. This included the Inter Faith Network for the UK (IFN), which was originally founded in 1987 to promote good relations between people of different faiths in Britain. Its member organisations include: national representative bodies of the Baha'i, Buddhist, Christian, Hindu, Jain, Jewish, Muslim, Sikh and Zoroastrian communities; national, regional and local interfaith organisations; and academic institutions and educational bodies concerned with interfaith issues. The emphasis is on linking, cooperation and communication. In the 2000s, a Faith Communities Forum was developed within the framework of the IFN to provide a mechanism for consultation between national faith community representative bodies on matters of mutual concern, including issues on the public agenda as well as the development of interfaith relations. Another key body was the Churches Community Work Alliance (CCWA), an infrastructure organisation with a remit to work across all parts of the UK and the Republic of Ireland to advance and encourage church-related community development work. It promotes community development values and principles as the most effective and authentic way to engage with communities, and it seeks to support front-line workers and organisations in delivering training and services. Substantial financial support was also provided for nine 'regional faith forums', performing similar functions at the regional level.

The extent to which this funding and infrastructure could genuinely be said to be interfaith or multi-faith has been questioned (Dinham and Lowndes, 2008). What is it about multi-faith working that can be said to underpin cohesion? The assumption is that where faith groups can mediate their differences by working together, cohesion will be promoted. Yet, no precise methods of multi-faith partnership have been demonstrated as resulting in cohesion, either qualitatively or quantitatively. Likewise, the participation of people of faith in multi-faith partnerships cannot be determined externally and participants will therefore self-select according to their openness and readiness to engaging with people different to themselves already. It is not clear how this will address cohesion where it is most needed since the policy aspiration is as much about reaching the marginal as it is about sustaining cohesion where it already exists. At least some of that marginality will preclude engagement precisely where it is most needed. It is also by no means clear that attempting partnership necessarily leads to greater understanding and mutuality. It might equally result in more informed strife and conflict as differences are surfaced and made obvious.

In this context, there is a risk that what emerges is, at best, a pragmatic cobbling together of people who see a promising source of funding and think that they could use this to do some work with people of other faiths that they were perhaps thinking of doing anyway. Whether this amounts to a multi-faith partnership is the central question. Policymakers and funders are often taking it on trust that the mix of participants is as described and that they are doing and achieving what they aim to do. At the same time, participants are unable to stand as representatives of anything. Multi-faith leaders (often the directors of faith forums) know that people may or may not bring with them 'constituencies' of faith. In this sense, as one faith forum head said: 'It works because of a willing suspension of disbelief' (private correspondence, July 2011).

Nevertheless, these infrastructures of interfaith and multi-faith work gave rise to questions about faith and the public realm, many of which had been thought to be settled. Some were about the legitimacy of public faith at all in a context that many had assumed to be both secular and neutral on matters religious. Others raised concerns about the enlistment or commodification of faith in pursuit of social or state aims (Bretherton, 2006). Some have challenged the distribution of capacity and power between faith traditions, asking how minority traditions or oppressed groups could participate, be represented and be voiced in public contexts in the civil society contest alongside larger, more organised and hierarchical faith groups, especially the Church of England (Dinham et al, 2009). After a change of government in 2010 in the UK, funding for cohesion work has been significantly reduced or removed but, having arisen, the questions persist: is this an issue of race or faith, and how do they differ? Is it a public problem in need of public funding, or private and unfunded? Is it best addressed via interfaith and multi-faith encounters, or are those merely conversations of the willing?

Prevention of extremism

A complicating dimension in the story of interfaith and multi-faith cohesion is the relationship between cohesion and the prevention of violent extremism. In interviews with directors of the nine now-defunct regional faith forums in 2009 (the year before they were closed under a new government), there was recognition that there was work to be done to engage with those on the margins and perhaps most vulnerable to extremism or radicalisation. However, in practice, multi-faith forum directors saw the 'Prevent' agenda as alienating both sides: "the government ... so far has potentially alienated ... both sides, the Muslim community because they see themselves being equated with terrorism ... and other communities thinking 'Why just the Muslim community? We are all affected by terrorism'" (anonymous). They also described a reluctance to bid for or accept Prevent funding, though some did so in the end: "it always seems that within different communities, there is ... a feeling that some of the others are getting things that we are not" (anonymous). In this sense, Prevent was widely seen as working *against* cohesion, relationality and trust.

What also emerges is that where people of many (multi-)faiths come together, they are labelled 'interfaith' or 'multi-faith' settings but only by consent and by participants who are already open to it. These are people whose attitudes to plurality and diversity are already open. They do not, on the whole, cohere in new meldings of organisation, money or leadership. In many cases, they do not even agree on goals and objectives, preferring to fudge specific, transparent aims in favour of rubbing along without having to face the process of identifying what is, and is not, really shared. As for questions of theology, belief and world views, these are largely left entirely out of the conversation. This may be pragmatic and even effective but how far can it go in building cohesion where potential participants are less liberal-minded, and where there is no cohesion as opposed to consolidating it where it already exists?

What 'prevention and promotion' strategies seem to have achieved most, Cantle argues, is a sense of separateness. It is feared that, in some cases, this separateness may result in the building of 'a common bond of disaffection, both within nation states and across national borders, embracing a transnational identity, rather than with their fellow citizens' (Cantle, 2005: 10). It is this that is primarily seen as the threat to cohesion. 'Prevent' also reflects competing strands within individual policy themes themselves: on the one hand, interfaith and multi-faith encounter is sought because of the assumed cohesion within and between faith groups; on the other, it is feared because of the threat of conflict arising out of religious difference. This matters because these policies play out in the same places at the same time in the real lives of participants. No wonder publics are confused.

Equality, diversity and inclusion

A third area of policy that confuses public understanding of religion and belief concerns equality, diversity and inclusion. In 2010, an overhaul of equality law in England and Wales produced a refreshed Single Equalities Framework, as expressed in the new Equality Act 2010. Before this, equality protections in the UK were fragmented across seven UK Acts of Parliament, one European Union (EU) directive and two UK regulations (in chronological order): the Equal Pay Act 1970; the Rehabilitation of Offenders Act 1974; the Sex Discrimination Act 1975 (and amended 2000); the Race Relations Act

1976 (and amended 2000); the Disability Discrimination Act 1997; the Human Rights Act 1998; the 2000 EU Employment Framework Directive on Religion or Belief; the 2003 Employment Equality (Sexual Orientation) Regulations; the 2003 Employment Equality (Religion or Belief) Regulations; and the Gender Recognition Act 2004. In addition, the Equalities Act 2006 established the Commission on Equalities and Human Rights (CEHR), now the Equality and Human Rights Commission (EHRC), which is an integrated equalities body covering sex, race, disability, criminal offending and sexual orientation.

While all these measures had implications for faith communities as employers and service providers, only two addressed themselves specifically to issues of religion and belief (the 2000 EU Employment Framework Directive on Religion or Belief and the 2003 UK Employment Equality [Religion or Belief] Regulations, which implements it). This means that the implications of each Act or regulation, and of the overall framework, were relatively unclear. The Equality Act 2010 was therefore highly significant, both in consolidating law in one place and in explicitly extending protection against discrimination to religion and belief. This measure prohibits discrimination on the grounds of religion or belief in employment and the provision of services. This effectively encompasses anyone who uses services and anyone who has or provides a job – which, in turn, includes almost all of any public.

There are exceptions that further complicate the picture: where an organisation has an ethos based on religion or belief, it may be able to apply a 'genuine occupational reason' (GOR) exclusion by demonstrating that such a religion or belief is a requirement to carry out a particular job. Examples include being a priest or a Muslim outreach worker. In these cases, it would almost certainly be regarded not as discrimination, but as an occupational requirement.

The 2010 Act also added a new public sector equality duty, supported by specific requirements. In summary, in the exercise of their functions, those subject to the equality duty must have due regard to the three 'arms' of the duty:

- to eliminate unlawful discrimination, harassment and victimisation and other conduct prohibited by the Act;
- to advance equality of opportunity between people who share a protected characteristic and those who do not; and
- to foster good relations between people who share a protected characteristic and those who do not.

The Act explains that having due regard to advancing equality involves:

- removing or minimising disadvantages suffered by people due to their protected characteristics;
- taking steps to meet the needs of people from protected groups where these are different from the needs of other people; and
- encouraging people from protected groups to participate in public life or in other activities where their participation is disproportionately low.

These are fiendishly difficult standards to meet in relation to religion and belief, as complex test cases have shown. Consolidating this, the Act defines religion or belief as 'any religious belief, provided the religion has a clear structure or belief system ... or a philosophical belief'. Within that, a philosophical belief must:

> be genuinely held; be a belief and not an opinion or viewpoint, based on the present state of information available; be a belief as to a weighty and substantial aspect of human life and behaviour; attain a certain level of cogency, seriousness, cohesion and importance; and be worthy of respect in a democratic society, compatible with human dignity and not conflict with the fundamental rights of others. (Equality Act, 2010)

The Act's elastic definition of religion or belief, to include non-religious beliefs and non-traditional ones too, perhaps comes closest in public policy terms to imagining religion and belief as they really exist in everyday life – as messy, fluid, broad and changing. However, the definitions are at once both complex and necessarily imprecise so as to be almost infinitely interpretable. The challenge, then, is to translate this well-imagined policy into practice in workplaces and professions. This has clear implications for education and training. The task has been presenting employers, providers and judges with some extremely interesting and difficult dilemmas. Research in 2012 (Dinham, 2013) indicated two key findings. First, employers and providers did not feel that the law had clarified matters; in fact, they found that it was adding to the confusion. For example, a court's finding in one legal case does not necessarily point to the answer – even the likely answer – in the next. Second, employers and providers had observed that a turn to law was leading to an assertion of rights over and above an engagement in dialogue, and that this was generally unhelpful.

Legal expressions of the public muddle

The difficulties have been expressed in a number of legal cases that even highly skilled lawyers admit to finding complex. They revolve around seven key themes: visible manifestations of belief in workplaces and schools; time off work for festivals, rites and regular practices; workplace opt-outs; freedom of expression, religious harassment and victimisation; the restriction of a service; and the nature of religion or belief. The problems and the findings in each case are complex and messy, reflecting the lived experiences that they address. Together, they shed light on how hard it can be to pick through the dilemmas, and how difficult it is to predict final outcomes.

In relation to visible manifestations of religion and belief, a pair of cases reveal the complexities of the law, making it very difficult to anticipate legal outcomes in different disputes. The first involves a member of the check-in staff at British Airways (BA), Nadia Eweida, who was a Coptic Christian. In 2004, a new uniform policy required female staff to wear an open-necked blouse and a cravat. Eweida began wearing a cross openly in 2006 to show her religious commitment. After initially agreeing to remove it, she later refused to do so and was sent home on unpaid leave, later rejecting an offer of an alternative administrative position on the same pay but without customer contact. She lodged a claim for direct and indirect discrimination and harassment in 2006 but all her claims were dismissed, first by the Employment Tribunal and the Employment Appeal Tribunal (EAT) in January and April 2008, and then by the Court of Appeal in February 2010. Eweida appealed to the European Court of Human Rights (ECtHR), which ruled in January 2013 that her Human Rights Act Article 9 right to manifest her belief had unjustifiably been breached. It stated that domestic courts had given too much weight to the employer's need to project a corporate image and not enough to the employee's right to wear a visible cross, which did not adversely affect that corporate image. The UK government accepted the judgment. In the meantime, BA amended its uniform policy from February 2007 to allow staff to display a faith or charity symbol while wearing the uniform. Eweida returned to work but BA did not compensate her for the earnings that she had lost since the previous September.

The second case in the pair involves Shirley Chaplin, a member of the Free Church of England and a nurse with 30 years' experience. Throughout her working life, she had worn a crucifix on a chain over her uniform as a manifestation of her religious beliefs. In June 2007, new uniforms were introduced at the NHS Trust that, for the first time, included a V-neck tunic for nurses. In June 2009, Chaplin's manager asked her to remove her 'necklace', stating that it contravened the new uniform policy restricting the wearing of jewellery. Her employer offered several alternative solutions, for example, that she wear the crucifix under a high-necked T-shirt or pinned inside a pocket, but Chaplin rejected them all. Consequently, she was removed from her nursing duties and redeployed to a post that did not have the same uniform restrictions. This post ceased to exist in July 2010. Supported by the Christian Legal Centre, Chaplin took her case to an Employment Tribunal which ruled that she had not been subjected either to direct or indirect religious discrimination. Chaplin's case went to the ECtHR in 2011, where it was linked with the Eweida case. The ECtHR ruled against Chaplin in January 2013. The key difference between this case and Eweida's was that the NHS Trust had imposed its restriction on health and safety grounds in order to reduce the risk of injury when handling patients, and that the policy applied equally to non-Christians and Christians because it related to jewellery, not the religious symbol itself.

This health and safety theme appeared in a case about the visible manifestation of religion in schools too. Here, Tamanna Begum, a Muslim woman, was interviewed for an apprenticeship as a trainee nursery assistant at the Barley Lane Montessori Day Nursery in Ilford, Essex, and offered the position. Begum believed that her religion required her to wear a long *jilbab* – a long, loose-fitting garment worn by some Muslim women – which covered her shoes when she was sitting. At the interview, the nursery asked if she could wear a shorter *jilbab* when she started the job as it considered that the garment might constitute a trip hazard. Begum did not take up the apprenticeship. She brought a claim for indirect discrimination on the grounds of her religious belief but the Employment Tribunal dismissed her claim in April 2013. It found that the requirement that staff should not wear any garment that constituted a trip hazard did not discriminate indirectly against Muslim women. The rule applied equally to staff of all religions, and if some Muslim women were put at a particular disadvantage, any indirect discrimination was justified as a proportionate means of achieving the legitimate aim of protecting the health and safety of staff and children.

In another schools case where a pupil had started to wear a ring to symbolise her new commitment to celibacy before marriage, the court found that in choosing to come to this school rather than another specifically Christian institution, she and her parents had voluntarily accepted the school uniform. In addition, the wearing of the ring was not considered to be a manifestation of her belief. Yet, a notable feature of the case was the support offered by various bishops and prominent politicians, including such former government ministers as Ann Widdecombe, David Willetts and Norman Tebbit. It is not clear whether they supported the moral or legal points at stake.

Conversely, in 2007, a Sikh girl was asked to remove her *kara* bangle at school because it contravened the school's uniform policy. She continued to wear it and was given a series of exclusions as a result, eventually leaving the school and enrolling at a different school where she was allowed to wear the *kara*. She challenged the decision to exclude her in the High Court with the support of Liberty. In July 2008, the High Court ruled in her favour, agreeing that her freedom to manifest her religion under Article 9 had been infringed on the grounds that she had been forbidden to wear an item that was exceptionally important to her religion. The High Court also found that the *kara* was a small and unostentatious symbol, and that wearing it did not undermine the aim of the uniform policy of fostering community spirit. This contrasts with the case involving the celibacy ring whose seriousness as a religious symbol was not accepted.

Other cases involve taking time off work. Jake Fugler, who was Jewish, was employed by a hairdressing salon in London. After four years there, Yom Kippur, the most important festival in Judaism, when many secular, as well as religious, Jews fast, refrain from work and attend a synagogue, fell on a Saturday. Fugler requested a day's holiday but this was refused as his employer had discouraged holiday requests on Saturdays, the salon's busiest day, and several other staff had already booked the day off. After arguing with the salon owner, Fugler walked out. He lodged a claim for religious discrimination, as well as race discrimination and constructive unfair dismissal. In June 2005, an Employment Tribunal found that the employer's provision indirectly discriminated against Jews and was not justified since the employer had failed to consider whether its staffing needs could have been accommodated in some other way.

In another case, a residential care worker who believed that Sunday was a day of rest, was issued a final warning for refusing work on occasional Sundays and resigned in May 2010. An Employment Tribunal found that her employer was not guilty of discrimination and was justified in requiring her to work on the occasional Sunday. The EAT supported this on the grounds that Sunday working was not a core element of the Christian faith, though the Court of Appeal, which agreed, refrained from making any such comment.

Another challenging area is around opting out of work duties. Lillian Ladele, who was a member of an Evangelical Anglican Church, was employed by a local council as a registrar of births, deaths and marriages. When the Civil Partnership Act 2004 allowed same-sex unions, Ladele refused to conduct them on the grounds that it was against her beliefs. At first, she could make informal arrangements with colleagues to avoid doing so but after two of them accused her of homophobia, the council took disciplinary action against her. She took the council to an Employment Tribunal, which found the council guilty of direct and indirect discrimination for not taking account of Ladele's conscientious objection. The EAT later ruled that the council's treatment of her was proportionate and that she *was not* discriminated against. The Court of Appeal upheld this decision. The ECtHR also ruled against Ladele.

Similarly, Gary McFarlane, a relationships counsellor and member of a Pentecostal Church, believed that homosexual activity was sinful. Although he was willing to counsel same-sex partners, he eventually asked his employer to be exempted from offering psychosexual therapy (PST) to same-sex couples. This request was refused. He then voluntarily signed up for Relate's postgraduate psychosexual counselling course and agreed to undertake PST with same-sex couples if asked. However, after complaints from other therapists and following an investigation, his employer found him reluctant to do so and he was summarily dismissed. His appeal was rejected by both the Employment Tribunal in January 2009 and by the EAT in November 2009, while in April 2010, the Court of Appeal refused to allow him to appeal to a higher court. Instead, he took his case to the ECtHR in 2011, which also ruled against McFarlane. He later stated on a website that the case had made him 'acutely aware of an increasing intolerance for Christian viewpoints in our society'.

Cases have also been bought that relate to freedom of expression. In 2003, an evangelical Christian distributed a document to various colleagues based on extracts from the New International Version of the Bible. The first two headings were: 'Sexual activity between the members of the same sex is universally condemned' and 'Male homosexuality is forbidden by law and punished by death'. The materials had not been distributed during a prayer group meeting and a number of the recipients were not members of the prayer group. The staff member was suspended on basic pay and a disciplinary hearing found him guilty of gross misconduct. He was dismissed with immediate effect. His appeal failed and he launched a claim for direct and indirect religious discrimination and unfair dismissal. He argued that because the material that he had distributed had come from the

Bible, he was protected by the prohibition against discrimination on the grounds of religion or belief. The tribunal found that, irrespective of its source, the material 'was hostile and offensive towards homosexuals and was thereby homophobic', and that he had been dismissed for distributing the literature 'outside the confines of the prayer group and its meeting place'.

Another case involved the use of a workplace email to send homophobic material. A staff member, Haye, used her work email address to email Reverend Sharon Ferguson, who was then head of the Lesbian and Gay Christian Movement (LGCM), condemning the organisation as sinful. Her comments included that:

> You should be ashamed of yourself, this type of sexualism is not normal and it's not of God, it's sin in itself, to perform such things and mock God.... God created men and women to be together. How can you be preaching and running a church in such mockery. What you're doing is your own man made religion and it's wrong. The Bible says the wages of sin is death. Your type of sexualism is a type of sexual spirit that you all need to be delivered from. It is not the spirit of God but of the enemy. We're living in the last days it's important to repent and turn from your sinful ways until it's too late. Hell is not a nice place.

When Ferguson complained about the email, Haye was first suspended for six months and then eventually dismissed for using the council's email system to state 'homophobic views'. These were in breach of the council's Wired Working policy, which prohibits distributing material that is racially, sexually or otherwise offensive, and had brought the council into disrepute. With the support of the Christian Legal Centre, she brought a claim of unfair dismissal against Lewisham Council. However, in June 2010, an Employment Tribunal upheld the dismissal, finding that any non-Christian employee would have been treated in the same way as Haye.

The combination of religion/belief complexity and legal complexity is also well revealed in a case concerning religious harassment and victimisation. Here, a Christian staff member was dismissed for gross misconduct after she accessed staff emails without authority and found that the deputy chief executive had mocked her religious beliefs, referring to her as 'Looney Tunes' and criticising her 'excessive religiosity' in the office, for example, by ending conversations with 'I'll pray for you'. The sacked staff member made 29 claims of direct discrimination, harassment or victimisation because of race and/or religion/belief. The Employment Tribunal dismissed most of these claims but upheld her claim of religious harassment since the manager's mocking email had created an intimidating, hostile, degrading, humiliating or offensive environment. It also agreed that the manager's comment about 'excessive religiosity' was religious harassment. He had failed to deal with the issue, instead poking fun at the staff member behind her back and then seeking to justify his comments. While the Employment Tribunal considered that the staff member's unauthorised accessing of emails was gross misconduct, the deputy chief executive was also guilty of this and had only not been suspended because he had not lodged a grievance or made allegations against senior managers, as the staff member had. It therefore found that she had been unfairly dismissed and also victimised because of race and religion or belief.

A number of cases have related to the restricting of a service. A well-known 'bed-and-breakfast' case involves Martyn Hall and Steven Preddy, civil partners who booked a room at a hotel in Marazion, Cornwall, in September 2008. When they arrived at the hotel, they were informed by the hotel owners, Peter and Hazelmary Bull, that the hotel did not allow unmarried persons to share a double room and that the couple would have to seek accommodation elsewhere. The hotel's online booking form stated that the Bulls preferred to let double accommodation to 'heterosexual married couples only' but Preddy had made the booking by telephone and had not been made aware of this provision. Supported by the EHRC, they brought a claim to the County Court against the Bulls (who were backed by the Christian Legal Centre) on the grounds of sexual orientation. It found in January 2011 that Hall and Preddy had suffered direct and indirect discrimination. The court stated that there was no material difference between marriage and a civil partnership. The Bulls's refusal to allow Hall and Preddy to occupy the double room that they had booked was because of their sexual orientation: this was direct discrimination.

Finally, cases on what constitutes the nature of a religion or belief have also been brought. Louisa Hodkin and Alessandro Calcioli from East Grinstead, Sussex, who were both members of the Church of Scientology, wished to get married in the London Church Chapel. The registrar general had refused to register the chapel for the solemnisation of marriages as it was not a place of worship under the relevant legislation. Hodkin challenged the decision and in July 2014, the Supreme Court ruled that Scientology should be classified as a religion as religions should not be restricted to faiths involving 'a supreme deity' since this would exclude Buddhism and Jainism, and also mean that the courts would be entering difficult theological territory. Hodkin and Calcioli married in the chapel in February 2014.

Some conclusions on a muddled context

Individuals almost always stand in several or many places simultaneously in relation to the issues described: sometimes as employers; at others as employees; as religious, non-religious, occasionally a bit religious or something else; and perhaps as part of minority or oppressed groups themselves, or occasionally even as oppressors. At other times, they may seek to work as promoters of rights. This applies to religion and belief communities as well as to individuals and other groupings, and poses a 'multiple perspectives' dilemma. From the various perspectives of religion and belief, the protections offered in law to minorities and the oppressed may sometimes appear just as much as challenges to their own perspectives and beliefs. This makes the identification of implications for religion and belief, and their secular contexts, all the more complex as they depend very much upon the perspective from which one starts.

This is capable of further complication in relation to the diverse moral, ethical and theological standpoints to which people of all religions, beliefs and none may be variously committed, some of which may cut against the trend of equalities legislation (though much is likely to support it). It should also be noted that there is much diversity within religion, belief and non-belief identities themselves, and most include a variety of denominations, traditions, practices, beliefs, values and world views, people of various ethnic origins and cultures, people with disabilities, people from a variety of social backgrounds, people of all ages, and people with diverse sexual orientations and gender identities. Homogeneity of perspective is impossible, yet policy and law seek definitions that they can work with. How can these translate into spaces of education and training such that they can make meaningful sense to publics, citizens and professionals? What does this look like in concrete encounters and practice?

3

Religion and belief in Religious Education

Introduction

Learning about religion and belief starts *in* school and even *before* school. Birth ceremonies are often obviously religious, while there appears to be an increasing tendency towards non-religious or pluralist 'naming ceremonies' (though there is little research in this area). Birth registrations themselves reflect essentially religious family normativities rooted in theology and natural law, despite the growing advent of families where gamete donors are not legal parents, and vice versa, or where an egg donor, surrogate, sperm donor and co-parent may all be involved in the creation of a pregnancy but not all be part of the child's new family, in biology, in parenting or in law. Nurseries and libraries may be packed full of little Noah's Arks. Sunday Schools and church playgroups tell many more stories than Noah's. Easter and Christmas set the dates of term, and the price of holidays, even when Ramadan, Diwali and Yom Kippur are also increasingly visible. At the same time, 'British values' are pinned up on nursery and school walls, and advertisements for everything from baby milk to vodka make for a subliminal backdrop of religiously rooted normativities, from whiteness and heterosexuality to able bodies and blue or pink gender types. From Mothercare to 'Music with Mummy', roles are implied, even now that sandwich shops and supermarkets embrace the Pride rainbow to 'queer' their products and consumers. This is the subconscious stuff of religion, belief and world views. It seeps into everything, even before we become conscious of learning or enter formal learning spaces. So, we arrive at school apparently fresh to learn but already full of deep expectations and atavisms. What happens next is critical to challenging those inheritances, and shaping our abilities to think, feel and live religion, belief and non-belief for the rest of life. Yet, policy and practice on religion and belief in schools, and on school RE, are themselves in a highly muddled state. This is a major factor in the widespread lack of religion and belief literacy, and in the broken chain of learning. This chapter will explore this in relation to

RE in particular. The following chapter will pick this up in relation to religion and belief in the wider life of schools.

RE

Under the Education Act 1944, it is a requirement in English law that learning about religion and belief must take place in all state-maintained schools, including those in reception classes and sixth forms (though not in further education colleges). The 1944 Act also makes it mandatory for fully funded state schools to follow an 'agreed syllabus' for what it called 'religious instruction', developed within each of England's 56 local educational authorities by a 'syllabus conference', consisting of representatives of the Church of England and other Christian denominations. Reflecting this, during the period up until 1988, teaching was almost entirely based on a Christian, scriptural approach, though increasingly with consideration of the other 'world religions'.

Although these provisions continue, the field, like society, has not been static. The Education Reform Act 1988 maintained the model of the local determination of RE, rooted in the local education authorities, but at the same time shifted the stated purpose of RE from 'teaching religion' to 'teaching *about* religion', and prohibited indoctrinatory teaching (Section 9 of the Education Act 1988). 'Religious education' replaced 'religious instruction' and multi-faith Standing Advisory Councils for Religious Education (SACREs) replaced the Christian 'syllabus conferences' to set curricula. Agreed syllabi are now required to 'reflect the fact that religious traditions in Great Britain are in the main Christian, whilst taking account of the teaching and practices of the other principal religions represented in Great Britain' (Section 8.3 of the Education Act 1988) – a situation that is at least questionable in relation to the religion and belief landscape as we actually find it.

In 1994, the School Curriculum and Assessment Authority (SCAA) introduced non-statutory model syllabuses that included six 'main' religions and used the two attainment targets of 'learning about' and 'learning from' religion. While this raises the unresolved question of what counts as a 'main' religion, these models were widely adopted in agreed syllabuses. In 2004, the successor Qualifications and Curriculum Authority (QCA) introduced another non-statutory national framework to support those responsible for syllabus development locally. The aim was to clarify the required standards in RE (see QCA, 2004). The range of religions to be studied was further widened and it was recommended that students also have the opportunity to study 'secular philosophies such as humanism' (QCA, 2004).

Alongside the 1988 Act and these non-statutory measures, the 1944 Act, which continues to be in effect, also mandates a daily act of collective worship in the Christian mode. Although this continues to be required, it is widely ignored in practice. At the same time, parents have a right to withdraw their children from the act of collective worship, as well as from RE itself. It has been suggested that collective worship and the right to withdraw further confuse the place of religion and belief in schools, both in the overall environment and within RE (see Clarke and Woodhead, 2015). It draws the religion and belief perceptions of parents and young people outside of schools into the heart of the policy and practice muddle within them.

Policy changes have resulted in changes in school structure too, which have also been important. New 'academy' schools introduced after 2000 are allowed to determine their own curricula, free of local authority, SACRE and national curricula requirements. The expansion of the 'academies' programme in the UK since 2010 has resulted in an increasing number of schools that are allowed to operate quasi-independently. In practice, this means that they are not required to follow agreed syllabuses on RE or the national curriculum more widely. New 'free schools' are also outside these requirements. The increase in free schools and academies has also permitted more schools to define for themselves 'a religious character' within the state system. There are now Jewish faith schools in Manchester, Liverpool, Birmingham and North-East and North-West London. Independent Muslim faith schools emerged in the 1950s and 1960s, and their number has grown rapidly since 1990. The first two Muslim state schools (one in North London and the other in Birmingham) became state-maintained in 1998. Since 2001, Muslim schools have been actively welcomed into the maintained sector, with the government giving the Association of Muslim Schools (AMS) financial support to facilitate their integration into the sector (Hewer, 2001). The first state-maintained Hindu school opened in September 2008 in Harrow, West London. The first state-funded Sikh school in Hillingdon, London, opened in 1999. In 2017, 35 per cent of maintained schools in England had a religious character (6,814 maintained faith schools out of a total of around 20,000 maintained schools), educating just under a quarter of all pupils. The majority are primary schools (6,177, or 37 per cent of all state-funded primaries), of which 26.1 per cent are Church of England and 9.8 per cent are Roman Catholic. There were 637 secondary schools with a religious character (19 per cent of all state-funded secondaries). Of other faiths, 48 (0.2 per cent) are Jewish, 27 (0.1 per cent) are Muslim, 11 are Sikh and five are Hindu.[1]

The impact on RE has been an increasing diversity of approaches in a context that was already complex. This is true in other mixes in other countries too (see Diaz, 2018). Much of this is lost in the detail and public awareness tends to revolve around an over-representation of a faith school 'problem' via news stories about Muslim 'takeovers' of values and curricula (as in the so-called 'Trojan Horse' scandal[2]) and controversies about perceived discriminatory admissions requirements. With greater curricular freedoms, many schools have taken to delivering RE through tutor time, or occasional 'RE days', so that RE is no longer a discrete regular subject on the timetable. Within this, there is concern that RE has increasingly been colonised by proxy themes such as ethics, citizenship and cohesion, which overlap with, but are not in themselves, religion or belief (see Gearon, 2013).

The 1944 settlement is now more than 70 years old and has been repeatedly amended in piecemeal ways, usually in the direction of trying to keep up with a changing religion and belief landscape. However, changes in the real religion and belief landscape have far outpaced changes in education about it. The real picture is made up of more believing without belonging (see Davie, 2015), as well as more non-believing (see Lee, 2015). It is a context that is Christian, plural and secular all at the same time (see Weller, 2007). The requirement for RE of a 'Christian character', the notion of 'six main religions', the continuing mandate for a daily act of collective worship, the right to withdraw and massive change in the real religion and belief landscape suggest that, in relation to religion and belief, we have a mid-20th-century settlement for an early-21st-century reality. This is likely to both reflect and reproduce a lack of religion and belief literacy among school leavers, who are confused by the religion and belief messages communicated in schools and, by extension, in wider society. That confusion all too often falls over into disinterest. Key questions are at stake about the purpose, content and structure of learning about religion and belief. What is it for? What should it include? Where should it happen?

What is RE for?

The purpose of teaching and learning about religion and belief in schools is hugely contested, though debate has not been especially focused, coherent or articulate. The policy muddle outlined has made it difficult to think systematically, and the variety of approaches that have emerged since 1944 have tended towards sedimentation and aggregation rather than clarification. The starting point of religious instruction in the Christian mode has given way to RE with a broadly Christian character, along with the emergence of a number of faiths that are newer to Britain, as well as non-religious beliefs such as humanism and secularism, and reports of no religion. As the categories blur and overlap, religion and belief are accidentally socialised as essentially difficult and confusing phenomena. A low priority for society, religion and belief have also become a low priority in schools, mandated but marginalised, and colonised by proxies about values, ethics and citizenship, which themselves have limited alternative space. How have these debates unfolded, and what do they imply?

Pedagogical debates

Following the contributions of Edwin Cox's (1966) important book *Changing Aims in Religious Education* and Ninian Smart's (1968) *Secular Education and the Logic of Religion*, there was a shift in pedagogical theory, and practice too, which moved towards an epistemological justification of RE based not on religion's publicly agreed truth, but on its role as a distinctive area of experience – a 'form of knowledge' or 'realm of meaning'. Thus, the influential report *Religious Education in Secondary Schools* (Schools Council, 1971) advocated a 'phenomenological' approach to RE, which saw the subject as developing an understanding of religions without promoting any particular religious stance.

A key divide has been between those who consider the main aim of the subject to be to help pupils develop their personal views or interpretation of life through the mode of RE and those who place greater emphasis on learning about the beliefs and practices of religions in themselves (Erricker, 1987). Wright (1993) describes this as a tension between implicit and explicit approaches. This finds its roots in experiential models, developed in the 1960s (Goldman, 1965), which attempted to dissociate experience-based teaching from a theological approach, viewing religion as a universal phenomenon embracing all aspects of human life and experience. Experiential teaching was seen as useful to prepare pupils for the later (from age 13) study of religions as phenomena that could be interestingly observed. Such models first encourage pupils to explore their own inner world of belief or spirituality as a basis for later relating this to the religion and belief experiences of others (Grimmit, 2010). The learning would reside in being ready from self-reflection to imagine the religion and belief realities of others. This has involved RE in ongoing debates about how to balance the experiential and the descriptive (Grimmit, 2010). It was hugely influenced by the Schools

Council Lancaster Secondary RE Project led by Ninian Smart in the late 1960s. This gave rise to the phenomenological approach, popularising the distinction between 'implicit' aspects (concerned with pupils' search for meaning) and 'explicit' aspects (concerned with detailed phenomena of religion). The phenomenological approach provided a broad framework for the study of the major world religions by focusing on key religious phenomena featuring across them, such as 'founding fathers', rites of passage, holy books and places of worship. The underlying pedagogical principle is that learning and teaching about religion and belief should promote both academic and personal forms of knowledge and understanding (Grimmit, 2010). It has been criticised for having, in practice, largely lost its liberal educational value of addressing the personal and existential concerns of the learner. Instead, it is thought to have become overly focused on a narrowly descriptive and content-centred approach that largely flattens the idea of religion and belief as lived phenomena, which are rather rendered monolithic and unchanging blocks of objective facts to be learnt.

In response, an 'interpretive' approach was developed in the 1980s and 1990s at the University of Warwick, UK, which reclaims and builds on the phenomenological approach. This focuses on pupils' interactions with religious content, examining the relationship between individuals, groups and the wider religions being studied (Jackson, 2014). It encourages learners to connect personal knowledge and experience to material from religious traditions as an interpretive tool. The goal is to make links between the religious lives of others and their own experiences and viewpoints. A key innovation is the importance given to the role that interpretation plays on both 'insiders', who are living their religion, and 'outsiders' (the learners), who are trying to understand it. Ipgrave and McKenna (2008: 114) comment on how this approach marks a shift away from 'phenomenological agnosticism, by which pupils temporarily suspend their judgement on the religious beliefs of others'.

At the same time, Wright is critical of how interpretivist approaches continue to accidentally restrict the focus to human experience to the detriment of belief systems. He dislikes what he calls the 'post-modern hermeneutics' at the heart of interpretivism, which he thinks is likely to give pupils the sense that their relatively unformed experiences or sense of religion and belief may already have similar epistemological status to the formal world religions. This he regards as doing both a disservice. Instead, he proposes a critical realist approach that favours the exploration of religious truth claims on their own terms, though from a critical perspective. He prefers this over the development of a generalised empathy towards religions and beliefs, regarding it as embracing the lived complexity and depth of religion while providing pupils with systematic alternatives. They can become both knowledgeable observers and critical choosers. Ipgrave and McKenna (2008: 115) themselves express concern that theology may be lost in the study of religion that focuses on an anthropological and experiential perspective, leading to a preoccupation with the inner self.

Others question the legitimacy of 'adopting any single monological framing of religion' (Freathy et al, 2017: 11), recognising rather that 'religions are contested, complex, diverse, multi-faceted, evolving and multi-dimensional phenomena (including, for example, doctrines, laws, literature, languages, narratives, traditions, histories, institutions, communities, people, places, practices and materialities)' (Freathy et al, 2017: 14). They promote a plurality of multidisciplinary approaches to teaching about religion and belief, suggesting that 'the search for a single "ground" needs to be replaced by a new metaphor that recognises dynamism, diversity, complexity, contestation, provisionality, flux, fluidity and uncertainty' (Freathy et al, 2017: 15).

This tussle between religion/belief experience and knowledge is ongoing, and has been summarised as follows: 'post-modernists say that religion is fluid to the point of non-existence; critical realists say that religions are stable social facts; and interpretivists say that religion exists but is fuzzy and disputed' (Iversen, 2013: 176). It plays out in how different schools pick different emphases, or sometimes fail to discern or express their stance at all clearly in the first place. Yet, there is a broad consensus that school RE can and should synthesise experience and knowledge.

Grimmit picks up on this, locating his work in theories of social constructivism, which again focus on pupils' own experiences. This 'deliberately seeks to accommodate the formal teachings of religion within the personal meaning constructs of pupils' (Grimmit, 2010: 47). Grimmit (2010: 34) places new emphasis on using the religious content of RE to illustrate what it means for humans to make a faith response to those 'fundamental, inescapable questions about the human condition'. This approach emphasises pupils' reflective and empathetic skills, and their personal development, alongside and in interaction with the development of their academic understanding of religions. Grimmit proposes a three-stage model. The first stage is 'preparatory pedagogical constructivism', in which pupils reflect on their own experience in order to prepare them for encounters with items from other religions and beliefs. The second is 'direct pedagogical constructivism', where pupils engage in direct contact with religious items without explanation or instruction so that they can act as stimuli for the construction of pupils' own meanings. The third stage is 'supplementary pedagogical constructivism', where additional information about religious items is provided so that pupils are confronted with the gaps between their own and alternative interpretations, which allows them to challenge themselves further. Here, interpretive pedagogy is combined with critical analysis. For Grimmit, the constructivist model thus combines a focus on 'learning from' with 'learning about' in a way that overcomes the narrowly descriptive nature of the one while bringing learning to life in the manner of the other. The extent to which pupils recognise the distinction and are able to draw the boundaries between them may be part of the muddle underpinning the religion and belief literacy problem. Certainly, these differences in approach are illustrated in widely varying approaches to RE practice in classrooms.

This connects these pedagogical considerations to the moment of practical application. It relates 'up the ladder' to structures of national and even international policy and pedagogy, and how this frames the practices of RE itself, but critically also downwards to the relationship between RE and school policy, and what then happens in classrooms. One key question is: how conscious are these processes in schools?

In these contested and muddled contexts, it might just be too hard to get clarity. Thus, Chater and Erricker (2013: 261) conclude that 'the most difficult questions in RE have been postponed in the interests of a unity of pedagogical purpose', though that pedagogical purpose itself fails the test of unity. In a summary of the state of RE, Chater and Erricker (2013: 261) observe that 'the definitions of learning in RE are a superstructure built upon shifting epistemological sands, and that the consequent muddle of the subject becomes apparent in its collapsing political structures and its weak and fragmented learning'.

A national curriculum

Despite its continuing to be a required subject under the Education Act 1944, RE was not included in a comprehensive government review of the statutory national curriculum in 2012. This is because it had not been included in the national curriculum when it was introduced in 1988. As a result, it was widely felt that 'The RE community has felt a sense of crisis despite government assurance' (REC, 2013: 8). In response, the RE Council – a highly reputable charitable educational body championing the professional teaching of RE – produced a new non-statutory framework for RE in parallel. It was hoped that this would help address the observation made in repeated reports from the Office for Standards in Education (Ofsted, 2015) that in the absence of a national framework, 'there are significant and well-founded concerns about the uneven quality of learning and teaching in RE across the country'. The adverse consequences of government policy on RE's place in schools were recognised by the then Secretary of State for Education on 3 July 2013. Addressing an event at Lambeth Palace, the formal home of the Archbishop of Canterbury, Michael Gove conceded that RE had been an 'unintended casualty' of recent curriculum reforms, and acknowledged that in thinking that RE's 'special status' was protected under the Education Act 1944, 'he had not done enough' (REC, 2013: 5). The REC non-statutory framework that emerged is accepted as having succeeded the QCA (2004) national framework and as supplementing the current government guidance, *Religious Education in English Schools: Non-Statutory Guidance* (DCSF, 2010). It encapsulates the ambiguous status of RE as both required and outside the national curriculum, and clarifies what an un-muddled RE could look like in schools.

The framework as a whole is an attempt to balance the various aims of RE. It introduces the concept of religious literacy (using this earlier language), defined as: 'investigating religions and worldviews through varied experiences, approaches and disciplines; reflecting on and expressing their own ideas and the ideas of others with increasing creativity and clarity; and becoming increasingly able to respond to religions and worldviews in an informed, rational and insightful way' (REC, 2013: 10). This immediately moves it away from instrumental policy goals and closer to critical disciplinary ones.

At the same time, the new framework certainly continues to reflect the wider policy focus on learning about religion and belief in order to engage with diversity, particularly in the lower key stages. Thus, all pupils are expected to develop their knowledge and understanding, develop their own values and identities, and have 'an aptitude for dialogue so that they can participate positively in our society with its diverse religions and worldviews' (REC, 2013: 14). However, it does so alongside a clear attempt to balance it with knowledge and understanding for its own sake, as well as personal development. This is seen particularly in the early years foundation stage, where personal, social and emotional development are framed in terms of understanding and responding to the 'other', with the emphasis on respect, sensitivity and harmony as general life skills, not in response to extremism. The emphasis on responding sensitively to difference extends throughout Key Stages 1 and 2. For example, in Key Stage

1, pupils are encouraged to: 'Observe and recount different ways of expressing identity and belonging, responding sensitively for themselves'; 'Notice and respond sensitively to some similarities between different religions and worldviews'; and 'Find out about and respond with ideas to examples of co-operation between people who are different' (REC, 2013: 19–20). Likewise, in Key Stage 2, they are called to be able to 'Explore and describe a range of beliefs, symbols and actions so that they can understand different ways of life and ways of expressing meaning' and to 'Consider and apply ideas about ways in which diverse communities can live together for the well-being of all, responding thoughtfully to ideas about community, values and respect' (REC, 2013: 23). A transformative addition is that this is accompanied by a developing focus on thinking critically, asking 'increasingly challenging questions about religion' (REC, 2013: 21) such that pupils can 'Observe and consider different dimensions of religion, so that they can explore and show understanding of similarities and differences within and between different religions and worldviews' (REC, 2013: 21–2). This underpins a more nuanced and sophisticated engagement with religion and belief as heterogeneous and fluid, rather than as a blunt category of 'religion' about which to feel somehow anxious.

Key Stage 3 also increases the focus on thinking critically, including philosophically, and thinking about controversies and the nature of religion in current affairs. As noted by Chater and Erricker (2013: 258), this also represents a 'slight but perceptible shift in RE thinking away from instrumental outcomes, such as community cohesion, towards a sense that the object of RE is worthy of study in its own right', though the focus on handling diversity is still evident. Key Stages 4 and 5 (ages 14–16 and 16–19, respectively) build on this further, focusing on systematic understandings of religions and world views, the nature of religion, their relation to current affairs, diverse interpretations, and skills for developing personal responses to ultimate questions. This includes being able to use different disciplines (textual analysis, sociology, philosophy) in the study of religion and belief.

In this vein, it is also stated that pupils should be able to 'appreciate and appraise varied dimensions of religion or a worldview', with the footnote that:

> Here, however, the aim is to consider religion and belief itself as a phenomenon which has both positive and negative features, and is open to many interpretations: in this aspect of the aims, pupils are to engage with the

concept of religion and non-religious belief, not merely with individual examples, and similar critiques should apply to both. (REC, 2013: 14)

Crucially, it is also suggested that pupils explore the connections between RE and other subject areas, namely, humanities, language, literature, technology and science.

REforREal

The 2013 review was followed by research that further explored these questions of the role of school RE in a project called REforREal (Dinham and Shaw, 2015). This involved interviews and focus groups with 331 participants – teachers, pupils, parents and employers – in 19 schools around England, with questions revolving around three key areas: understandings of the purposes of RE; aspirations regarding content; and thoughts about the structures of teaching and learning of religion and belief. The project found that students, teachers and parents alike thought that RE was important. They wanted young people to learn about religions and beliefs, and they recognised that they are important parts of many people's identities and lives. However, they wanted to learn about a broader canvas of experiences and outlooks, which would include not only Christianity and the world religions, but also non-traditional forms like Paganism and Wicca, and non-religious beliefs like humanism and secularism. They also wanted a focus on how religion and belief are lived as fluid experience rather than fixed identity, and how they are internally differentiated rather than homogeneous, as well as to focus on real-world dilemmas and controversies, such as 'gaycake' (legal cases concerning bakeries refusing to provide cakes celebrating same sex weddings or the right to them) and the banning of minarets and hijabs. Thus, students in the study widely recognised the relevance and importance of religion and belief in the world, and felt that this makes it something they need to know about:

> 'I'd say as Britain is becoming more multi-faith and multicultural, it's important to learn about it because it's becoming more and more relevant.... I think it's important so you can understand what other people believe in life.' (Student)

> 'You're going to meet all kinds of people, you don't know what the future holds, and it's important that you have at

least awareness and consideration for everything that you might come across.' (Student)

For teachers, a key concern was how to balance engagement with both breadth and depth. This was partly a response to time constraints, though there was also broad agreement that the focus on one or two traditions at GCSE level is too narrow. This points to a key dilemma for the reform of RE: how much can be done, and when? This is illustrated in the following quotes:

> 'I'd learn the different sects and denominations but you can't spend much time talking about differences between individuals because there's not enough time.' (Teacher)

> 'I think it is important that they do obviously understand the ones that a majority of the people in the world follow but there are also other belief systems out there as well that they should be learning about.' (Teacher)

As well as the diversity of traditions, participants felt it important to explore diversity within traditions and diversity at the individual level in terms of interpretation:

> 'It's such a broad thing, so to say, like, Christians believe that, like, having women bishops is wrong ... is a really difficult thing to say ... there could be some people who are Christian who completely don't think that.' (Pupil)

> 'It's important for pupils to know that there are lots of people that would tick a religious box but not practise it, and that that doesn't make their religion any less valid than those following it more closely.... There are spectrums everywhere.' (Teacher)

> 'It's not something you can just learn as a block. It's individual what you believe.' (Pupil)

To add to the time pressure, all groups showed an interest in learning about informal, non-traditional religion and belief, as well as the traditions. That curricula are often restricted to two, let alone the 'big six', was evident in participants' appetite for the study of other, non-traditional world views that do not easily fit into the current RE framework:

> 'Obviously, you can't look at them all, but I think it is important to look at how people have beliefs but they may not be within a formal religion.' (Parent)

> 'It's like a mind map of religion because within that, you've got religions that aren't necessarily religious but are spiritual.' (Teacher)

Likewise, all groups agreed that non-religion and non-religious beliefs should be studied, with humanism and atheism most referred to:

> 'I would hope that RE would include units on atheism and agnosticism, not just as footnotes, but as important sets of beliefs in themselves.' (Teacher)

> 'They don't like to say that they are a religion, but they are a set of beliefs and so they should be learnt in the same way.' (Student)

At the same time, all groups emphasised the importance of learning about 'lived' religion. Within this, teachers observed an oversimplification in the GCSE, which sets up religion and belief as unchanging blocks of tradition, rather than fluid identities: "You're not going to meet a Christian and start talking about how Jesus was born, or Adam and Eve, which is something we cover a lot in RE ... you should learn more about what people do in everyday lives" (student). This naturally leads to an emphasis among all groups that RE should also address the contemporary, including controversies and dilemmas. Students particularly prioritise the contemporary over the historical and are especially keen to study real-world controversies:

> 'I think it's interesting when we look at the big disasters and the terrorists ... then we look at why they did it, from their religion, what were their reasons, what we've done to them.... I find that more interesting.' (Student)

> 'You're not really doing RE unless you lift up the rug. If we teach them Christians are all kind people, then they'll

get to history and hear about the crusades or slavery and go, "What?"' (Teacher)

'They need to know about Jihadi John, and that sort of thing.' (Parent)

These responses suggest the need to challenge existing orthodoxies and that reformed RE should reflect the religious landscape as we really find it, as revealed by cutting-edge theory and data on the study of contemporary religion and belief. This would mean finding room for: the study of a broad range of religions, beliefs and non-religion; the exploration of religion, belief and non-belief as a category; the exploration of the changing religion and belief landscape and its impacts on contemporary society; a focus on contemporary issues and the role of religion and belief in current affairs and controversies; a focus on the relevance of religion and belief for workplaces and working life; and an exploration of religion and belief as lived identity as well as tradition.

Within this, the study also looked at what school RE should be for. It found that, whether in inner-city or more rural schools, participants were concerned about engagement with diversity. They felt that RE should help them to manage difference positively and to avoid offence:

'It's for our future as well because if you're not used to being around them sort of people now ... when you're older and working and you come across one of them, you know what to say and what not to say ... so you don't accidentally say something they could be offended by.' (Student)

Students also had a developed sense of how religion and belief may manifest itself in the workplace, and they see RE as key to preparing them for this:

'Understanding why, if you're an employer, why different people might have to do things slightly different to others, so when they have to take more time off for religious reasons, why they work a certain amount of hours, why they have to work differently, speak to people differently. And some Muslims have to pray a certain amount of times and people need to understand that.' (Student)

However, there was also a perception that there has been a colonisation of the RE space, particularly where RE is combined with personal, social, health and economic education (PSHE) or citizenship education. The majority wanted RE as a separate lesson:

> 'We're supposed to be doing RE and then we're doing global warming.' (Student)

> 'Quite often, we're not really looking at religion. It's just different opinions.' (Student)

> 'You couldn't learn the core things about belief and worship anywhere else. In other lessons, you might see the social side, but the core is RE.' (Student)

> 'You might cover it briefly in other subjects, like in history when you cover other religions, but then you move onto something else ... you need RE to focus on the religion.' (Student)

Crucially, the study found that specialist RE teachers emphasised the intrinsic value of religion and belief learning while non-specialists emphasised its role in cohesion:

> 'The academic study of religion as a phenomenon in the world.' (Specialist RE teacher)

> 'It's more to do with education for education's sake. It should be exciting to go out and engage with difference.' (Specialist RE teacher)

> 'Particularly here because it's not a very diverse community and some of our students may go on to university or they might go to cities to work and not be prepared for anyone that's different.' (Non-specialist teacher of RE)

> 'Ultimately, it's not about someone who can answer the pub question on Hinduism; it's about someone who can go out there and relate to someone of the Hindu faith.' (Non-specialist teacher of RE)

Specialist RE teachers were rather troubled by a lack of shared aims and purposes for RE, and many felt that there is simply not the time to do all that is asked of RE:

> 'Make it an academic subject, be honest about it. If it's about holistic development, be honest about it. But it can't be both. Not in an hour a week.' (Teacher)

> 'It's almost like two different subjects within RS [religious studies].' (Teacher)

> 'It's very confused. One of the issues in RE generally is it isn't a thing. It's a strange collective of subjects, which, depending what your own background is, you come at from your own way.' (Teacher)

> 'It does feel like you are being pulled in lots of different directions.' (Teacher)

There was a broad consensus that learning about religion and belief should play a role in developing students' spirituality – the development of a non-materialistic, spiritual side to life, including a sense of identity, self-worth and personal insight, and the development of a pupil's soul, personality or character. Although the RE classroom is considered an explicit space for this, there is significant insistence that this should not be the sole responsibility of RE:

> 'They need to work out what their own beliefs are.' (Teacher)

> 'It's one of the few subjects you can delve, beyond academia ... how [young people] think and how they feel and allow them also to have a spiritual response. That doesn't have to be [a response] around the world faith, but to have a response that comes from deep within.' (Teacher)

Of 90 teachers who expressed an opinion, 86 per cent said that RE should be included in the national curriculum:

> 'I think that like the rest of the national curriculum, these are essential bits of knowledge and skills that equip someone to live in our modern world.' (Teacher)

> 'It's very diverse; the youngsters' experiences can be very different from class to class, or from school to school. Therefore, if there was a national curriculum and there

was a requirement for these skills to be covered and these topic areas to be covered, at least you would know that youngsters have that basic knowledge going through to 16–18. At the moment, it is too diverse and too unpredictable.' (Teacher)

Of those teachers who expressed an opinion, 99 per cent favoured compulsory 'religious education' (of whom 11 per cent specified to age 14, 34 per cent to age 16 and another 38 per cent to age 18). Only one teacher thought that 'religious education' should not be compulsory:

'The level of importance that it has around the planet means we should keep it.' (Teacher)

'I think if it's not taught, I don't think it's something students would otherwise think about or consider.' (Teacher)

'all the way through because some of the things you discuss require a level of maturity that you can only discuss later. The fact-gathering is done in lower school but the application takes time.' (Teacher)

One possible solution to the problem of instrumentalisation may lie in a distinction being drawn between 'vocational' and 'academic' strands in the study of religion and belief, with an emphasis on vocational elements for everybody and academic elements within the GCSE:

'something that was really tailored for preparation in the workplace of multi-faith people, something like that, then that kind of a key skills unit, that could be really helpful. What are the rights of people with religion? How do you need to act towards these people? What it's not okay for you to say or do in the workplace.' (Teacher)

'We're supposed to be preparing them for life and that means encountering these things, so I definitely think it should be in a classroom dedicated to it. But it's useful to have it in those other areas so they can see how it applies and why we learn it.' (Teacher)

'The ethical and moral side of it should be fostered across the curriculum and then leave the actual teaching about [religion and belief] to RE.' (Teacher)

'RE as a standalone subject is something that is quite powerful; I think it sends out a powerful message as well to the students. So, it's not RE and PSHE, it's not RE as part of humanities or citizenship, it's RE as a credible subject.' (Teacher)

Conclusions

These findings, and the reflections before them, imply the need for a reconsideration of the context in which religion and belief learning takes place in schools in order to clarify the muddles, especially in the relationship between learning inside RE, outside in other subjects and in the wider life of schools (as Chapter 4 will consider). There are likely to be particularly challenging implications for the amount of time that might be needed – and found – to do religion and belief justice. Based on the research findings, wherever religion and belief learning occurs, content should reflect the breadth of the religion and belief landscape and focus not solely, or even primarily, on traditions. Nor should it overemphasise instrumental concerns about cohesion and citizenship. Rather, religion and belief learning should be concerned with preparing students for the practical task of engagement with the rich variety of religion and belief encounters in everyday, ordinary life. It seems especially important to model the distinctions within and between religions and beliefs, and to be clear about their differences and overlaps with other school concerns around ethics, morals, values and spirituality. Clarity of purpose, content and structure seems essential to the goal of socialising young people to do likewise.

4

Religion and belief across schools

Introduction

Religion and belief are not simply the preserve of RE in schools, though they may be most obvious there. They also appear in the requirement of the act of daily worship, as well as in the right to withdraw – a right belonging only to this sphere and to sex education, apparently two areas in need of more than usually sensitive handling. However, religion and belief are implied, and have implications, throughout the whole life of schools. The muddle spills over throughout. A number of spaces complement, supplement, overlap with and even colonise the formal business of 'religious education'. 'Spiritual, moral, social and cultural education' (SMSC), 'British values', the 'Prevent duty', 'citizenship education', Personal, Social, Health and Economic education (PSHE) and 'relationships and sex education' (RSE) are all interrelated parts of socialising pupils in religion and belief in schools, and each does so from its own epistemological and normative starting points, which do not necessarily line up. This brings its own layer of confusion. This chapter examines each of these spaces in turn, as well as in relation to each other and RE.

SMSC

The Education Act 2002 includes for the first time the requirement that all schools promote the 'spiritual, moral, social and cultural' development of pupils. This is part of a trend since the early 1980s towards measurement, and Rees (2017) notes that it is 'a sad indictment of education in the UK, especially England, that we have narrowed the success indicators for organisations and individuals to a few things that we (think we) can measure'. Nevertheless, he sees the introduction of SMSC as broadly positive, in that it challenges a narrowly understood knowledge-based education that valorises 'subjects' over the development of the person and community. Indeed, this is a plank in the Education Act 1944, which gave local education authorities the duty to contribute towards 'the spiritual, moral, mental, and physical development of the community'. More contemporary legislation has added a statutory obligation to promote pupils' well-being (Children Act 2004), and to prepare children and young people for the challenges, opportunities and responsibilities of adult life (Education Act 1996). It is also the case that all state-funded schools must meet the expectations of the national curriculum: 'Every state-funded school must offer a curriculum which is balanced and broadly based and which promotes the spiritual, moral, cultural, mental and physical development of pupils at the school and of society [and] prepares pupils at the school for the opportunities, responsibilities and experiences of later life' (DfE, 2013). Schools also have a duty under the Equality Act 2010 to ensure that teaching is accessible to all, including those who are lesbian, gay, bisexual and transgender (LGBT+). It has been argued that 'High quality SMSC … can help to foster good relations between pupils, tackle prejudice – including trans and homophobia – and promote understanding and respect, to enable all members of the school community to flourish' (Rees 2017: 27). Yet, at the same time, schools do not have to teach specific lessons on SMSC development, and the language within it is fiendishly difficult to pin down once closely scrutinised.

Thus, 'spiritual development' is defined in terms of competences and themes: exploring beliefs and experience; respecting faiths, feelings and values; enjoying learning about oneself, others and the surrounding world; using imagination and creativity; and reflecting. Ofsted (2015) assesses pupils' spiritual development in terms of their:

> ability to be reflective about their own beliefs, religious or otherwise, that inform their perspective on life and their interest in and respect for different people's faiths, feelings and values; sense of enjoyment and fascination in learning about themselves, others and the world around them; and use of imagination and creativity in their learning willingness to reflect on their experiences.

Moral development describes being able to: 'recognise right and wrong; respect the law; understand consequences; investigate moral and ethical issues; offer reasoned views' (Ofsted, 2015). This is assessed by Ofsted (2015) in terms of their:

> ability to recognise the difference between right and wrong and to readily apply this understanding in their own lives, recognise legal boundaries and, in so doing, respect the civil and criminal law of England; understanding of the consequences of their behaviour and actions; interest in

investigating and offering reasoned views about moral and ethical issues and ability to understand and appreciate the viewpoints of others on these issues.

Social development is defined as being able to: 'use a range of social skills; participate in the local community; appreciate diverse viewpoints; participate, volunteer and cooperate; resolve conflict; engage with the "British values" of democracy, the rule of law, liberty, and respect and tolerance' (Ofsted, 2015). It is assessed by Ofsted (2015) in terms of being able to:

> use of a range of social skills in different contexts, for example working and socialising with other pupils, including those from different religious, ethnic and socio-economic backgrounds; willingness to participate in a variety of communities and social settings, including by volunteering, cooperating well with others and being able to resolve conflicts effectively; acceptance and engagement with the fundamental British values of democracy, the rule of law, individual liberty and mutual respect and tolerance of those with different faiths and beliefs; they can develop and demonstrate skills and attitudes that will allow them to participate fully in and contribute positively to life in modern Britain.

Cultural development is being able to: 'appreciate cultural influences; appreciate the role of Britain's parliamentary system; participate in culture/cultural opportunities; and understand, accept, respect and celebrate diversity' (Ofsted, 2015). Ofsted (2015) assesses this in schools in terms of:

> understanding and appreciation of the wide range of cultural influences that have shaped their own heritage and those of others; understanding and appreciation of the range of different cultures within school and further afield as an essential element of their preparation for life in modern Britain; knowledge of Britain's democratic parliamentary system and its central role in shaping our history and values, and in continuing to develop Britain; willingness to participate in and respond positively to artistic, musical, sporting and cultural opportunities; interest in exploring, improving understanding of and showing respect for

different faiths and cultural diversity and the extent to which they understand, accept, respect and celebrate diversity, as shown by their tolerance and attitudes towards different religious, ethnic and socio-economic groups in the local, national and global communities.

Here, culture and religion are elided such that they could be construed as interchangeable. According to Ofsted (2015), an 'outstanding' school will have a 'thoughtful and wide-ranging promotion of pupils' spiritual, moral, social and cultural development', while an 'inadequate' school will have 'serious weaknesses in the overall promotion of pupils' spiritual, moral, social and cultural development'.

It is difficult to argue with the aims described but this is largely because they fall into the category of what has been called elsewhere 'cosy ideas', such as 'community' and 'empowerment' (Demaine and Entwistle, 1996). At best, they provide a sense of aspiration; at worst, they are vague to the point of meaninglessness. This reveals a critical problem with SMSC in its lack of tangible definitions. This is highlighted by the attempt to assess it in school inspections. It is unclear how inspectors will know whether they have seen any of what is set out. What does it look like to 'be reflective about their own beliefs, religious or otherwise, that inform their perspective on life and their interest in and respect for different people's faiths, feelings and values' (Ofsted, 2015)? What actually is the 'difference between right and wrong' (Ofsted, 2015)? What is it to succeed in 'working and socialising with other pupils, including those from different religious, ethnic and socio-economic backgrounds' (Ofsted, 2015)? What is an 'interest in exploring, improving understanding of and showing respect for different faiths and cultural diversity' (Ofsted, 2015)?

This highlights a challenge for the religion and belief literacy of inspectors, let alone for the teachers and school leaders who are expected to operationalise these terms and ideas for children. At another level, it is notable that the SMSC approach, while including religion and belief, does not draw the distinction between the categories that it entails: religion and belief, spirituality, morality, sociality, and culture. These are difficult boundaries to draw, and elements certainly overlap. However, the absence even of a critical acknowledgement of the difficulties in pinning them down and distinguishing them makes it all the harder for pupils, teachers and parents to tell the differences themselves. Certainly, female genital mutilation is one example of a confusion of cultural norms with religious ones, which encapsulates the importance of being able to tell the difference. It is simply not the case that all Muslims do *this*, or all Christians do *that*. They are culturally inflected, as well as having some dimensions in common. Yet, SMSC risks socialising pupils in the same conceptual muddles that it tries to address. There is a probability that pupils will leave school unclear about the differences and overlaps between religion, morality, values, ethnicity and culture.

British values

As of November 2014, all British schools have a duty to promote defined 'British values'. These are described as 'democracy, the rule of law, individual liberty, and mutual respect for and tolerance of those with different faiths and beliefs' (DfE, 2014). They are set out in the Department for Education's document *Promoting Fundamental British Values as Part of SMSC in Schools* (DfE, 2014) and Part 2 of the Education (Independent School Standards) Regulations 2014 for academies and independent schools.[1] 'British values' are thus located at the heart of SMSC. The introduction to the guidance makes clear that:

> It is expected that pupils should understand that while different people may hold different views about what is 'right' and 'wrong', all people living in England are subject to its law. The school's ethos and teaching, which schools should make parents aware of, should support the rule of English civil and criminal law and schools should not teach anything that undermines it. If schools teach about religious law, particular care should be taken to explore the relationship between state and religious law. Pupils should be made aware of the difference between the law of the land and religious law. (DfE, 2014: 4)

The knowledge and understanding expected of pupils is set out. They must obtain:

> an understanding of how citizens can influence decision-making through the democratic process; an appreciation that living under the rule of law protects individual citizens and is essential for their wellbeing and safety; an understanding that there is a separation of power between the executive and the judiciary, and that while some public bodies such as the police and the army can be held to account through Parliament, others such as the courts maintain independence;

an understanding that the freedom to choose and hold other faiths and beliefs is protected in law; an acceptance that other people having different faiths or beliefs to oneself (or having none) should be accepted and tolerated, and should not be the cause of prejudicial or discriminatory behaviour; and an understanding of the importance of identifying and combating discrimination. (DfE, 2014)

The guidance is both uncomfortably broad (in the generality of the values themselves) and narrowly focused (in its anxiety to promote state law against the Aunt Sally of an assertion of religious law, by which it primarily implies sharia). It is highly notable that respect and tolerance for different faiths or beliefs is one of just five British values at all. It suggests that governments are highly conscious of and concerned with the role of religion and belief in the public square sphere. The implied policy goal already imbues a sense of risk while failing to engage with religious systems of jurisprudence as potentially interesting and important objects of study themselves. They are circumscribed as problematic before any exploration even begins. Whatever the rights and wrongs of this, the normativities are there, and they contribute to the muddle. The message is both that religions must be *respected* and *suspected* because they are sometimes at odds with the state – and, on occasion, can be viciously violent. This is also true of a range of beliefs and world views, including Far Right nationalism and racism, but these are not singled out in this way or in this context (though this is now acknowledged in 'Prevent' documents). This suggests that there may be better ways of having this important conversation more directly. After all, almost everybody agrees that extremism is dangerous and undesirable, and that toleration and respect are positive and helpful. However, implying rather than expressing the distinction is unhelpful. Yet, the political underpinnings are clear. They are set out in an explanatory note to the Education Select Committee in 2014 from the Parliamentary Under Secretary of State for Schools. He said that the changes were designed to 'tighten up the standards on pupil welfare to improve safeguarding, and the standards on spiritual, moral, social and cultural development of pupils *to strengthen the barriers to extremism*' (DfE, 2014: emphasis added).

Prevent in schools

This implied emphasis on religious extremism as a driver of learning about religion and belief in schools is also apparent in 'Prevent'.

Since July 2015, the 'Prevent duty' means that schools have a legal duty to prevent pupils from being radicalised into extremism. The Department for Education recommends addressing this through citizenship teaching in secondary schools, and stresses that this should be regarded as a child protection issue and treated as part of schools' wider safeguarding duties.

This has been widely criticised for the resulting 'securitisation' of religion in the school space, with examples from the US, Europe and the United Nations being used to illustrate an emergent interface of religion, education and security (see Gearon, 2013). Religion is thus implicated in a new and explicit way for political and security purposes, marking a new connection of the political with the religious. This also renders RE itself susceptible to colonisation as learning is increasingly circumscribed by political and social agendas that squeeze out the intellectual curiosity of the subject. Paradoxically, in the context of this squeeze, it has been suggested that 'Many religious educators are content to comply with seemingly benign political agendas that, to put it crudely, have provided a post-9/11 boon for their subject' (Gearon, 2013: 130).

It has also been noted in international contexts that the Organisation for Security and Cooperation in Europe (OSCE) has centralised religion in education post-9/11, as exemplified in the Toledo Guiding Principles on Teaching about Religions and Beliefs in Public Schools (OSCE, 2017). This states that 'It is important for young people to acquire a better understanding of the role that religions play in today's pluralistic world. The need for such education will continue to grow as different cultures and identities interact with each other through travel, commerce, media or migration' (OSCE, 2017: 9). One critic observes that 'The idea that a former Cold War security organization should be interested in developing teaching and learning materials does not seem to have struck many as anything out of the ordinary' (Gearon, 2013: 134). Gearon also notes other international examples of the growing intersection between religion and security in education: in Afghanistan, a review of materials on religion in education underpins new approaches to teaching as an instrument in countering insurgency (Borchgrevink and Berg Karpviken, 2010); and in Pakistan, Fair's (2008) *Madrassah Challenge: Militancy and Religious Education in Pakistan* explicitly links religion, education and security. Likewise, the REsilience initiative of the Religious Education Council of England and Wales aimed to counter extremism through religious education.[2] Gearon observes an expanding market in educational materials in this area.

Prevent thus intertwines education and security, and has been criticised for failing to solve the problem of Muslim stigmatisation already present in community Prevent programmes outside of schools (Davies, 2014). Thus, 'Arab and Muslim youth are presumed to be a vulnerable population, predisposed to extremism and needing guidance to overcome "the trap of radicalization" ... to become modern, moderate, and democratic subjects' (Shirazi, 2017: 3). This approach has been described as a strategy of overly simple 'net widening' and of having 'fallen into the political trap set up by Islamist terrorists ... [fuelling] the rhetoric of a domestic clash of civilisations' (Bonino, 2016: 241). Indeed, literature across the disciplines of sociology, criminology and security studies has extensively criticised the British government for widening the net beyond terrorist groups to target Muslim communities at large, just in case (Pantazis and Pemberton, 2009), as well as stigmatising and alienating Muslims qua Muslims (Bartlett and Birdwell, 2010) through extensive surveillance (Thomas, 2012). In this context, the organisation Families Against Stress and Trauma (FAST), which works with schools and the families of radicalised British Muslims, reports that Prevent does not give teachers sufficient training and its approach could be superficial and counterproductive.[3]

Research has also examined the experiences of education professionals and found that the majority report feeling fairly confident to deliver Prevent in their schools (Busher et al, 2017). However, it also found that teachers believe that Prevent should be more fully expressed as relating to all forms of extremism, not only religious. It also finds 'widespread – and in some cases very acute – concerns about increased stigmatisation of Muslim students in the context of the Prevent duty' (Busher et al, 2017: 7). It concludes that 'the Prevent Duty is making it more difficult to foster an environment in which students from different backgrounds get on well with one another' (Busher et al, 2017: 6). Clearly, this stands in direct contradiction to the goals of British values, SMSC and Prevent itself.

Jackson also highlights widespread concern among teachers around Prevent, citing the General Secretary of the National Union of Teachers, who commented that 'the Prevent counter-extremism strategy was causing significant nervousness and confusion among teachers and that concerns over extremism could close down classroom debate designed to encourage democracy and human rights' (Jackson, 2016). He refers to a newspaper article heading: 'Jesus Would Have Been Done for Extremism under This Government'.[4] He contrasts the UK's focus on British values and SMSC as a counterterrorism strategy with the approach of the Council of Europe. This is grounded in human rights values described as 'a positive emphasis on learning to live together within societies that are inclusive, rather than a preoccupation with identifying remarks and actions that could be considered as potentially extremist' (Council of Europe, 2015).

Jackson (2016: 23) also makes the point that anti-extremism education 'potentially, and inadvertently, undermines the "democratic" justification that it claims to uphold' and warns of a danger of 'slippage towards authoritarianism'. He advocates for 'a more nuanced form of "dialogical liberalism" which seeks a greater degree of dialogue between values as expressed in the human rights codes, and values that are rooted in particular religious and cultural contexts, than is to be found in some of the rhetoric of the UK Government' (Jackson, 2016: 23).

Citizenship education

A new subject called 'citizenship' was included for the first time in England from September 2002. This followed a review by what was called the Crick Group, which was established in 1997 to develop a working definition of citizenship education and to make recommendations for how to deliver it in schools. The review noted that there is no real tradition of dedicated teaching of this kind in English schools and no consistent framework for discussion in this area. Concomitantly, there is no solid knowledge and research base. It also noted that attempts to shape citizenship are themselves often the result of perceived crises in wider society, and that, to this extent, this represents another aspect of the instrumentalisation of education for political aims. Kerr (2003: 9) thus recalls that 'The Conservative Government urged individuals to take up actively their civic responsibilities rather than leave it to the government to carry them out.' Conversely, he notes that 'The new Labour Government, which came to power in May 1997, championed a different approach to citizenship and citizenship education. This was a definition associated with the communitarian movement with a particular emphasis on "civic morality"' (Kerr, 2003: 11). He sees this as 'part of the wider philosophy of "new Labour" based on the civic responsibilities of the individual in partnership with the state' (Kerr, 2003: 14).

The definition adopted by the Crick Group was centred on 'civic participation' and based on a 'civic republican' concept of citizenship deriving from the Athenian polis, wherein civic life is understood in terms of community and the political obligations of individuals to it. Thus, Aristotle defines the citizen as 'someone who participates in public affairs' through the innate natural order of homo politicus, which ethically requires it (Germino, 2000). Such a conception focuses on the mutuality of membership and the shared life of the polis, and is understood as citizenship by practice. This conception aimed to synthesise 'liberal-individualist' and 'communitarian' concepts of citizenship rooted in 'the three elements of citizenship – namely the civil, the political and the social – contained in T.H. Marshall's classic definition ... The definition reinstated the second element – the political – which had been strangely silent in the Conservative government's "active citizenship" in the early 1990s' (Kerr, 2003: 14). Citizenship is taught as part of a non-statutory framework for PSHE (see later) at Key Stages 1 and 2 (pupils aged 5–11), and as a new statutory foundation subject at Key Stages 3 and 4 (pupils aged 11–16). Schools have been legally required to deliver citizenship education at Key Stages 3 and 4 since September 2002.

Government guidance for citizenship is available in the national curriculum guidance for Key Stages 3 and 4 (ages 11–16) and for citizenship within PSHE at Key Stages 1 and 2 (ages 5–11). In relation to Key Stages 1 and 2 (ages 5–11), the government provides non-statutory programmes of study.[5] At Key Stage 1 (ages 5–7), these state that 'pupils learn about themselves as developing individuals and as members of their communities, building on their own experiences and on the early learning goals for personal, social and emotional development' (DfE, 2014). There are references to 'knowing what is right and wrong' and to being able to 'identify and respect the differences and similarities between people', as well as to 'consider social and moral dilemmas' (DfE, 2014: 1–2). None of this is unpacked in any way and these complex ideas of community, right and wrong, difference, and morality are left hanging, rather than being connected to the study of them that goes on in the RE space. Thus, they are taught in RE as religion and belief and socialised here as secular. Then, at Key Stage 2 (ages 7–11), the goal is that 'pupils learn about themselves as growing and changing individuals with their own experiences and ideas, and as members of their communities' (DfE, 2014: 3). Crucially, they are also to learn about 'moral responsibility' and to 'reflect on spiritual, moral, social, and cultural issues, using imagination to understand other people's experiences' (DfE, 2014: 3). At this stage, they are also encouraged to 'appreciate the range of national, regional, religious and ethnic identities in the United Kingdom' (DfE, 2014: 4). In a section headed 'Developing Good Relationships and Respecting the Differences between People', they are encouraged to learn that 'differences and similarities between people arise from a number of factors, including cultural, ethnic, racial and religious diversity, gender and disability' (DfE, 2014: 4). They are also asked to 'meet and talk with people ... who contribute to society ... for example ... religious leaders' (DfE, 2014: 5).

Yet, in guidance for Key Stage 3 (ages 11–14) and Key Stage 4 (ages 14–16), religion and belief are not mentioned or even implied at all.[6] This guidance states that 'citizenship education should foster pupils' keen awareness and understanding of democracy, government and how laws are made and upheld' (DfE, 2013). It should also 'prepare pupils to take their place in society as responsible citizens, manage their money well and make sound financial decisions' (DfE, 2013). This has been followed up with more detailed, separate, 'schemes of work' for citizenship at Key Stage 3 (pupils aged 11–14), Key Stage 4 (pupils aged 14–16) and one for Key Stages 1 and 2 (pupils aged 5–11). In the 2010 QCA scheme of work, pupils are invited merely to 'consider their identities and the different national, cultural, religious, regional and ethnic identities and communities to which they belong', and the scheme states that 'the focus of this unit is on respect for diversity in our society'.[7] Thus, pupils' journeys through their understanding of religion and belief as an aspect of citizenship is not only minimal, but also internally incoherent, as well as making no necessary connection with RE, SMSC, PSHE or other appearances of religion and belief in the wider life of the school.

Key debates around the role of religion in relation to citizenship education include discussion of why religion was not there in the first place despite Jackson's (2003: 67) argument that RE 'complements citizenship education through the process of helping children debate issues relevant to plural society'. In contrast, he recalls the alignment of Christian and moral education in the early half of the 20th century, quoting the Institute of Christian Education in 1954: 'The Ministry of Education Pamphlet No.16, *Citizens Growing Up*, plainly says (p.10) that Christian belief and practice are the most secure foundations for the building of a true and enduring citizenship' (Jackson, 2003: 68). Jackson goes on to track the effects of secularisation, plurality and globalisation leading to the separation of religious, moral and political education. He argues that the debate about the relationship between religious, moral and citizenship education was reopened in the 1990s, though the Crick Report (DfEE, 1998) did not discuss the relationship between citizenship and religion. Jackson sees the agency of policy secularism in this, arguing that David Hargreaves, Professor of Education at Cambridge and until 2001 Chief Executive of the QCA, was very influential on New Labour policy and had widely argued that 'in a secular, plural society, religion can no longer be the basis of a socially cohesive civic education' (quoted in Jackson, 2003: 70). Hargreaves had proposed an expansion of faith schools that nurtured a shared moral and religious culture, and that in secular schools, RE should be abolished and *replaced* with citizenship. This was based on the premise that 'whereas Christianity formerly provided a moral basis for civic life, now the public language of citizenship provides the necessary social cement, also functioning as a bridge to the "second languages" of the distinct moralities of the various religions now actively present in society' (quoted in Jackson, 2003: 71). Thus, for Hargreaves, religion was seen as a force to be moderated rather than as a tool to support understanding of global citizenship. Its bracketing off into a small number of faith schools was his proposed answer.

Despite this, within citizenship policy, there seems to be a growing recognition of the importance of religion and belief, but it is largely located within somewhat anxious discourse around cohesion. The National Foundation for Educational Research (NFER) was commissioned by the former Department for Education and Skills (DfES) to conduct a longitudinal study on citizenship provision and its impact (through 2001–10). While an interim report documents the addition of a new strand that pays attention to 'critical thinking about ethnicity, religion and race' (DfE, 2007), it does not discuss it further and the final report understands citizenship only as political literacy and civic participation, with the only mention of religion being in relation to 'participation in community groups'.

In this vacuum, Gearon (2013) produced a guidance paper on RE and citizenship in 2009. In this, he charts the historical neglect of religion in citizenship education and the increased focus in recent times on human rights, along with the 'reciprocal neglect of citizenship within religious education' (Gearon, 2013: 9). He presents 'pathways' to support teachers in RE and citizenship to 'bridge as well as demarcate the differences' between the two subjects (Gearon, 2013: 30). The 'pathways' are suggestions of how to explore the relationship between religion and politics, including explorations of religion and human rights. A key message from this is that 'however much we explore the relationships between religion and politics and education, religion can never be reduced to politics' (Gearon, 2013: 44). Gearon (2013: 45) argues that while 'a self-critical appreciation of religion's political role here is important, it also potentially risks reducing religion's broader theological, metaphysical and existential scope'.

This is echoed in EU commitments to citizenship education, where religion is not mentioned specifically, but assumed to be part of 'cultural diversity'. In an attempt to rescue this religion–citizenship breach, Jackson's work with the Council of Europe has been path-breaking. In 2008, the Council of Europe (2008) called on member states to 'pursue initiatives in the field of intercultural education relating to the diversity of religions and non-religious convictions in order to promote tolerance and the development of a culture of "living together"'. Jackson's response was *Signposts*, which emerged out of a 2008 report by the Children's Identity & Citizenship in Europe (CiCe) working group and places learning about religion at the heart of citizenship. The report is based on the premise that religion and civic education have been historically entwined and then forcibly divorced from one another in the late 20th century. Using Ireland as an example, the report sees this trend across Europe. The report documents the 'recovery of the religious roots of citizenship' within the EU in the 21st century due to 'an enhanced sense of the significance of religion as a cultural phenomenon and as a significant feature of civilisation' (CiCe, 2008: 6). It calls for the 'recognition of religion as a source of positive civic values … [and] the need to be able to understand religion as a feature of social diversity' (CiCe, 2008: 6). Religion also features in a section on school culture and student participation, where meeting representatives of various religions is given as an example of intercultural dialogue. It quotes the Council of Europe policy document on religious knowledge as being 'an integral part of the knowledge of the history of mankind and civilisation' (Council of Europe, 2005: clause 8, quoted in CiCe, 2008: 9). In relation to religion as a source of moral good, the report cites the recommendation of the Norwegian Ministry of Education that 'Biblical similes as well as illustrations from other religions, from history, fiction, biography, and from legends, parables, myths and fables be used as part of moral and civic education' (Royal Ministry of Education, Research and Church Affairs, 1997: 9, quoted in CiCe, 2008: 8). Thus, while the 'the fundamental rationale for including religion in the Council of Europe's educational work relates to human rights, citizenship and intercultural education', Jackson (2016: 6) is careful to state that it does not ignore aspects of personal development related to learning about religion(s) or reduce religion to culture.

In 2010, the Council of Europe and the European Wergeland Centre in Oslo established a joint committee to investigate how to support policymakers and practitioners in taking forward the 2008 recommendations. A survey was conducted of member states around the potential challenges of meeting the recommendations and the issues raised. Common themes were: ambiguity and a lack of clarity in terminology associated with teaching about religions and beliefs;

a need to understand the component elements of 'competence' for understanding religions; how to make the classroom a 'safe space' for discussion and dialogue by students; how to help students to analyse representations of religions in the media; how to integrate a study of non-religious convictions and world views with the study of religions; how to tackle human rights issues in relation to religion and belief in schools and classrooms; and how to link schools to wider communities and organisations, with the goal of increasing students' knowledge about and understanding of religions and non-religious philosophies, such as secular humanism (Jackson, 2016: 9). *Signposts* (Jackson, 2014) was written in response to this. There is a strong emphasis in *Signposts* on 'intercultural encounter between different faiths and worldviews, the importance of learning about the internal diversity of religions, as well as gaining a sense of religions as distinct phenomena' (Jackson, 2016: 14). *Signposts* has now been translated into 11 languages (Arabic, Dutch, English, French, German, Greek, Norwegian, Romanian, Russian, Spanish, Swedish and Ukrainian, with more to follow), and is being used in various initial teacher-training courses across Europe.

PSHE

PSHE is another element in schools that contributes to children's ideas of religion and belief. This had been a non-statutory subject, though PSHE education is compulsory in all state-maintained schools from 2020. The overall goal is 'making sure children and learners are taught how to keep themselves safe' (PSHE Association, 2014). It is expected to form part of the SMSC provision, and within that, inspectors are required to evaluate the effectiveness and impact of the provision 'for pupils' spiritual, moral, social and cultural (SMSC) development, with PSHE education playing a key role in this' (PSHE Association, 2014). PSHE is expressly regarded as a central part of schools' duties in relation to promoting pupil well-being and pupil safeguarding (Children Act 2004) and community cohesion (Education Act 2006). Thus, in paragraph 41 of statutory guidance on *Keeping Children Safe in Education*, the Department for Education (DfE, 2018: 22) states that 'schools should consider how children may be taught about safeguarding, including online, through teaching and learning opportunities. This may include covering relevant issues through PSHE'. Thus, the PSHE space is trying to do a lot of heavy lifting in terms of child protection as well as overall SMSC development. Relevant issues that may be covered in PSHE education include child sexual exploitation and other forms of abuse, the sharing of sexual images, the impact of online pornography on pupils, the dangers of extremism and radicalisation, forced marriage, and honour-based violence and female genital mutilation (FGM). In this, it locates religion and belief within a distinctively risk-oriented milieu.

The PSHE space is also full of internal inconsistencies, and it muddles the messages coming in from other parts of the school. Overall, it is located as key to providing a 'balanced and broadly-based curriculum' that promotes 'the spiritual, moral, cultural, mental and physical development of pupils at the school and of society, and prepares pupils at the school for the opportunities, responsibilities and experiences of later life' (Section 78 of the Education Act 2002). Schools are also required to provide 'opportunities to explore, clarify and if necessary challenge their own and others' values, attitudes, beliefs, rights and responsibilities' (PSHE Association, 2014).

The UK government funds the PSHE Association to support PSHE teaching and learning, and their advice states that 'We recommend that PSHE education should be taught in discrete lessons, supported by other learning opportunities across the curriculum, including the use of enhancement days where possible' (PSHE Association, 2014). In practice, this often means that PSHE themes appear in subjects that are seen to be overlapping, including RE. Despite this – and the headline references to 'spiritual' and 'moral' learning – of 262 learning items across the PSHE scheme of work, only 13 (5 per cent) relate to issues that share major and obvious overlapping themes with religion and belief (extremism and cohesion, honour-based violence, same-sex marriage, FGM, forced marriage, and shame). A further 11 *imply* religion and belief but do not state the relationship. Only two (0.8 per cent) mention religion or belief directly. Thus, the boundaries between the wider issues included in PSHE in general and those about religion and belief in particular are permeable, to say the least. It could be argued that this socialises children to be unable to tell the difference between religion, morality, culture and ethnicity.

For example, guidance in Key Stage 2 on health and well-being calls for 'understanding that actions such as female genital mutilation (FGM) constitute abuse, are a crime and how to get support if they have fears for themselves or their peers' (PSHE Association, 2014: 9). This comes up again at Item 5 in Key Stage 3 on 'living in the wider world', where children are required 'to know that there are some cultural practices which are against British law and universal human rights, such as female genital mutilation' (PSHE Association, 2014: 13), and again at Item 6 in Key Stages 3 and 4 on health and well-being, which refers to 'the risks associated with female genital mutilation (FGM), its status as a criminal act and sources of support for themselves or their peers who they believe may be at risk, or who may have already been subject to FGM' (PSHE Association, 2014: 15). While these may be laudable aims in themselves, it is not clear from the guidance that either teachers or pupils will be equipped to tell the differences between the cultural, ethnic and religious aspects of FGM, in which FGM is often perceived to be a 'Muslim problem' but is, in fact, overwhelmingly cultural (happening in certain places rather than religions).

Likewise, Item 5 in Key Stage 2 on relationships states 'that civil partnerships and marriage are examples of stable, loving relationships and a public demonstration of the commitment made between two people who love and care for each other and want to spend their lives together and who are of the legal age to make that commitment' (PSHE Association, 2014: 10), and Item 6 in Key Stage 2 calls for pupils 'to be aware that marriage is a commitment freely entered into by both people, that no one should enter into a marriage if they don't absolutely want to do so' (PSHE Association, 2014: 11). Item 5 here addresses same-sex relationships, on which there is considerable controversy across and within the religious traditions, some of which has spilled over into protest actions and that therefore touch on religion, British values, citizenship and sex and relationship education (SRE). Item 6 implies the problem of forced marriage, which again has apparent overlaps with religion and belief (often regarded as a 'Hindu problem') but is actually predominantly cultural.

Again, at Item 8 in Key Stage 3 on 'relationships', pupils are expected to learn about 'different types of relationships, including those within families, friendships, romantic or intimate relationships and the factors that can affect these (including age, gender, power and interests)', and at Item 9, pupils are expected to understand 'the nature and importance of marriage, civil partnerships and other stable, long-term relationships for family life and bringing up children' (PSHE Association, 2014: 18). Again, same-sex relationships are implied here but without a critical framing in relationship to religion and belief, or to culture. At Item 10, the issue of forced marriage is again implied in the requirement that pupils should learn 'that marriage is a commitment, entered into freely, never forced through threat or coercion and how to safely access sources of support for themselves or their peers should they feel vulnerable' (PSHE Association, 2014: 18). This arises again at Item 5 in Key Stage 4 on relationships in relation to 'honour based violence, forced marriage' (PSHE Association, 2014: 18).

Notably, Item 3 in Key Stage 3 on 'living in the wider world' omits religion from a list of 'the similarities, differences and diversity among people of different race, culture, ability, disability, sex, gender identity, age and sexual orientation and the impact of stereotyping, prejudice, bullying, discrimination on individuals and communities' (PSHE Association, 2014: 20), though religion is mentioned in Item 4 about 'the potential tensions between human rights, British law and cultural and religious expectations and practices' (PSHE Association, 2014: 20).

Then, at Item 3 in Key Stage 4, there is a requirement that pupils be prepared to 'think critically about extremism and intolerance in whatever forms they take (including the concept of "shame" and "honour based" violence)' (PSHE Association, 2014: 20), and 'to recognise the shared responsibility to protect the community from violent extremism and how to respond to anything that causes anxiety or concern' (PSHE Association, 2014: 20). Finally, Item 13 states that pupils should learn that 'differences and similarities between people arise from a number of factors, including family, cultural, ethnic, racial and religious diversity, age, sex, gender identity, sexual orientation, and disability (see 'protected characteristics' in the Equality Act 2010)' (PSHE Association, 2014: 11).

Across PSHE, there is no critical acknowledgement of the overlaps or differences, and pupils are left to work out the boundaries for themselves. Moreover, the key messages that *do* appear revolve around problems – mainly of extremism but also of homophobia, honour, shame-based violence and genital mutilation. While these are clearly legitimate concerns, there is no context by which to balance the idea of religion and belief. Likewise, there is no boundary setting between identity categories that could help children and young people to tell the difference between a problem that is cultural and one that is religious. No wonder publics are muddled about religion and belief.

RSE

Another curricula area that overlaps with religion and belief is RSE. The Children and Social Work Act 2017 commits to compulsory 'relationships education' in all primary schools and 'relationships and sex education (RSE)' in all state-maintained secondary schools (except academies, which do not have to provide RSE, but must have regard to the Secretary of State's guidance when they do). The 2019 RSE guidance replaces that of 2000 and is required to be reviewed three years from first becoming required teaching in September 2020, and then every three years after that. Right at the start, it states that 'all of the compulsory subject content must be age appropriate and developmentally appropriate. It must be taught sensitively and inclusively, with respect to the backgrounds and beliefs of pupils and parents while always with the aim of providing pupils with the knowledge they need of the law'.[8] It goes on to refer to its role in 'the spiritual, moral, social, cultural, mental and physical development of pupils, at school and in society'.[9] Yet, here again, despite framing the overall area in relation to religion and belief, it goes on to mention them very sparsely, and almost entirely in terms of risks and problems. Thus, it rather obliquely states that 'Schools must consult parents in developing and reviewing their policy ... [and] should ensure that the policy ... reflects the community they serve'. It also suggests that 'A good understanding of pupils' faith backgrounds and positive relationships between the school and local faith communities help to create a constructive context for the teaching of these subjects'. It continues:

> In all schools, when teaching these subjects, the religious background of all pupils must be taken into account when planning teaching, so that the topics that are included in the core content in this guidance are appropriately handled. Schools must ensure they comply with the relevant provisions of the Equality Act 2010, under which religion or belief are amongst the protected characteristics.[10]

This seems a somewhat tangential, if tactful, way of addressing the highly controversial issue of how religious groups have sometimes clashed with sexual orientation issues, notably, for example, in protests against LGBT+-inclusive teaching in schools in Birmingham. At the same time, the guidance says that 'All schools may teach about faith perspectives. In particular, schools with a religious character may teach the distinctive faith perspective on relationships, and balanced debate may take place about issues that are seen as contentious'.[11] It adds that 'the school may wish to reflect on faith teachings about certain topics as well as how their faith institutions may support people in matters of relationships and sex' but notes that 'In all schools, teaching should reflect the law (including the Equality Act 2010) as it applies to relationships, so that young people clearly understand what the law allows and does not allow, and the wider legal implications of decisions they may make'.[12] Thus, it reminds schools that under the provisions of the Equality Act, they must not 'unlawfully discriminate against pupils because of their age, sex, race, disability, religion or belief, gender reassignment, pregnancy or maternity, marriage or civil partnership, or sexual orientation (collectively known as the protected characteristics)'.[13]

The guidance also makes the interesting observation that 'Provisions within the Equality Act allow schools to take positive action, where it can be shown that it is proportionate, to deal with particular disadvantages affecting one group because of a protected characteristic. This should be taken into consideration in designing and teaching these subjects'.[14] Schools are also guided to ensure that all of their teaching is sensitive and age appropriate in approach and content. At the point at which schools consider it appropriate to teach their pupils about LGBT+ :

> they should ensure that this content is fully integrated into their programmes of study for this area of the curriculum rather than delivered as a standalone unit or lesson. Schools are free to determine how they do this, and we expect all pupils to have been taught LGBT content at a timely point as part of this area of the curriculum.[15]

The guidance oscillates between clarity about the equality duty, on the one hand, and highly diplomatic language verging on the oblique, on the other. It amounts to a gentle reminder of the law, drawing attention to the highly contested nature of debate in this area. It appears to boil down to schools being left to decide, within the law, how best to proceed given their own situations and communities. This approach has been criticised by one head teacher at the heart of the Birmingham protests in 2019, who was damning about an insistence in a 'frequently asked questions' document and in statements by ministers that although primary schools are 'enabled and encouraged' to cover LGBT+ content if they 'consider it age-appropriate to do so', there is no requirement for them to teach it. She believes that this contradiction amounts to discrimination and has fuelled homophobia because a single protected characteristic is singled out for exemption, saying: 'the bottom line is "I'll leave it up to headteachers". That's wrong'.[16]

This area is also further complicated by having in common with RE that parents have the right to withdraw their children from all or part of RSE (excluding withdrawal from learning about reproduction and human development within national curriculum science). To mitigate this, many schools build a relationship with parents on these subjects over time, for example, by inviting parents into school to discuss what will be taught, address any concerns and help support parents in managing conversations with their children on these issues. The guidance encourages this, noting that it 'can be an important opportunity to talk about how these subjects contribute to wider support in terms of pupil wellbeing and keeping children safe. It is important through such processes to reach out to all parents, recognising that a range of approaches may be needed for doing so'.[17] It is also noted that 'Before granting any such request it would be good practice for the head teacher to discuss the request with parents and, as appropriate, with the child to ensure that their wishes are understood and to clarify the nature and purpose of the curriculum'.[18] Part of an effective relational approach, the guidance explains, would include explaining that:

> Families of many forms provide a nurturing environment for children. (Families can include for example, single parent families, LGBT parents, families headed by grandparents, adoptive parents, foster parents/carers amongst other structures.) Care needs to be taken to ensure that there is no stigmatisation of children based on their home circumstances and needs, to reflect sensitively that some children may have a different structure of support around them; e.g. looked after children or young carers.[19]

The RSE guidance ends with a clutch of advice referring somewhat randomly to elements relating to aspects of religion and belief. Thus, 'Schools must also ensure that their teaching and materials are appropriate having regard to the age and religious backgrounds of their pupils'; furthermore, they may 'choose to explore faith, or other perspectives, on some of these issues in other subjects such as Religious Education'.[20] This is the only reference to connections to RE; they should also 'be taught where to find support and that it is a criminal offence to perform or assist in the performance of FGM or fail to protect a person for whom you are responsible from FGM', and that 'pupils may also need support to recognise when relationships (including family relationships) are unhealthy or abusive (including the unacceptability of neglect, emotional, sexual and physical abuse and violence, including honour-based violence and forced marriage)'.[21] In a summary of what pupils should know by the end of secondary school, the guidance states:

> what marriage is, including their legal status e.g. that marriage carries legal rights and protections not available

to couples who are cohabiting or who have married, for example, in an unregistered religious ceremony ... how stereotypes, in particular stereotypes based on sex, gender, race, religion, sexual orientation or disability, can cause damage (e.g. how they might normalise non-consensual behaviour or encourage prejudice).[22]

Yet, in sections on well-being and menstruation,[23] where religion and belief may well be expected to be referenced, they are not mentioned at all. Finally, in a section called 'Subjects Complementing RSE', the guidance lists citizenship, science, computing and physical education (PE); RE is not mentioned.[24]

Collective worship

Another key space in which children and young people learn about religion and belief in schools is in the daily act of collective worship. This is a requirement, alongside RE, under the Education Act 1944, as well as in relation to the 1994 government circular 1/94. Both the 1988 Act and the 1994 circular elide RE and collective worship, stating that:

> Religious education and collective worship make an important, although not exclusive, contribution to spiritual, moral and cultural development. These activities offer explicit opportunities for pupils to consider the response of religion to fundamental questions about the purpose of being, morality and ethical standards, and to develop their own response to such matters.[25]

In practice, the daily act of collective worship is widely varied or even ignored. It should also be noted that the most recent guidance was published 25 years ago and so could hardly be regarded as a policy priority. Also of note is that 'worship' is not defined in the legislation, and in the absence of any such definition, it is advised that 'it should be taken to have its natural and ordinary meaning'.[26] That is, it must in some sense reflect something special or separate from ordinary school activities and it should be concerned with reverence or veneration paid to a divine being or power. However, 'worship in schools will necessarily be of a different character from worship amongst a group with beliefs in common. The legislation reflects this difference in referring to "collective worship" rather than "corporate worship"'.[27]

The given purpose is:

> to provide the opportunity for pupils to worship God, to consider spiritual and moral issues and to explore their own beliefs; to encourage participation and response, whether through active involvement in the presentation of worship or through listening to and joining in the worship offered; and to develop community spirit, promote a common ethos and shared values, and reinforce positive attitudes.[28]

In these ways, collective worship is supposed to be educational, intended to give pupils the opportunity to worship or to have an experience of worship to evaluate or perhaps assimilate. The extent to which this is the case is difficult to assess.

Critically, the guidance goes on to require (as does the original 1944 Act) that 'Collective worship ... must be wholly or mainly of a broadly Christian character, though not distinctive of any particular Christian denomination'.[29] This clearly implies that Britain is a self-evidently Christian-majority country, though the data are clear that there is somewhere between 25 per cent (2011 Census) and 52 per cent (British Social Attitudes Survey, 2019) of people in Britain having 'no religion', as well as a significant degree of continuing Christianity and a growing mix of faiths that are newer to Britain. This is not the message communicated by the requirement for a daily act of collective worship in the Christian mode. The guidance also states that it is open to a school:

> to have acts of worship that are wholly of a broadly Christian character, acts of worship that are broadly in the tradition of another religion, and acts of worship which contain elements drawn from a number of different faiths. Provided that, taken as a whole, an act of worship which is broadly Christian reflects the traditions of Christian belief, it need not contain only Christian material.[30]

While the guidance notes that the *majority* need be of Christian character, Humanists UK thus wryly observe that, 'Technically, this means that only 51% of school days each term need have an act of worship of a broadly Christian character.'[31]

There are also a number of specific opt-outs. Schools are able to 'apply for a determination' that the requirement for a Christian character be lifted in a school where this may be appropriate. There is no definition of what would be appropriate, and the application for a determination is made to the SACRE, possibly in consultation with the governing body, who may, in turn, wish to consult parents. It is explained that 'One factor which may inform a head teacher's decision to make an application to the SACRE is the extent of withdrawals from broadly Christian collective worship'.[32] The Secretary of State for Education nevertheless retains the power to revoke a determination to vary the Christian character requirement.

The involvement of SACREs is also a complicating issue in itself. They have an advisory role in which they are entitled 'to support the effective provision of RE and collective worship in schools'.[33] SACREs are required in their composition to include 'Christian denominations and other religions and religious denominations', and should 'reflect broadly the proportionate strength of that denomination or religion in the area'.[34] They should also always include the Church of England as well as 'such associations representing teachers as, in the opinion of the authority, ought to be represented, having regard to the circumstances of the area ... [and] the local education authority'.[35] The inclusion of religious groups and representatives has been criticised as a key part of the muddle in teaching and learning about religion and belief in schools. One issue concerns the degree to which participants can be said to be representatives of the religious groups for whom they speak. Another questions the involvement of religious figures as vested interests in what children and young people learn about them. REforREal (Dinham and Shaw, 2015) recommends a review of the role of SACREs, arguing that the status quo on both RE and the daily act of collective worship make for a confusion of educational, confessional and formational elements such that children and young people are unable to tell the difference. The perception of vested interests also adds to the muddle and could be easily clarified by the abolition of SACREs altogether.

Finally, collective worship is also subject to a right of withdrawal,[36] which parents can exercise on behalf of their children. This also implies for religion the status of some kind of special problem.

Conclusions

Every subject and setting has its quiet normativities, as revealed by the recent reform of the teaching of history in England (to make it more chronological and more 'British'). However, as revealed here, the policy muddle and its implications question whether teaching and learning about religion and belief in schools can make any sense to children and young people. The evidence suggests that RE bears too much of an instrumental responsibility, not only in England, but also across Western societies, where secular assumptions predominate but are largely only dimly thought through. Other spaces in which religion and belief come up reproduce and consolidate the muddle by failing to connect or distinguish between themselves. In doing so, they fail to socialise the differences between religion and belief, on the one hand, and their overlapping proxies in culture, ethnicity, spirituality and morality, on the other. The risk is that, alongside the instrumental focus on cohesion (and extremism) and a desire to support the formation of personal development and spirituality, this produces muddled learning about religion and belief. This reproduces shallow or partial understandings, alongside anxieties about religion and belief as forces for division, violence and oppression. At the same time, it risks failing to engage with the ordinary pervasiveness of lived religion and belief, which evidence suggests looks nothing like these concerns. Clarification of the purpose and content of religion and belief inside RE is important, as is its part in the wider school environment. This may underpin clarification of the conversation about religion and belief more broadly; as such, getting it right in schools is an important space for the renewal of religion and belief literacy in wider society.

5

Religion and belief in university practices

Introduction

Unlike schools, universities seem at first glance to have broken off their relationship with religion and belief, largely appearing to have expelled them from both curricula and operations. Many fancy themselves secular. Yet, the medieval universities were an essentially Christian settlement, organised monastically, in which the primary subjects read were theology and medicine. In them, it was the *nature* of God that was questioned, not God's *existence*. In many ways, universities continue to reflect their Christian medieval roots (directly or by pastiche), hanging on to the gowns and hoods, titles, and roles of a Christian age. This legacy is deep in the contemporary higher education landscape.

This acts out a tension for religion and belief in universities because things have changed. In 1700, there were seven universities in Britain (just two in England). In 2019, there are 133 members of Universities UK, the main representative body for higher education institutions (HEIs). The relationship between British universities and religion changed dramatically over that period too. It was not until 1871 that religious tests were fully abolished at Oxford and Cambridge, and the Victorian expansion of the university sector was, in part, motivated by the goal of establishing countermanding secular centres of higher learning that would be open to everyone, notably, University College London (UCL), the first consciously secular university (Gilliat-Ray, 2000: 22; Rüegg, 2004: 61–4; Graham, 2005: 7–9). Anglican chaplaincies remain a strong feature of higher education in this milieu. Up until the 1950s, there was a widespread view that the primary reason for making most chaplaincy appointments was to serve the interests of the Anglican Church (Gilliat-Ray, 2000: 29). This model of chaplaincy has since given way to one in which chaplains are understood to serve the whole university and frequently define themselves as 'multi-faith'.

In teaching and learning too, there has been considerable change. In all the British Commonwealth countries, the presence of theology courses reduced by 60 per cent between 1915 and 1995. However, in some contexts, they underwent revival from the 1980s on, though this time in new forms focusing especially on Islam, or the intersection between religion and public life (Frank and Gabler, 2006: 92–116). In Britain in particular, the link has been largely broken between the study of theology (formerly in a degree called Bachelor of Divinity) and ordination as a priest in the Church of England. Almost all theology students in the UK now study theology and/or religious studies, and obtain a Bachelor of Arts (BA) degree, locating them firmly in the humanities, like any other subject.

Crucially, the apparent retreat of religion in universities has been linked to the ways in which academic disciplines and their attendant communities of scholars have emerged precisely in contradistinction to theology (Edwards, 2006: 84). According to Edwards, each discipline has developed its own procedures and vocabularies for understanding its subject matter, and has usually done so as alternatives to the dominant forms of theological knowledge that preceded them. The sciences, the social sciences and then the humanities in turn 'declared their independence from religion' (Edwards, 2006: 84). The old centrality of religion as the major mode of study in the universities, and understanding of the world, has largely been forgotten.

Yet, increasing awareness of religion, driven largely by anxieties about extremism, sex and money, have prompted some to suggest that 'religion is back' (Micklethwaite and Wooldridge, 2009), for universities as for other institutions and public spaces. A crucial challenge is how to work out a place for education – in universities, as for schools – which emerges out of a Christian past, and to some extent present, while at the same time taking fully and authentically on board the contemporary religion and belief landscape, which is Christian, secular, plural and non-religious all at once. The problem is that universities tend to pick up where schools leave off, continuing the confusion with a subtextual replaying in both teaching and operations of old binaries and tropes about science versus religion, secular versus sacred, private versus public and resource versus risk. These are all built deeply into the epistemologies of disciplines, as well as reflected in the day-to-day operations of institutions.

A paucity of attention to religion and belief in the academy

Reflecting this, there has been little attention paid to religion and belief in higher education. Strands that have emerged examine the *history* of religion in higher education (Reuben, 1996; Hart, 1999;

Roberts and Turner, 2000), the supposed 're-emergence' of religion on university campuses in the 21st century (Edwards, 2008) and the implications of increasing religion and belief diversity for teaching and research (Edwards, 2006; Tisdell, 2008). Partly inspired by the widely discussed 'de-privatisation' of religious traditions and communities of faith since the end of the Cold War (Casanova, 1994; Berger, 1999; Habermas, 2007), this literature has tended to renew an old debate about the responsibilities of universities in a world marked by the 'complex co-presence' (Ford, 2004: 24) of a variety of often competing religious and secular philosophical traditions.

Recognising the muddle, a number of scholars based in the UK (Gilliat-Ray, 2000; Ford, 2004; Woodhead and Catto, 2012) and the US (Prothero, 2008) have argued that the education system, and particularly universities, could play a vital role in improving the quality of these vexed conversations. For example, as part of a comprehensive rationale for the public role of universities in relation to religious faith, Ford (2004: 25) has contended that higher education institutions 'ought to be taking far more seriously than they do their responsibility to contribute to the coming century by engaging with the issues arising from the simultaneously religious and secular character of our world'. Similarly, Graham (2005: 243–61) has argued that universities have a vital role to play as part of a society's cultural infrastructure, and that one part of this role is consideration of both religious and secular spiritual values. A different take on the same issue is provided by Gilliat-Ray, who chooses to stress not the role that universities can have in educating about religion, but bringing young people from diverse backgrounds into contact with each other. She observes that 'Universities are sites of cultural engagement and exploration, and if issues of religious diversity, rights and representation cannot be debated and explored in this context, then where else?' (Gilliat-Ray, 2000: 59).

Another important strand has been reconsidering the place of Christians in universities, as in Guest et al's (2013) study *Christianity and the University Experience*. This examines the beliefs, values and social lives of Christian undergraduate students in particular, both noting and challenging two stereotype models: a 'conflict model', which assumes that students will experience cognitive dissonance as their faith comes up against their learning (Schietle, 2011); and a 'compartmentalisation model', which brackets religion and belief off as a distinct, private and unrelated dimension (Guest et al, 2013). In a survey of 4,500 undergraduates from 13 universities, students were asked 'to what religion or spiritual tradition do you currently belong?' (Guest et al, 2013: 212–13). To the surprise of some, this found a simple majority of 51.4 per cent of Christian students (Guest et al, 2013 p214), alongside 'None' (34 per cent), Buddhism (2.2 per cent), Hinduism (2.0 per cent), Islam (4.9 per cent), Judaism (0.5 per cent), Sikhism (0.3 per cent) and 'Other' (4.7 per cent). In addition, 73.1 per cent of the Christian students said that their faith had remained the same at university, while 11.9 per cent said that they had become less religious and 15.1 per cent said that they had become more religious (Guest et al, 2013: 104). Thus, for a small minority, academic studies led to a gradual move away from their faith positions; for some others, it led to a strengthening. However, for the majority, academic study did not challenge their faith (Guest et al, 2013: 127). The authors conclude that 'the recasting of faith identity in non-cerebral terms, as a combination of experience, participation and personal spirituality, seems to have rendered Christian identity fairly immune to intellectual crises generated by academic study' (Guest et al, 2013: 131). In other words, students' Christianity appears to be bracketed off from their intellectual curiosity. One reviewer's interpretation is that 'there are many "hidden Christians" in English universities and that university studies and life do not have the secularizing influence upon them that we might expect' (Shortt, 2014: 366). An alternative conclusion is that in largely ignoring religion and belief in curricula, universities accidentally surrender the critical ground, rendering religion and belief, at best, irrelevant. This may be a crucial gap in graduates' abilities to encounter religion and belief diversity well.

University chaplaincy

Another revealing strand concerns the changing role of university chaplaincy. Up until the 1950s, there was a widespread view in England that the primary reason for making most chaplaincy appointments was to serve the interests of the Anglican Church (Gilliat-Ray, 2000: 29). However, this model of chaplaincy began to give way in the 1960s and 1970s, with chaplains starting to serve the whole university. Aune et al (2019) have focused on this in their 2019 study. They found that of 1,032 chaplains, 63 per cent were Christian (including Quakers), 9 per cent were Muslim, 8 per cent were Jewish, 5 per cent were Buddhist, 4 per cent were Hindu, 2 per cent were Sikh, 2 per cent were Baha'i and 7 per cent were 'other', In the 'other' category, the largest groups are humanist (1.6 per cent), interfaith (1.4 per cent) and Pagan (1.4 per cent) chaplains. The study finds that one third of chaplains see their primary aim as pastoral, and only one sixth as religious, and that they spend 71 per cent of their time on pastoral work. A great deal of the work of chaplains is voluntary, though universities do fund chaplaincy to a significant, if patchy, degree and frequently locate chaplaincy in wider student services teams. The study notes that the term 'chaplain' is now used to describe pretty much anyone contributing to a university team of religion and belief actors, whether or not their own tradition uses the term 'chaplain' and whether or not that actor is actually religious. For example, it might include a mindfulness practitioner, and almost always includes a humanist. Likewise, the assumption is widespread that any chaplain is available for any person on any matter. In practice, the boundaries between traditions, as well as between traditions, the secular and the non-religious, are permeable or even invisible. What is not clear is the extent to which universities intend this and how much is by accident.

'Prevent' in the universities

In these ways, mixed messages are rooted in ideas of foundation, mixed historical relationships with churches and state, the continuing presence of chaplaincies, and the ongoing and pluralising presence of religious, secular and non-religious students. Alongside this, the place and treatment of Islam has been adding a particular layer of complexity. Interest in Islam since 9/11 prompted the UK government to name Islamic studies – which has seen a sharp rise in student numbers – as a 'strategically important subject' in 2007 (Higher Education Funding Council for England, 2008: 4). Following the Siddiqui's (2007) report, the Higher Education Academy has also been exploring the possibility of building formal links between the UK's private centres of Islamic education and its largest public universities. These reflect an anxiety about religion in general and Islam in particular, which is most explicit in the relationship between universities and 'Prevent'.

The Prevent strategy, published by the UK government in 2011, is part of the overall counterterrorism strategy 'CONTEST'.[1] Extremism is defined in the 2011 strategy as 'vocal or active opposition to fundamental British values, including democracy, the rule of law, individual liberty and mutual respect and tolerance of different faiths and beliefs'.[2] The guidance explains that:

> Islamist extremists regard Western intervention in Muslim-majority countries as a 'war with Islam', creating a narrative of 'them' and 'us'. Their ideology includes the uncompromising belief that people cannot be both

Muslim and British, and that Muslims living here should not participate in our democracy. Islamist extremists specifically attack the principles of civic participation and social cohesion.[3]

Section 26(1) of the Counter-Terrorism and Security Act 2015 imposes a duty on 'specified authorities', which includes universities, to have due regard to the need to prevent people from being drawn into terrorism. Universities are singled out for their own Prevent guidance, while police, prisons, schools and local authorities are subject only to general guidance. The reason given is universities' 'commitment to freedom of speech and the rationality underpinning the advancement of knowledge [which] means that they represent one of our most important arenas for challenging extremist views and ideologies' (Her Majesty's Government, no date: 2015 3).

The guidance states that 'We do not envisage the new duty creating large new burdens on institutions and intend it to be implemented in a proportionate and risk-based way', and that 'Compliance with the Prevent duty requires that properly thought through procedures and policies are in place' (Her Majesty's Government, no date:2015 3). In practice, this foregrounds a culture of religion as risk, and the policies that result are almost always drawn up in isolation from chaplaincies and equality offices, and certainly without the input of academic departments, even where they may have expertise, as in theology, religious studies, sociology and social policy. Once devised, awareness of them is often very limited, while controversy about embroilment in surveillance and security dimensions is high.

Nevertheless, certain areas within universities are specified for attention. Thus, HEIs are expected to specify their positions on external speakers, balancing 'legal duties in terms of both ensuring freedom of speech and academic freedom, and also protecting student and staff welfare' (Her Majesty's Government, no date: 2015 4). This is tempered by the reminder that 'where any event is being allowed to proceed, speakers with extremist views that could draw people into terrorism [must be] challenged with opposing views as part of that same event' (Her Majesty's Government, no date:2015 4). In this space, there has also been much debate about 'no platforming', in which students unions and universities themselves have sometimes excluded a speaker on the grounds that their views are already settled as in some way unacceptable. This has been particularly contentious in relation to anti-Semitism, where some settings have been unable to distinguish between criticism of Israel (anti-Zionism) and anti-Semitism, despite internationally agreed definitions, which are sometimes debated and even eschewed.

HEIs are also required to pay regard 'to their existing responsibilities in relation to gender segregation', as outlined in the guidance produced in 2014 by the EHRC (2014: 5). This advises that gender segregation is not permitted in any academic meetings or at events, lectures or meetings provided for students, or at events attended by members of the public or employees of the university or the students' union, though it is permissible during collective religious worship because it is not subject to equality law. Staff involved in the physical security of the institution's estate are also required to have an awareness of the Prevent duty.[4]

The Prevent Duty Guidance also requires 'institutional policies regarding the campus and student welfare, including equality and diversity and the safety and welfare of students and staff'. The development of policies is expected to enjoin 'active engagement from senior management of the university (including, where appropriate, vice chancellors) with other partners including police and BIS [Bureau of Investigative Services, since replaced with the Insolvency Service criminal enforcement team] regional higher and further education Prevent Duty Guidance'.[5] Universities are also expected to: carry out a risk assessment, which includes not just violent extremism, but also non-violent extremism; make arrangements for managing prayer and faith facilities (for example, an oversight committee); and have clear policies and procedures for students and staff working on sensitive or extremism-related research.[6] Yet, research suggests that policy on religion and belief in universities is haphazard, patchy or missing altogether (Dinham et al, 2017). It is likely that in many universities, 'Prevent' may be the *only* explicit policy, as well as being narrowly produced and shared. Its biggest impact is likely to be in the headline controversies about Islamophobia and religious 'othering', which add to a sense that religion and belief are problems for university operations and distract from academic disciplines.

A changing religion and belief landscape

This analysis, in turn, gives way to an engagement with findings in the sociology of religion, drawing attention to a context that seems both post-religious and post-secular, as well as to dramatic changes in the religion and belief landscape, and how to think about it. Thus, the 2011 UK Census suggests that Christianity remains the largest religion in England and Wales but is down from 71 per cent (in 2001) to 59 per cent. Muslims are the next biggest religious group at 4.8 per cent, and this is the most increasing group, up from 3.0 per cent in 2001. Meanwhile, the proportion of the population who report that they have no religion has now reached a quarter in the UK, which is an increase from 14.8 per cent in 2001 to 25.1 per cent. According to the British Social Attitudes Survey (2019) this 'no religion' figure is much higher, at 52 per cent. According to other sources and other questions, *what* we believe has changed too. Belief in 'a personal God' roughly halved between 1961 and 2000: from 57 per cent of the population to 26 per cent. However, over exactly the same period, belief in a 'spirit or life force' doubled: from 22 per cent in 1961 to 44 per cent in 2000 (see Woodhead and Catto, 2012).

Of course, the data are hugely debatable but the trends are clear enough: society continues to be Christian, as well as plural, non-religious and less formal. At the same time, while there may be a decline in religion, this is not necessarily the case for belief. Critically, all of these things are happening together. It is important that universities grasp and reflect this because there appears to be a *real* religion and belief landscape and one imagined by policymakers, professions and publics, as well as a growing gap between the two (see Dinham, 2012a).

Changes in the higher education sector

In England, the last 30 years have also been a period of profound and sometimes traumatic change within higher education itself: the number of students entering university – and, indeed, the number of universities – has risen sharply; new indicators of performance have been introduced (Breakwell and Tytherleigh, 2010); and huge changes have been made to the way in which HEIs are funded (Graham, 2005: 15–22). So far-reaching have these changes been that some have gone so far as to suggest that the university as an institution is going through an acute crisis, or even a terminal decline (Blackmore, 2002). The conception of the university popularised by individuals such as Humboldt, Schleiermacher and Newman, in which a community of scholars engage in intellectual pursuits for no overriding reason other than to provide a broad, liberal education, is 'being challenged by globalisation, the high demand for access, public sector management and financial reform that links allocation of resources to the achievement of defined measures of productivity and excellence' (Bosetti and Walker, 2009: 4).

In a study published just after the turn of the millennium, Gilliat-Ray (2000: 25) summarised one of the common responses to these changes using a quote from a former chaplain at a university in the North of England: 'It all went wrong during the '80s. Education is no longer about developing the individual or building a person; it's about finding a job. [Universities have] become part of the economic machine.' This interpretation of events is by no means universally shared (see Bosetti and Walker, 2009: 8–9), but there is some consensus that personal formation has been pushed to the side as the main aim of higher education. Instead, successive government publications have prioritised the kind of skills and qualifications that are believed to encourage economic competitiveness (see DTI, 1998; DBIS, 2009). The latest of these, the Browne Review (Browne, 2010), pushed higher education in England further in this direction: over the following two years, a system was introduced in which almost all funding for university teaching was replaced by fees, paid initially by government-secured loans, and the failure to attract students was thought likely to lead to courses or even whole universities being forced to close. This latest shift towards a higher education system modelled as a transaction between consumer and service provider has put what Bartram (2009: 309) calls 'the classical humanistic ideology that has underpinned English educational traditions' in peril, and threatens to weaken the associated objectives of developing the student as an individual still further. Many vice chancellors and academics have spoken out against the Browne Review's recommendations and the free-market ethos that informs them (Collini, 2010; Eagleton, 2010), indicating a desire to do more than provide bankable qualifications.

Yet, at the same time, universities have been incentivised to pay greater attention to the personal beliefs and identities of students (Dinham and Jones 2010) through an increased emphasis on student satisfaction (NUS, 2008), broadening access to traditionally under-represented groups (Greenbank, 2006; Modood, 2006) and the importance of attracting international students. This has all placed pressure on HEIs to respond to students' religion and belief backgrounds. New legislation to prevent discrimination and harassment on the grounds of religion or belief, and elevated anxiety about the perceived threat of religiously inspired extremism (DCLG, 2007; DIUS, 2007), have also added to the pressure.

The Religious Literacy Leadership in Higher Education programme

One response has been the Religious Literacy Leadership in Higher Education programme (2009–14). This focuses on what universities do about religion and belief in their day-to-day operations – from admissions to catering. It also picks up the critical question of whether and how to take religion seriously in curricula.

Research was conducted to address these issues as part of a national Religious Literacy Leadership programme between 2009 and 2014 (Dinham and Jones, 2010; Dinham et al, 2017). First, a needs analysis of the English higher education sector was conducted. This was followed by a series of workshops: one for vice chancellors and another for any other university staff who wished to attend. By the end of the programme, there had been 19 vice chancellors and 600 other participants. A further 30 participants took part in a semi-structured interview after they had attended, which asked about their reasons for attending and any dilemmas that had emerged in their own university relating to religion and belief.

The findings cannot be considered representative of the higher education sector. However, they are indicative, taking in a wide range of staff at all levels of higher education in England and across the full range of mission groups of university affiliation: the Russell Group of the 20 larger research-intensive universities; the 1994 Group, a now-defunct grouping of 19 smaller research-intensive institutions; the Million+ Group, a group of 28 former polytechnic institutions given university status in 1992 and that aspire to research strength; University Alliance, made up of 22 former polytechnic universities with an emerging research track record; GuildHE, the 21 remaining former polytechnic universities; and the Cathedrals Group, comprised of 15 former church foundations that are now universities. The study identifies two overarching themes (see Dinham and Jones, 2012): the first is about the sort of stances that universities think they take in relation to religion and belief; and the second is what motivates practical action in relation to religion and belief.

In relation to the first, four university stances, or 'types', were identified (Dinham and Jones, 2012). In the first type, the university is conceived of as a self-consciously secular space that should remain as far as possible 'neutral' on religion and belief, and in which education would largely avoid reference to them. This group was labelled 'soft neutral', and it is noted that the neutrality in the label is never defined and is undercut anyway by the liberal normativity of universities, which makes them far from normative. A similar but firmer line sees universities as actively seeking the protection of the university space from religion and belief, asserting a duty to preserve public bodies, including universities, as 'secular'. Here too, the secularity in question is almost never explained or understood, and is frequently elided with neutrality. This group was called 'hard neutral'. Others saw religion and belief as a valuable aspect of identity and as a potential resource for academic learning and personal formation. This was the stance of the largest group of vice chancellors, with many stressing that their campus is friendly to religions and religious people, and comfortable with religion and belief diversity. The emphasis here was on religion and belief identity as an important *object* of study (in order to engage with them when they are encountered in daily life). This group was called 'repositories of resource'. The fourth approach identified aims to offer education 'for the whole person', incorporating a specifically religion or belief dimension in teaching and learning, and in day-to-day operations. This perspective was more common in universities that were founded as religious institutions. This group was called 'formative-collegial' (see Dinham and Jones, 2010). It emphasised religion and belief as a *subject* of reflection, that is, a valued aspect of students' overall formation that should not be left out, just as ethnicity or gender would not be.

The second strand addresses what sorts of religion and belief matters preoccupy vice chancellors and other university leaders. The study found that practical and policy concerns overwhelmingly dominate. Vice chancellors were concerned about four key areas, in the following order of intensity: possible legal action arising out of discrimination on the grounds of religion and belief (especially since the Equality Act 2010, which prohibits discrimination in the provision of services – including in universities – on the grounds of religion or belief); campus extremism and violence; the 'student experience' of students of all religion and belief backgrounds and none (which has been measured against the National Student Survey and fed into crucial league tables for students and parents since 2005); and the recruitment of international students from all parts of the world, and therefore from all religions and beliefs. These concerns blend risk (being sued and being bombed) with opportunity (providing a well-received and attractive environment to students), though the risk side is more prominent and defined than the opportunity side from the outset.

The programme also looked at who attended the original series of training events (in 2010/11) and found that the majority (71 per cent overall) were from chaplaincies (26 per cent), student services (24 per cent) and equalities teams (21 per cent). Only 1 per cent came from academic departments (Dinham and Jones, 2011). This reflects a widespread assumption that religion and belief is something that is bracketed off from the wider life of universities. It is largely done primarily in the chaplaincy, and elsewhere takes a risk-management focus located within equality and student experience settings, where religion and belief identity might translate into problems for the institution.

The programme also undertook case-study research in three universities to understand the narratives of religion and belief as they are experienced by students and staff. This enabled an exploration of the many practical ways in which religion and belief play out in universities much more widely. This found students who had not felt able to attend interviews, exams or Saturday lectures because of clashes with religious events. There were anxieties and controversies about public speakers and what to 'allow' them to say on topics like Israel and Zionism. Timetabling staff were worried about how to handle the exam period for the several years after 2014 when Ramadan coincided with it. Canteens and bars were taking all sorts of stands for or against halal food, alcohol-free events and single-sex socials, and there were bitter rumours in one institution that Muslims were receiving subsidised lunches. There were sports societies whose members were ribbing a Sikh for wearing the five K's (worn by orthodox Sikhs: *kesh* – uncut hair; *kara* – armband; *kangha* – comb; *kacchera* – knee-length shorts; and *kirpan* – sword). Residences were struggling with kosher kitchens and women-only halls. Campus banks either could or could not handle the requests of Muslim students regarding halal borrowing for student fees, while counselling services felt that they could not discuss religion with religious students. The strong impression was of institutions that are far from comfortable talking about religion and belief, and in which responses are patchy (even random), predominantly reactive rather than proactive and highly focused on risk.

For example, three of the HEIs in the study were making significant changes to the built environment and support mechanisms of the university, at least in part, because of an effort to improve student satisfaction. In two cases, the conventional chaplaincy systems were being overhauled and incorporated into a far broader framework of health and well-being, with religious observances being provided for along with leisure and fitness. At another, the university was making connections with a local Chinese church after some of the international students provided particularly poor feedback, feeling that, as the Chaplain at the university observed, "the college and the students' union centred around the bar" and "hospitality-wise, the interests of overseas students could be cared for better". Here, one pro-vice-chancellor regarded student experience as a way of engaging with religion and belief differences that went beyond compliance with anti-discrimination legislation. As he observed:

> 'I personally think the whole kind of student experience agenda which has taken off lends itself to partnership working; and if you are engaged in partnership working, one of your tasks is to understand who your partners are, what your partner's world view is, and to seek to engage with that in terms of moving forward.'

Others were introducing initiatives on internationalisation, with religion and belief differences and needs again being an important part of that:

> 'Obviously, one of the objectives I have is internationalisation, so I hope I can attract more international students, creating an even more diverse campus and so on ... and obviously a Muslim student coming from Bangladesh or Pakistan, they will have a different background and different expectations, and I think that will again mean facing new challenges: how we integrate them, for instance, vis-a-vis the ... Muslim students [from this city]. Even in Catholicism, I want to attract Catholics from Asia but, again, they will come from different traditions.' (Vice chancellor at a post-1992 university, religious foundation)

> 'We recruit, and obviously, like other universities, we're looking to recruit as many as we can of international students and many of them come from countries of the Muslim faith, and clearly there are many from that faith position [in the UK] as well now. So, the numbers [from different faiths] are simply becoming greater in this university.' (Head of student services at a pre-1992 university, secular foundation)

At the same time, some universities founded with an explicit religious ethos, particularly the new universities that were formerly church colleges, were stressing their status as religious institutions precisely to develop a distinctive 'brand' that would have appeal for Christian overseas students. Two of the chaplains interviewed, for example, made the following comments:

> 'I think it would be true to say [this university has] become a more [self-consciously religious institution] because of

the need to be distinctive.... That's not the way that the chaplaincy sees it, but I think it's fair to say that's the way the institution [as a whole] sees it.'

'[There was] a lack of confidence about what [being a religious foundation] meant, not necessarily within the chaplaincy, but within the institution, a sense almost of embarrassment at the church origins.... [But] one of the things that we've begun to realise is that having a religious foundation can be a positive, and while it may not be at the top of the list for why someone chooses an institution ... it can certainly add value.'

Similarly, the director of international partnerships at another religious foundation said the following about his current aims: "The issue for us is how, whether, where and when to play the [Christian] card in terms of whether we target [Christian] countries or do we target [Christian] schools in other countries and so forth" (director of international partnerships, pre-1992 university). Although this effort to appeal to transnational religion and belief identities does not appear to be as common among the secular foundations, new challenges emerged for them too as a result of internationalisation. In some cases, universities described becoming more aware of the values and intellectual traditions that they embody institutionally as a result of negotiations with students and institutions from abroad. One pro-vice-chancellor at a secular institution founded in the Victorian period, for example, had been involved with the development of a three-way international partnership with a university in the Middle East and another Christian university based in the US that requires all its students to take a compulsory theology course. The experience of working with these institutions had led to a reconsideration of the secular identity of the university. It had been necessary, he observed, to separate "points that are non-negotiable", such as the co-educational nature of the university, from those alternative norms that could be respected and accommodated. These changes, the pro-vice-chancellor thus commented, "are helping us to work out what exactly our position on faith is".

Yet, in such self-defining 'secular' foundations, the limits and form of secularity, and what that means for the mission, can shift:

'he wants to find a way of discussing the nature of the "secular" within the university, and at present he does not know of a way to do this, either because he is unaware of the places where the discussion can take place or because they *cannot* take place.' (Deputy academic registrar, pre-1992 university)

'I can remember when I was writing our international strategy back in 2003 and I was using terms such as moral responsibility, social good and so on, and people were saying, "This is not appropriate for our university." And yet now, a few years on, virtually everyone who is drafting [a strategy] will talk about moral responsibility ... the issue of faith becomes part of that.' (Pro-vice-chancellor at a pre-1992 university, secular foundation)

This is certainly supported by the views of students too. In one case study, approximately 16 per cent of students said that they wanted the institution to 'provide better opportunities for religious and spiritual development'. This constitutes a significantly larger minority group than for ethnicity; yet, while many institutions have highly developed policy and practice on that aspect of identity, very few have equivalents for religion and belief (Dinham et al, 2017: 8). This study also found a considerable degree of internal diversity in response to religion and belief, and that the approach taken quite often appears to be a product of individual staff members' own outlooks, attitudes, sympathies or beliefs, rather than part of an institutional stance (Dinham et al, 2017: 8). It was also notable for 'student experience' that twice the number of students than staff thought that religion was accommodated 'not very well' and 'poorly' (12 per cent of students and 6 per cent of staff) (Dinham et al, 2017).

The university muddle

Three important features appear in relation to religion and belief. First, there is a clear attitudinal divide between university operations and curricula. In operations, religion and belief are largely bracketed off to chaplaincies (where the focus is on pastoral care, spiritual life and practice), equality teams (where the emphasis is on ensuring accommodation and compliance within the law) and student experience teams (responding to the religion and belief identities of a significant number of students that are likely to translate into their evaluations of their courses). A fourth location is 'Prevent', which hugely magnifies the idea of religion and belief as risk, and of Islam as 'other'.

Second, there is a lack of knowledge, let alone understanding, of the religion and belief landscape within many institutions, and a reluctance to monitor it, despite the majority of staff and students (more than 80 per cent) being relaxed about these data being gathered. While ethnicity is almost always measured, religion and belief are rarely counted. It will be very challenging for universities to act in relation to religion and belief in the absence of this knowledge, and its absence itself is an indication of the lack of seriousness or confidence in addressing it.

Third, there are differing, patchy and localised responses to religion and belief within and between university departments. One key distinction is between academic and professional services departments, where the former tend to act out a number of almost-unconscious post-religious tropes, while the latter tend towards pragmatism. Responses also appear to depend partly on personalities rather than being carefully and consciously thought through in policies and strategy. This lack of coherence is likely to translate into a lack of coherence on religion and belief among students as they progress through the university and beyond.

Conclusions

The combination of higher education reforms, changes in the religion and belief landscape, and a wider social emphasis on religion and belief in recent years has certainly resulted in interesting shifts and debates. Perhaps this represents not the *marginalisation* of religion and belief in universities, as happened in the early 20th century, as much as a *reconstitution* of the relationship between them.

Nevertheless, this shifting context struggles to think and act strategically and consistently on religion and belief, and continues to enjoin a somewhat vague idea of secularity, as well as religion, which it often responds to with a stance of 'neutrality', without necessarily understanding what that could mean. There is evidence of much liberal sentiment among staff regarding issues of religion and belief, revolving around patchy notions and enactments of tolerance and respect but lacking in direction and surety as to how such sentiment should be made coherently tangible. Universities have an instrumental interest in responding to the religion and belief identities of students but have less of an interest in shaping them through educational formation. There is an incentive to accommodate all forms of religion and belief and practice but not to try and bring them into contact with modern scholarship and science. Universities are also tasked with responsibility for the prevention of extremism, which is an element that stresses the risk dimension of religion and belief. Ultimately, the concern is that universities accidentally split their student into parts that learn and parts that experience. The ability to think and feel critically about religion and belief is confused in this milieu.

6

Religion and belief in university teaching and learning

Introduction

Debate about the role of religion in operations has been widespread and visible. A conversation about religion and belief in teaching and learning is also starting to emerge, and some disciplines appear to engage with this more than others. In some subjects, of course, religion is simply a topic of relevance, as in history and in religious studies itself. In others, it is a cultural legacy to be decoded and understood, as revealed in the growing tendency to teach 'Introduction to the Bible' to students of English literature so that they can manage Milton or Donne. In others again, it embodies the opposite of the rational, scientific method that predominates in higher education, and in relation to which practically all other disciplines have cut their teeth. As such, it is an utter irrelevance, as in Richard Dawkins's (2010) disparaging contrast of theology as being like astrology in relation to astronomy. In some cases, this produces hostility against all religious ideas. This is likely to feel painful for some students, who can feel uncomfortable when hearing lecturers be rude or offensive about their beliefs or about belief in general. In the social sciences, unlike race, gender or sexual orientation, religion has rarely been a variable.

The professional subjects like social work and education studies seem to have a somewhat better understanding that many of their stakeholders are religious and that they need to equip professionals to handle this. Others remain entirely uninterested, or even dismissive. This reflects a contention in the rest of society about the re-emergence of religion and belief as a public category. Are society and its institutions secular or sacred, or complexly both? To what extent should religion be private or public? Can we leave religious identity at the university door? If so, which door: the canteen, the chapel, the quiet room, the students' union or the lecture hall (see Dinham, 2015a, cited in Day and Lovheim, 2015)?

The question of the place of religion and belief in university disciplines was explored in the project Reimagining Religion and

Belief for Policy and Practice (Baker and Dinham, 2017). This started with the observation that religion and belief were cropping up across a wide range of academic disciplines, many of which had never, or not recently, been interested in them. The aim was to critically map this and then to connect the findings to policymakers in service provision settings of varying kinds. The study analysed nine arts, humanities and social science disciplines, including anthropology, cultural studies, geography, philosophy, religious studies, social policy, social work, sociology and theology. 'Landmark' interviews were undertaken with 18 leading thinkers across these fields, selected not only for their global reputation, but also because they are considered to be public intellectuals, transcending as well as epitomising key thinking in their disciplines. Each responded to three questions: 'How do you characterise the present conversation about religion and belief in your field?'; 'What are the key pinch points and new insights?'; 'Where is the conversation going in the next five to ten years?'

This was followed by an intensive three-day residential colloquium in which the findings from the landmark interviews were deepened and extended by a multidisciplinary group of 15 further academics, including five international participants (from Australia, Canada, Finland, Norway and the US), as well as seven doctoral or early-career researchers who were selected because they were doing innovative cross-disciplinary work in their own studies of religions and beliefs. A third phase focused on policy engagement. A group of eight participants, drawn from the fields of government and civil service, local authorities, faith-based social action, and councils of voluntary service, met for a one-day workshop at the House of Lords in the UK Parliament. Each participant was asked to give a 'lightning' presentation outlining the ways in which religions and beliefs 'bite' in their setting. They then identified and prioritised a shortlist of five potential practical changes to public policy in relation to religions and beliefs in these policy areas.

The final phase was an international roadshow to test out how the ideas emerging in a UK context might translate into public policy contexts elsewhere. One-day events were held in Ottawa, Canada (in May 2016), Oslo, Norway (in June 2016), and Melbourne, Australia (in November 2016). These combined the formats of the colloquia and the policy workshop, to include a presentation of findings from the landmark interviews and a discussion of their translatability, though this time transnationally.

The study indicated four preoccupations in contemporary thinking about religions and beliefs, which are largely shared across these nine disciplines and in international perspective: the role of religion and belief in welfare services; their relationship to cohesion, integration and violence; the impacts on, and of, equality law; and their part in new forms of participative governance (Baker and Dinham, 2017). The complexity and variety of these discourses across disciplines indicates a liminality: a moment of change in which the relationship between disciplines may be newly permeable, just as the boundaries around a 'secular' public sphere are also giving way. How much is this translating into what universities teach and what students learn?

Anthropology

Anthropology identifies stereotypical and negative assumptions as making it difficult for more nuanced and complex views on religion and belief to be heard. The subject's commitment to ethnographic fieldwork is seen as a crucial part of breaking open often dense and abstract debates about the post-secular into its lived-out complexities and particularities. It is also seen as enabling new sorts of questions and debate in some areas of academia. As one respondent said: "I think that one of the most interesting things that has developed in anthropology in religion has been … the willingness to look out for new questions, and not be satisfied with a priori positions." As a fuller spectrum of lived religion and belief becomes more apparent through fieldwork, anthropology is asking whether the West can discover more effective forms of coexistence. One interviewee asks: "Can religious traditions and the language that different people have inherited in different ways from those traditions … contribute to enlightening us in ways that help us both to resolve and to accommodate each other, but also to challenge each other?" This stands in the tradition of Hannah Arendt, who wondered similarly in the 1920s, but a key difference is in the contemporary commitment to engaging with religion and belief here, and now, rather than as exotic 'others'.

Geography

In Geography, the focus is on human geographies of care. Debate largely adopts a narrative that sees religious welfare, social care and justice movements as compensating for the gaps left behind by a retreating state. In this, it echoes the instrumentalisation of religion and belief across the public sphere. Geographers also note the 'spatial' turn within sociology and religious studies, which they regard as 'borrowed' from geography. This reflects on the increasingly significant role played by individuals and communities in the creation of flourishing and resilient localities, especially in contexts of poverty and marginalisation. One contributor reflected that the decline of the political Left in these communities has created new opportunities for religion to step into the vacuum:

> 'When I was growing up, you could change the world through Left politics. It's now short-changed. It's much harder to do it through the secular, political tradition. It's been defeated time and time again. And so religion stands out more because there's a kind of vacuum all around … not just because it's there, but also because it has a strong value base, and it offers people … an anti-materialist analysis of the world in terms of having a good life, a community, solidarity. So it's some of the space the Left used to fill.'

Geography is also interested in religion's ability to flourish in an increasingly globalised and urbanised world, and how this challenges one of the basic assumptions of the 'secularisation thesis': that processes of modernisation and technological innovation are supposed to render religious practices and discourses increasingly redundant and obsolete. Geography is recognising that religion and modernity not only coexist, but are symbolically intertwined.

Political philosophy

The question of coexistence arises in philosophy too, where the preoccupation is with the power of globalisation and the plurality of religion and belief that comes about as a result. Migration and trade are highlighted as spaces for the exchange of people, goods and *ideas*. Within this, a major question concerns the implications of the 'hushed-up' voice of religion (Eder, 2006: 1) coming back into the public square. A Rawlsian and Habermasian settlement is regarded as largely *unsettled*, though the direction of travel is seen as not fully determined. There is much interest in how the flux and intense changes that have emerged since the 2008 financial crash, and the political charge being increasingly attached to religion, are challenging to any idea of religion and belief as private. The knock-on effects on philosophies of the public sphere are deep, particularly in relation to secularity and post-secularity, both of which are contested and neither of which is regarded as a satisfactory pointer to the future.

Religious studies

In religious studies, there is a sense of being taken newly seriously and of renewed recognition and visibility, though what that recognition is, and what the response should be, may not yet have come into focus. Responses suggest that religious studies has been something of a 'Cinderella' discipline in many institutions (a distant relation, sidelined from the mainstream life of universities) but that lots of universities are now sensing a need to engage with the study of religion, even if they have not yet worked out how or where. There is a sense that religious studies is itself recognising that this is being driven by certain newly hard-edged and visible aspects of religion and belief, such as law, radicalisation and the growth of black-majority churches, which are making religion – and therefore religious studies – more prominent than they had expected. In many departments, new modules and courses have been appearing, revolving around the theme of 'religion and society'. This also draws attention to the risk that this leads to talk confined only to controversies, which could accidentally reproduce negative tropes and a focus on religion as risk.

Religious studies is also challenging the notion that public bodies themselves sit on one side of a secular–sacred divide – or that there even is such a divide. Likewise, nor do religions sit on one side or the other of the public–private divide. These are binaries that religious studies thinks are dissolving.

There is also a sense of relief that there is a widespread recognition that religion and belief never went away. Crucially, religious studies is looking to other disciplines – especially sociology and social policy – as it hardens up its questions. Importantly, it was also noted that, for the first time, other disciplines are also looking to religious studies. This raises the question of how these disciplines respond to each other, and whether there will be mutual respect, which is an important issue after a period when the status of religious studies has been in question. It might also imply a collusion of religious studies with the instrumentalising concerns emerging across the other university disciplines when it might perhaps play a more constructive role in pushing some of that back.

Social policy

Social and public policy are also beginning to be busy on religions and beliefs, though at least two of the interviewees said either that not enough is happening or that it is nothing but trouble. Welfare, violent extremism and cohesion are the three issues that are most apparent. These issues present themselves in the form of tricky dilemmas that policymakers have to deal with and that the study of policy can help with – key among them being how to handle visible manifestations of religions and beliefs, especially the hijab. Violent extremism is also an obvious and prominent theme.

More visible plurality is regarded as another key driver, playing out in the policy arena in anxiety and muddle about which approaches to follow and which words to use – 'multiculturalism', 'tolerance' and so on? There is a perception that these debates have been spilling over into debates about how policymakers can be helped to understand the contemporary religion and belief that they encounter. Political questions about religion and belief are also raised in the context of the study of policy – key among them being what is the place of an established church if society is multicultural, or at least plural? More broadly, the study of policy is exploring questions about the extent to which society is really secular, post-secular or something else. How should policymakers think about religion, belief and the secular, and what practices should change as a result?

Sociology and cultural studies

Two big narratives emerge in sociology. First is the problem of the long-term marginalisation of the sociology of religion from the wider sociology community, and therefore its relative silence in public debate. As one respondent said:

> 'Our debates about religion happen within the community of sociology of religion. This is all very interesting but who are we talking to? It results in a lack of analytical frameworks within which the commentariat can engage in this. They've no idea what the questions should be. This hasn't changed, but the interest in religion has.'

The other big narrative is about change. This, itself, breaks down in two ways. First, there is interest in what has changed in wider society to make it suddenly interested in religion again. Here, the same themes come up again: violence, law and plurality. Some new ones appear too, namely: the marketisation and consumerisation of religions and beliefs, in common with other aspects of the public sphere; the collapse of old political narratives (for example, Left–Right giving way to leave–remain) and meta-narratives of other kinds, including religious ones; and the move online, which is seen as highly democratising and flattening of the sorts of hierarchies that formal religion has previously depended upon.

Second, there is interest in how the religion and beliefs landscape itself has changed. This is not just about the facts and figures – plurality, decline and growth – but also about the quality of religion and beliefs. There is a discourse about their de-formalisation. There is an emphasis on the embodied and lived, as well as on the material. There is also a rapidly growing interest in religion and belief as dimensions of health and well-being, frequently couched in the language of mindfulness, and spirit. This adds up to a stretchier notion of religions and beliefs as including not only the 'old forms', but also now: informal, non-creedal forms; rejigged expressions of ancient ones, like Wicca and Paganism; and consumerised, fluid ones that are something of a pick and mix. Non-religion (secularism, humanism) and non-religious beliefs are also prominent. These interests see religion and belief in functional terms, that is, as social activism and individualised modes of meaning-making. This is contrasted with a continuing and widespread view of religion as narrow and top down, still interested in hierarchies and leadership structures.

In cultural studies too, there is an emphasis on the observation that there is far too much focus on religions as structures of belief. There is a call to move on to a focus on structures of *meaning* that cut across religious boundaries. The idea is that this will help the discourse to move on – from arid new atheism, which sees religions in this old way as structures of belief that are easily dismissible, to focusing on their morally and existentially charged meanings, which can be seen to continue to have traction *with* or, more probably, *without* the belief or practice commitments that used to pertain.

Theology

The responses of the theologians in the study can be grouped into two categories. The first could be labelled as reflecting a pessimistic response regarding the current role of religion and belief in the public sphere. This position sees religion, but particularly Christianity, as being driven out of the public square by an aggressive secularism, often sponsored by the state and abetted by certain sections of the media, opinion formers and academia. The second category, which might be labelled 'realist', was more sanguine, seeing at least as many opportunities as challenges in harnessing a renewed interest in religion and belief towards a new ethical consensus on the nature and purpose of the public square. In this, the religious and the secular are increasingly less differentiated and, instead, more co-mingled spatially, culturally and intellectually. The public space is one in which different constructions of religion and belief, and therefore different constructions of secularity, are now bumping up against each other in shared space or shared territory. How we learn to share such territory is the major challenge.

Another theological strand suggests that Western popular culture shows a persistent search for a magical or transcendent reality that exists beneath, or is intertwined with, the material and empirical realities of everyday life. The cultural representations of these existential questions offer important opportunities for public discourse shaped by theological ideas and motifs.

A third strand observes a decline in meta-narratives, and instead of looking for a way forward, appeals to a return to a religious past in which natural law, a strong church and doctrine are once again allowed to provide a telos for a public sphere that is regarded as having lost its way. This strand, sometimes referred to as 'radical orthodoxy', is prominent though highly controversial and largely dismissed for its inherent conservatism.

Conclusions: issues for universities

Some common and strong preoccupations are emerging across the disciplines, which present a number of challenges. Key among them are widely held but shallow assumptions about secularism right across the universities, which are regarded as an obstacle to a good quality of conversation about religion and belief. These are rooted in misplaced ideas of the simple decline of religion, rather than change. The secularisation story has been so dominant in the university landscape that it appears to continue to resonate even if and when it is expressly challenged, and there is a strong sense that the notion clings on despite a good deal of intellectual work that challenges it. Thus, much of the intellectual innovation found in this study is yet to make it into the mainstreams of their disciplines, let alone into lecture halls and seminars with students.

At the same time, there is a sense that the boundaries between disciplines are liquidating, and many universities are emphasising their interdisciplinarity in much of their rhetoric. There is even an interdisciplinary cross-referral process in the national research assessment, the Research Excellence Framework (REF), which prizes interdisciplinary approaches. However, this raises the question as to how to make disciplinary incursions well, and it seems that many, if not most, attempts are, at best, in their very early stages. Key connections are ripe to be made between theology, religious studies and the social sciences, as well as between sociology and the sociology of religion, where breaches are especially noted. In particular, there seem to be powerful echoes of classic epistemologies, some of which may well have themselves become subconscious – for example, religious studies, which has tended to think of religions as coherent blocks to be studied, rather than lived, transactional and steeped in fluid, located meanings and beliefs. How does it talk best to sociology, or theology, which may be caught in their own epistemological webs, preoccupied with dichotomies about science–religion (theology) and sacred–secular (sociology), for example? Moreover, how might disciplines that have previously had little or no connection – some of which may even have scoffed at one another – overcome their prejudices and talk well to each other, and how do university structures enable them to?

These debates are complicated by the ways in which functionalist and instrumental perspectives prevail. The tension between the usefulness and the experience of religion and belief is well felt at the grass roots, where faith communities often talk about being 'used' by government policy – and sometimes abused, as in policies to prevent violent extremism. This will not suffice in a globalised and de-boundaried intellectual and actual world. However, there is often a lack of ability to recognise, let alone acknowledge, the religion and belief roots and connections.

The challenge posed by this analysis of religion and belief in these university subjects is both practical and conceptual. At the level of practice, it is about how to engage well with the greater secularity, plurality, informality and diversity of religion and belief as they present and are encountered. However, this presents a conceptual challenge too: how do these disciplines and practices communicate with each other authentically? Religion and belief pose a uniquely interdisciplinary challenge to the old and new disciplines that are engaging them. It will be necessary to learn how to bridge the classic epistemologies and binaries in each: science–religion, secular–sacred, private–public and formal–informal. Another challenge is methodological: working out ways of asking questions of and reaching constituencies that can be mutually recognisable.

Where universities can or will not talk about religion and belief as a legitimate focus of academic attention, such nuanced and important ideas remain unengaged, and the practical and instrumental dimensions risk going largely unaddressed. Blurry thinking, which colludes with old binaries, also risks a lazy stereotyping of religion and belief as simply problematic in a public sphere that should be 'neutral'. The knowledge that resides in the disciplines shows this to be redundant, yet little of this has made it into curricula for students, who continue to be widely socialised in the notion that religion is the past, even when it appears very vividly in the present.

At the same time, as Taylor suggests, many people are also instinctively dissatisfied with a thin vision of human life, and are seeking a 're-enchantment of the world' (Landy and Saler, 2009). The potentially formational contribution of the study of religion and belief as identity, across university life, seems as crucial a space for exploration as ethnicity, gender and sexuality, as well as of values and wider existential questions. This is a space in which students might find so much more than the gaining of a bankable qualification in pursuit of instrumental aims. Yet, it still feels that universities struggle to see ways in which they might 'release religion from the constraints of the personal sphere and the container of the secular nation-state' (Vasquez, 2011: 264). At this liminal threshold, universities have the opportunity to engage with the new intellectual spaces that are opening up and to take their place in shaping the way in which religion and belief are imagined.

7

Religion and belief in professional education and workplaces

Introduction

Alongside schools and universities, vocations, professions and workplaces are themselves full of ideas about religion and belief. Some are explicit; many are not. These are spaces in which adults learn and relearn religion and belief, often for the first time since school. Here, the messages have their own flavour, once again distinctive from what may have come before. One dominant framing in workplaces is equality and diversity. This constructs religion and belief as potentially discriminatory and discriminated against. In doing so, religion and belief are once again thought of primarily in terms of risk. Another growing preoccupation is with spirituality and well-being in workplaces, often associated with the benefits of bringing the 'whole person' to work and engaging with the full scope of identities among service users. Within this, one suggestion is that 'survey after management survey affirms that a majority wants to find meaning in their work' (Garcia-Zamor, 2003: 360). This is especially prominent in health and social care, where religion and belief are manifest both in professional trainings and in regulatory standards for the professions. This chapter will explore both framings and consider how they connect and confuse.

Equality and diversity

The evidence on workplace religion and belief is very limited, though there is considerable work in relation to other identities, characterised as the 'protected characteristics' in equality law (ethnicity, age, gender, sexual orientation, disability and 'religion or belief'). A key principle is engagement with every aspect of the person at work to ensure diverse recruitment, retention and career progression, as well as yielding income, market-reach and reputational benefits. The research most often cited is provided by the global consultancy firm McKinsey. This compares the financial performance of large organisations according to gender diversity at senior levels, and finds that high returns on equity are correlated with greater diversity. It also claims that ethnically diverse companies are 35 per cent more likely to outperform on outputs and gender-diverse ones are 15 per cent more likely to do so (McKinsey Analysis, 2010). It is notable that there are implications for religion and belief but that they are not acknowledged or addressed.

The Center for Talent Innovation (CTI) in New York takes a step closer. It identifies the importance of 'two-dimensional diversity', by which it means combining *inherent* diversity, such as gender and ethnicity, with *acquired* diversity, such as global work experience and language skills. It found that publicly traded companies with two-dimensional diversity were 45 per cent more likely than those without to have expanded their market share in the past year and 70 per cent more likely to have captured a new market (Hewlett et al, 2013). A report from Deloitte similarly identifies an 80 per cent improvement in business performance when levels of diversity and inclusion are high (Toohey & Sweigers, 2013). It also found that 'If just 10% more employees feel included, the company will increase work attendance by almost one day per year per employee' (Toohey & Sweigers, 2013: 9). Likewise, Horwitz and Horwitz (2007) reviewed 20 years of research on team diversity and identified a positive relationship between diversity and team performance. Widely cited research on 506 US organisations also shows that organisations with greater ethnic and gender diversity performed better in terms of sales revenues, the number of customers and market share. For example, a one-unit increase in, respectively, ethnic diversity and gender diversity was shown to increase the number of customers by more than 400 and 200, and to increase sales revenue by 9 per cent and 3 per cent (Herring, 2009).

Similarly, an experiment at Tufts University, Massachussets, USA, demonstrated that diverse groups perform better than homogeneous ones. Researchers deployed 200 people in mock juries. The mixed juries all performed better than those comprising only white or only black jurors. This suggests that homogeneous 'groupthink' may lead to a cohesive team, though one that will also happily agree on the same potentially costly mistake. It was also the case that white participants in diverse groups were more lenient towards black defendants, indicating effects that go beyond simple information exchange. This appears to connect with the CTI study (Hewlett et al, 2013), which also found that 'ideas from women, people of colour, LGBTs, and Generation Y's are less likely to win the endorsement they need to go forward, because 56% of leaders don't value ideas they don't personally see a need for … the data strongly suggest that homogeneity stifles innovation' (Hewlett et al, 2013). Nevertheless, Stephen Frost, head of diversity and inclusion for the London Olympics and now for KPMG, writes in *The Inclusion Imperative* that discrimination against women, gay people and disabled people is estimated to cost US$64 billion a year in the US alone. He adds that 'When gay people remain in the closet, they are 10% less productive than when they feel able to be themselves' (Frost, 2014: 75).

Almost all the research on workplace diversity is unanimous on one thing: it can go wrong. Organisations without management and staff understanding of diversity are regarded as being at risk of heightened conflict and reduced productivity. As Deloitte's (2011: 7) 'Only Skin Deep?' report suggests, 'it is not enough to create a corporate version of Noah's Ark bringing in "two of each kind"'; rather, they observe that 'Inclusion increases the total human energy available to the organisation. People can bring far more of themselves to their jobs because they are required to suppress far less.' The report concludes that:

> The story is *not* about the increased representation of a particular demographic group bringing extra 'sparkle' to the workplace because of their special skills and talents. Rather, the story is about organisations with a more diverse talent pool, especially at senior levels, manifesting a workplace culture of openness, merit and rational decision-making. (Deloitte, 2011: 10)

The question of how to achieve this is addressed by the same report, which describes a number of key actions for getting there. Central is the argument that 'there is a clear business case for diversity but it is one which requires intentional acts of inclusion and adaptation as well as leadership capability' (Deloitte, 2011: 15). Key among them is the recommendation to 'develop metrics to hold leaders to account for implementing the business case' (Deloitte, 2011: 17). There are several such schemes that measure or benchmark employers in relation to other equality and diversity identities but not religion and belief.

The lack of explicit connection between equality and religion and belief in workplaces is striking, despite a number of workplace legal cases (as explored in Chapter 2). That said, there are a small number of initiatives that attempt to bridge this. One, in the US, is the Tanenbaum Centre for Interreligious Understanding, based in New York. This is a not-for-profit organisation that presents itself as a secular, non-sectarian initiative aimed at promoting mutual respect with practical programmes that bridge religious difference and combat prejudice in schools, workplaces, health care settings and areas of armed conflict.

These are aimed towards training future leaders in business, and their interventions are focused on training and educational resources in preparation for entering workplaces rather than taking place within them. They also offer online resources for employers and employees to raise awareness and help them deal with religious issues more effectively. The focus is strongly on diversity, which is targeted as a human resources issue. On offer are 'management briefings', 'skill building to handle religious diversity' and 'policy reviews to meet your legal obligations'. The website also advertises a training strand called 'Religion at Work', stating: 'From issues of workplace attire to conflicts between religious and LGBT interests, *Religion at Work* guides you through today's most common and most pressing religious diversity issues.'[1]

Similarly, the Global Business & Interfaith Peace Awards recognise business leaders who have demonstrated leadership in championing interfaith understanding and peace. The awards are an initiative of the Religious Freedom & Business Foundation (RFBF) in collaboration with the United Nations Global Compact Business for Peace (B4P) platform, the Global Compact Network Korea and the UN Alliance of Civilizations (UNAOC). The driving critique is rooted in the idea that denials of religious freedom are associated with poorer economic performance and lower global competitiveness.[2]

Such programmes imply a somewhat narrow idea of religion and belief. In Tanenbaum's training, this includes 'extensive information on world religions' and 'tools for establishing a respectful environment'. This stands in contrast to contemporary sociological research which suggests that a focus on the world religions fails to engage with important shifts towards non-traditional forms of religion and belief, as well as a dramatic increase in non-religious beliefs and non-religion. At the same time, this approach has been criticised for implying that religions can be understood as monolithic blocks of unchanging facts that can be learnt. The focus on 'information' reinforces this implication, whereas contemporary understandings tend to emphasise religion and belief as messy, fluid and lived. It also normalises understandings of religion and belief within a 'respect' narrative. This enjoins anxiety about how to get on with each other at the same time as implying that knowing about each other leads to respecting each other. This has been criticised as a liberal assumption without evidence (Parekh, 2000). Nevertheless, it is consolidated in Tanenbaum's work in a strand called 'Peacemakers', which is a facilitated international network of religious figures running 'peace' initiatives in their settings.

In the UK, a similar initiative takes a practical approach but engages with this more contemporary view of religion and belief as elastic, fluid and lived identity rather than fixed tradition. This is a partnership between a charity called the Coexist Foundation, a company spin-off of the Religious Literacy Leadership in Higher Education programme (see Chapter 5) called the Religious Literacy Partnership and the international consultancy firm EY. Together, they have developed an online training module as part of EY's equality and diversity provision, called 'Religious Literacy in Workplaces'. It is rooted in the 'religious literacy' concept developed by Dinham (see Dinham and Francis, 2015) and now evolved into 'religion and belief literacy'. This understands religion or belief as pervasive, ordinary and fluid, and in need of workplace attention. Risk-based dimensions include avoiding litigation, workplace conflict and even violence, and managing conditions that inhibit effective working and provision. However, it also urges a reframing towards a focus on workplace opportunities, which includes strong cooperation and teamwork, better engagement in diverse markets and settings, the better recruitment and retaining of new staff and users, and an enhanced brand and reputation.

Another initiative is the Canary Wharf Chaplaincy in London, UK. This offers chaplaincy services to both individuals and companies in the Canary Wharf community in the heart of London's business community. It is made up of Anglican, Catholic, Muslim and Jewish chaplains, who present themselves as offering a non-judgemental and safe place to help people discuss personal matters of worry or concern, explore how beliefs can inform or give meaning to their values at work (including the way in which they do business), and help them to make the changes they seek to make in their professional and personal lives. This certainly suggests a pastoral role for religion and belief in workplaces, though one that seems to stress spiritual and existential aspects rather than doctrinal or ritualistic ones.

There have also been initiatives in the armed forces, prisons and the civil service, though these have been patchy. For example, the publication *Religion in the Military Worldwide* (Hassner, 2013) provides a 'thick reading' of the role and significance of religion in the armed forces of Japan, Canada, the UK, Pakistan, Israel, Iran, India, the US and Turkey, including detailed case studies of the religiosity of soldiers, as well as the influence of religion on military organisation, its history and ongoing procedures and performances. Yet, the UK army website says only that 'The Army will always try to help you observe the customs of your faith'. Ministry of Defence policy is to help observe religion 'where circumstances allow'. In the civil service, the UK Foreign and Commonwealth Office (FCO) and Department for International Development (DfID) have each had occasional 'religious literacy' training events for selected staff. There is a strong sense that religion and belief are recognised as being in some way important, though these settings are largely unsure why.

Yet, the underlying assumption across this arena is that there is an inherently positive relationship between paying closer attention to religion and belief, on the one hand, and the benefits of this to particular sectors, on the other. The logic is that allowing for greater space for expressing personal religion and belief can improve the productivity of the labour force (Garcia-Zamor, 2003; Jurkiewicz and Giacalone, 2004), raise levels of job satisfaction (King and Williamson, 2005) and benefit career development (Duffy, 2006). Fernando and Jackson's (2006) study of Sri Lankan business leaders (including Buddhists, Christians, Hindus and Muslims) highlights ways of openly engaging in workplace spirituality, finding that this has greatly helped in dealing with 'difficult' situations, including major management decisions. These claims remain rather general and somewhat unevidenced.

This also appears to be the message of a report on belief at work (ComRes, 2017), aimed at shedding further light on the widely overlooked role of religion and belief in the workplace. The study involved interviews with 251 human resources managers in British companies with 50 or more employees, plus 984 British workers. One of the most significant findings was that almost one in five (17 per cent) of all British workers interviewed said that they themselves had experienced, or had seen someone else experience, at least one form of bullying, harassment or discrimination in the workplace, of which 3 per cent related to religion and belief. While this may seem like a small percentage, it can be extrapolated to approximately 1 million of the entire working population of the UK (ComRes, 2017). The report argues that most businesses place religion in the 'threat' box; however, it suggests that there is great potential for religion to be moved into the 'opportunity' box instead.

Workplace mindfulness

Picking up on this workplace-benefits framing, another significant area of growth has been in workplace mindfulness practices. The government-led Mindfulness Initiative is the main representative body in the UK, which published *Building the Case for Mindfulness in the Workplace* (Mindfulness Initiative, 2016). This starts with the premise that 'We spend more of our time working than doing anything else, and researchers have found that these hours are on average the least happy of our lives' (Mindfulness Initiative, 2016). The report adds that 'Although the research referenced in the report is promising, it is still considered to be in its infancy' (Mindfulness Initiative, 2016: 14). Nevertheless, studies have shown that those practising mindfulness report lower levels of stress and are able to concentrate longer without their attention being diverted. The research also suggests that employees of leaders who practise mindfulness have less emotional exhaustion, a better work–life balance and better job performance ratings. Effects are reported in relation to well-being, resilience, stress, workplace relationships, performance, leadership, decision-making, creativity and innovation.

A key feature of mindfulness work is that it is predominantly regarded as a secular pursuit, as explicitly stated throughout all of the professional institutions offering mindfulness training (for example, the Oxford Mindfulness Centre, Sussex Mindfulness Centre and Bangor Centre for Mindfulness Research and Practice). It also operates ubiquitously across both the public and private spheres, including and beyond the professions and workplaces (Brown and Ryan, 2003; Grossman et al, 2004). Its strongly secular self-identity appears to largely enable it to sidestep many of the taboos and limitations related to dealings with religion and belief in the public sphere. However, this also sidesteps the case for challenging the private–public and secular–sacred binaries that continue to contribute to the muddle on religion and belief. It is questionable whether mindfulness is thought of at all within the 'religion and belief' umbrella in workplaces, despite its very deep roots in Buddhism and its obvious connections to existential and spiritual dimensions. This may not matter except in so far as it perpetuates an implicit binary idea of 'acceptable spirituality' and 'unacceptable religion'. This risks the further bracketing off of religion. Greater future focus on spirituality may also lead towards a renewed focus on the spiritual authority of those who will be expected to become the main teachers, leaders and charismatics in the field (Arat, 2016).

Adult and further education

Within adult education, roughly 50 per cent takes place in further education settings and the rest among training providers and adult education and community settings (Skills Funding Agency, 2012: 26). The Skills Funding Agency acknowledges that very little is known about religion and belief in adult and further education, especially by contrast with the other protected characteristics in the Equality Act 2010. It nevertheless concludes that 'the Agency does not propose any systematic collection of data about learners' religion/belief as it does not consider the case for doing so is currently strong enough to outweigh the degree of intrusion ... and bureaucracy ... it would entail' (Skills Funding Agency, 2012). Instead, the Agency commissioned research 'to quantify the issues faced by learners' (Skills Funding Agency, 2012: 10), which provides a useful insight into constructions of religion and belief in this sector. The research focused on ten key issues. The first is 'barriers to participation and success'. This is indicative of the framing of the overall exercise as an equalities issue. Second is whether religion and belief should be monitored. Third is whether curricula provide safe spaces for religion and belief to be encountered and explored. Implicit in this focus is the idea that encounter is both legitimate and valuable. Although no explanation is given of how research questions were arrived at, this suggests that the notion of cohesion through encounter may be seen as important. Fourth, the research asks whether learning spaces are making accommodations for learners on grounds of religion and belief, listing as examples: 'clothing and symbols; prayer and chaplaincy facilities; dietary requirements; festivals and holy days' (Skills Funding Agency, 2012: 10). Fifth, it asks whether 'facilities for prayer, worship, meditation and celebration exist, are they appropriate to the full range of religions and beliefs?' (Skills Funding Agency, 2012: 10). This indicates a broad understanding of religion and belief that goes beyond the world religions and traditions. Sixth, the research is interested in learners' experiences of discrimination and likewise, and seventh, in how learning providers respond. Eighth, it wants to understand how experiences in adult and further education compare to those in school and university. Ninth, the focus is on whether there are 'good relations between learners with different religions' and, tenth, whether there are tensions, particularly between religion/belief and sexual orientation (Skills Funding Agency, 2012: 10). The questions suggest a relatively sophisticated understanding of religion and belief as broad categories, and a disposition towards inclusiveness of the 'full range' (Skills Funding Agency, 2012: 10).

Of respondents, 53 per cent said that they had a religion and 10 per cent said that they had a non-religious belief. A total of 38 per cent said that they did not have a religion or belief that affects their lives, though the researchers consider this to be under-reported (Skills Funding Agency, 2012: 18). Of the 'religious' group, 27 per cent were Muslim. Of the 'non-religious' group, 28 per cent described their belief as 'agnostic', 25 per cent as humanist and 21 per cent as atheist. Strikingly, while 79 per cent of respondents said that they are fully open about their religion or belief when they are at home, this drops down to less than 35 per cent when they are in their learning environment

(Skills Funding Agency, 2012: 24). Nevertheless, two thirds of religious learners give a score of at least eight out of ten in terms of perceptions of welcome in their setting (Skills Funding Agency, 2012: 28). On the other hand, around 5 per cent of respondents said that they felt 'totally unsafe' in the learning environment, with the library scoring worst for this group. A total of 40 per cent of learners said that there is some opportunity to discuss religion and belief. Similar percentages felt that their learning space was accommodating of their religion and belief, especially in relation to safe spaces, sensitive course content and timetabling (Skills Funding Agency, 2012: 33). At the same time, 10 per cent reported having experienced bullying or harassment in the learning space as a result of their religion or belief (Skills Funding Agency, 2012: 39), mostly in the form of verbal abuse and pressure to transgress beliefs and practices, or to miss prayer. Overall, while 50 per cent of learners were sure that their setting had policies relating to religion or belief, only 47 per cent of that group felt that policies translated into reality (Skills Funding Agency, 2012: 45). At the same time, 70 per cent of learners report no positive experiences in learning due to their religion or belief (Skills Funding Agency, 2012: 50).

The picture that emerges is one of learning settings in which learners feel broadly welcome, and where there are widespread commitments to the values of inclusion and good relations. This implies a preoccupation with the inverse – division and exclusion – and this dark side of the framing is important. What also emerges is a gap between policy and practice in which the great majority of learners feel that they must keep their religion or beliefs private.

Health and social care

A field that appears to be more advanced than others on religion and belief is health and social care. This area demonstrates a degree of preoccupation with religion, belief and spirituality issues going back some time, though there is little consensus or evidence of sophistication of practice to date. A study comparing the British Association of Social Workers (BASW) and the National Association of Social Workers (NASW) in the US, for instance, shows that the Americans look more favourably at the role and significance of religion and belief in their profession than their British counterparts (Furman et al, 2005). Furman also cites a survey by Moss (2003) on the extent to which social work training programmes are preparing social workers to understand the role and impact of religion and belief in society in the UK. Among the 30 social work training programmes willing to discuss these issues,

26 per cent reported that their syllabus did not cover these issues at all, 46 per cent reported that these issues were included very minimally (usually once in the entire programme) and then only in modules on diversity, and 36 per cent included these issues only in training on death and dying or the elderly (Furman et al, 2005: 833).

Nevertheless, the need to effectively respond to religion and belief diversity has been widely proposed as a strategy for managing tensions between individuals and groups who have different beliefs (Ezzy, 2013; Hovdelian, 2015), particularly in contexts of migration and globalisation. For example, a 2003 EU directive on refugees included the following definition:

> The concept of religion shall in particular include the holding of theistic, non-theistic and atheistic beliefs, the participation in, or abstention from, formal worship in private or public, either alone or in community with others, other religious acts or expressions of view, or forms of personal or communal conduct based on or mandated by any religious belief. (Quoted in Doe, 2009: 148)

For health and social care professionals in the UK, there has been a growing sense that they should be able to engage with the religion and belief of the individuals and communities with whom they work (Furness and Gilligan, 2010). However, many report feeling inadequately prepared to discuss religion and belief with service users (Horwath and Lees, 2010), or even knowing how to refer to religious celebrations in ways that will avoid offending people of varying religions (Bradstock, 2015).

At the same time, health and social care professionals also increasingly work within frameworks of regulatory standards. It has been suggested that the development of standards of practice has been essential to the modernisation of health and social care in the UK over the last two decades (Humphrey, 2003). This is accompanied by a perception of growing mistrust in the capacity of professions to self-regulate (Moran, 2001), contributing to several professions having moved from relative informal self-regulation by peers (Jha and Robinson, 2016) to becoming subject to statutory regulatory bodies (Speed and Gabe, 2013).

Alongside this, there is also a growing acceptance that identity issues matter, and this has been extended to explicitly include religion and belief. For example, it is noted in relation to nursing that a professional's 'ethnicity, gender, spiritual values, sexuality, culture, religion, upbringing, education and age have the capacity to influence his or her ethical sensitivity to moral issues' (Schluter et al, 2008: 306).

In recent research on religion and belief in health and social care (Crisp and Dinham, 2019), regulatory standards across 19 health and social care professions in the UK were examined in terms of what they say about religion and belief. The regulatory organisations examined were: the General Dental Council (GDC), which is responsible for the regulation of dental staff across the UK, including dentists, dental nurses, dental hygienists, dental therapists, orthodontic therapists, dental technicians and clinical dental technicians; the General Medical Council (GMC), which is responsible for the regulation of medical practitioners across the UK; the General Optical Council (GOC), which is responsible for the regulation of optometrists and dispensing opticians across the UK; the General Pharmaceutical Council (GPC), which is responsible for the regulation of pharmacists and pharmacy technicians in Great Britain; the Health and Care Professions Council (HCPC), which is the UK regulator for art therapists, chiropodists/podiatrists, dieticians, hearing aid dispensers, occupational therapists, orthoptists, paramedics, physiotherapists, practitioner psychologists, prosthetists/orthotists, radiographers and speech and language therapists (at the time of data collection, it was also the regulatory authority for social workers in England); the Nursing and Midwifery Council (NMC), which is responsible for the regulation of nurses and midwives across the UK; the Northern Ireland Social Care Council (NISCC), which is responsible for the regulation of social care workers and social workers in Northern Ireland; the Scottish Social Services Council (SSSC), which is responsible for the regulation of social workers, social care workers and other social service workers working with children and young people in Scotland; and Social Care Wales (SCW), which is responsible for the regulation of domiciliary care workers, residential childcare workers, social care workers, social care managers and social workers in Wales.

Each regulatory standard was searched electronically using the keywords 'beliefs', 'religion' and 'spirituality'. All documents were also read in entirety for context. One or more statements associated with religion and belief were found in the standards for every occupational group, except for those whose work is regulated by the SSSC in Scotland (SSSC, 2016). While there were some standards that were designed for specific professions, the standards produced by the HCPC mention religion or belief only generally in relation to art therapists, chiropodists and podiatrists, dieticians, hearing aid dispensers, orthoptists, paramedics, physiotherapists, radiographers, and speech and language therapists. These professions are required to 'be aware of the characteristics and consequences of verbal and non-verbal communication and how this can be affected by factors such as age, culture, ethnicity, gender, socio-economic status and spiritual or religious beliefs' (HCPC, 2013a–i, 2014a, 2014b, 2015, 2017).

Crucially, the study found that none of the standards include any definition as to what is meant by terms such as 'religion', 'belief' or 'spirituality'. Instead, they are most frequently mentioned as parts of long lists of factors that contribute to diversity within communities. For example, it is an expectation that medical graduates will 'respect all patients, colleagues and others regardless of their age, colour, culture, disability, ethnic or national origin, gender, lifestyle, marital or parental status, race, *religion or beliefs*, sex, sexual orientation, or social or economic status' (GMC, 2015a: 8). The NISCC standards for social care workers (NISCC, 2015[BIB]: 32) and social workers (NISCC, 2015: 38) take this further with a 'Glossary' that defines 'Equality' as 'Treating everyone fairly and ensuring they have access to the same opportunities irrespective of their race, gender, disability, age, sexual orientation, religion or belief'.

Likewise, only three of the regulatory bodies include guidance in respect of awareness of their stance or disposition in relation to religion and belief. Pharmacy professionals in Great Britain (but not Northern Ireland) should 'recognise their own values and beliefs but do not impose them on other people [and] take responsibility for ensuring that person-centred care is not compromised because of personal values and beliefs' (GPC, 2017: 8). Additionally, optometrists and dispensing opticians are told to 'ensure that your own religious, moral, political or personal beliefs and values do not prejudice patients' care. If these prevent you from providing a service, ensure that you refer patients to other appropriate providers' (GOC, 2016: 21).

The consequences of imposing personal views on service users is more strongly emphasised by SCW in a section on 'Professional Boundaries' in each of its standards documents. While the wording differs slightly, the message to all workers is the same: 'Some things clearly breach acceptable boundaries. Whilst not a complete list, unacceptable things include … using your personal beliefs, for example, political, religious or moral, in a way which exploits or causes distress' (SCW, 2018: 9–10). The need to avoid distress was also a requirement for dental workers, who are instructed that 'You must not express your personal beliefs (including political, religious or moral beliefs) to patients in any way that exploits their vulnerability or could cause them distress' (GDC, 2013: 15).

The most extensive guidance in respect of disposition was found in the regulations of the NMC, which expired at the end of 2018. It was expected of all nurses that:

> They must be aware of their own values and beliefs and the impact this may have on their communication with others. They must take account of the many different ways in which people communicate and how these may be influenced by ill health, disability and other factors, and be able to recognise and respond effectively when a person finds it hard to communicate. (NMC, 2015: 9)

For mental health nurses, this also includes the expectation that that they will use supervision to explore the impact of their own beliefs on their professional practice:

> [They must] have and value an awareness of their own mental health and wellbeing. They must also engage in reflection and supervision to explore the emotional impact on self of working in mental health; how personal values, beliefs and emotions impact on practice, and how their own practice aligns with mental health legislation, policy and values-based frameworks. (NMC, 2015: 17)

This also applies to the managers of clinical staff, who should 'actively promote and participate in clinical supervision and reflection, within a values-based mental health framework, to explore how their values, beliefs and emotions affect their leadership, management and practice' (NMC, 2015: 19).

However the explicit requirement for nurses and midwives to reflect on their own beliefs was removed by the NMC in its revised standards coming into effect in 2019. The requirement since then is that 'At the point of registration the registered nurse will be able to ... provide and promote non-discriminatory, person centred and sensitive care at all times, reflecting on people's values and beliefs, diverse backgrounds, cultural characteristics, language requirements, needs and preferences, taking account of any need for adjustments' (NMC, 2015: 8–9).

In terms of what knowledge professionals need, the requirement again remains very general. Thus, the common standard for all professions regulated by the HCPC, except social work in England, is a need for knowledge of 'religious and spiritual beliefs'. For many professions, this is the only regulation relating to religion and beliefs, and no definition is given. It is also notable that in the most recent standards for English social workers, the words 'and spiritual' have been deleted (HCPC, 2017: 9).

In respect of practitioner psychologists, the HCPC published two additional standards. The first calls for the need to 'understand the impact of differences such as gender, sexuality, ethnicity, culture, religion and age on psychological wellbeing or behaviour' (HCPC, 2015: 8). The second, for counselling psychologists only, is a requirement to 'understand the spiritual and cultural traditions relevant' (HCPC, 2015: 15).

Likewise, medical practitioners should be able to 'interpret findings from the history, physical examination and mental-state examination, appreciating the importance of clinical, psychological, spiritual, religious, social and cultural factors' (GMC, 2015a: 5), whereas midwives are expected to 'act on their understanding of psychological, social, emotional and spiritual factors that may positively or adversely influence normal physiology, and be competent in applying this in practice' (NMC, 2015: 4). Subsequent, more detailed guidance for midwives notes a requirement that they:

> Practise in a way which respects, promotes and supports individuals' rights, interests, offering culturally sensitive family planning advice; ensuring that women's labour is consistent with their religious and cultural beliefs and preferences; and the different roles and relationships in families, and reflecting different religious and cultural beliefs, preferences and experience. (NMC, 2015: 10)

In these ways, this study found that there are widespread requirements that UK health and social care workers need to engage with religion and belief, with all regulators except the SSSC making some reference to them. Yet, the language appears to be largely interchangeable and undefined, incorporating varying combinations of 'religion', 'belief', 'spiritual', 'values' and 'world views', with no critical engagement with their meanings and differences. At the same time, there are no stated rationales for why and where these terms are included or used, and on what basis. Likewise, the knowledge that is needed is not specified, such that calls for knowledge of 'beliefs', 'practices' and 'differences' are not fleshed out in any way. The requirement for knowledge of 'effective practices' and 'legislation' is more concrete but mostly still fails to point to which practices and laws in particular, and professional training in universities does almost nothing to illuminate these or the wider points. Thus, the standards in respect of religion and beliefs are characterised by a lack of clarity and specificity (Leka et al, 2011), and are open to interpretation by individual practitioners.

Thus, the standards end up randomly paying attention to religion and belief in health and social care, and much further thinking is required. For example, why is it that only mental health nurses are expected to be aware of the impact of their own beliefs on their practice, and not all nurses and midwives? Likewise, why do only learning disability nurses need to take account of the spiritual needs of individual service users (NMC, 2015) but not nurses more generally? There are also some important and obvious omissions, such as no recognition of religious issues in respect of diet, food and drink. These can be highly significant issues for patients and service users. At the very least, one might expect that there might be a standard for dieticians.

In the health and social care field, these issues play out in relation to counselling and psychotherapy in particular, which lean heavily towards 'spirituality' rather than 'religion', perhaps as a way of sidestepping perceptions of religion as controversial. While the topic of religion/spirituality is covered to some degree in most accredited clinical programmes, only a minority of these programmes approach this training in a systematic fashion, with the remainder offering no educational opportunities in this area at all. Instead, they recommend that training programmes are encouraged to increase their sensitivity to this topic, provide more opportunities for student growth in this area, and incorporate religious and spiritual issues into course work.

This is well illustrated in West's (2010) influential edited collection *Exploring Therapy, Spirituality, and Healing*, which draws on first-hand experiences of both clients and practitioners to explore how therapists deal with both their own and their clients' spiritualities in the context of professional practice. Similarly, there is important work on therapeutic approaches to spiritual abuse (Oakley and Kinmond, 2013), which adds a new layer to the idea of the spiritual as 'coercion and control of one individual by another in a spiritual context' (Oakley and Kinmond, 2013: 21). In a chapter titled 'What Does It Look Like?', there are illustrations of spiritual abuse that link it to forms of psychological and emotional abuse associated with churches. While this is helpful, it nevertheless describes rather than analyses the phenomenon, though in light of the relative dearth of similar frameworks elsewhere, this remains one of the few attempts at pinning down the term 'spiritual'.

These issues of lack of definition are meted out internationally too, as shown by research about religion and belief in social work education globally (Crisp and Dinham, 2019). This explores guidance across a set of countries that have English in common as an official language and for which a degree of shared histories and ideologies have resulted in many commonalities in respect of social work education (Williams and Sewpaul, 2004). This research explored the regulations or standards for social work education for Australia, Canada, Hong Kong, Ireland, New Zealand, South Africa, the UK and the US, as well as the 'Global Standards for the Education and Training of the Social Work Profession' (IFSW and IASSW, 2004). Again, each document was searched electronically, this time using the keywords 'beliefs', 'faith', 'religion', 'secular' and 'spirituality'. One or more statements associated with religion and belief were found in documents from all jurisdictions except for Hong Kong (SWRB, 2015) and Wales (CCfW, 2013). Again, religion is often one of several items on a list of factors that contribute to diversity within communities. The Northern Ireland document is (understandably) unique in that it is the only one that lists religion first: 'Social workers practise in a society of complexity, change and diversity. This diversity is reflected through religion, ethnicity, culture, language, sexual orientation, social status, family structure and lifestyle' (NISCC, 2015: 6). More often, religion tends to come near the end of a long list of factors contributing to diversity. However, while religion is often linked with a wide range of beliefs and characteristics, it is generally not defined, with an assumption made that the meaning of religion and its proxies is self-evident. A notable exception is in relation to working with indigenous Australians. One reference concerns 'Ways of Knowing': 'Ways of Knowing is specific to ontology and Entities of Land, Animals, Plants, Waterways, Skies, Climate and Spiritual systems of Aboriginal groups. Knowledge about ontology and Entities is learned and reproduced through processes of: listening, sensing, viewing, reviewing, reading, watching, waiting, observing, exchanging, sharing, conceptualising, assessing, modelling, engaging, applying' (AASW, 2012: 20). Following on from this is 'Ways of Being':

> We are part of the world as much as it is part of us, existing within a network of relations amongst Entities that are reciprocal and occur in certain contexts. This determines and defines for us rights to be earned and bestowed as we carry out rites to country, self and others – our Ways of Being. (AASW, 2012: 21)

Understanding how 'Ways of Knowing' and 'Ways of Being' are understood underpins 'Ways of Doing':

> Our Ways of Doing are a synthesis and an articulation of our Ways of Knowing and Ways of Being. These are seen in our: languages, art, imagery, technology, traditions and ceremonies, land management practices, social organisation and social control.... Our Ways of Doing express our individual and group identities, and our individual and group roles. Our behaviour and actions are a matter of subsequent evolvement and growth in our individual Ways of Knowing and Ways of Being. (AASW, 2012: 21)

This seems almost to model the possibilities for framing and articulating religion and belief more meaningfully for health and social care professionals. However, it also challenges a tendency in social work, as in other disciplines and professions, to fall into 'reducing the religion being discussed to the concepts and approaches of Western scholarship alone' (Joy, 2012: 103).

Other notable features of this international research include: changes proposed in Scotland in 2016 to delete any reference to 'beliefs', calling instead for 'respecting diversity within different cultures, ethnicities and lifestyle choices' (SSSC, 2016); the 'Social Work Field Education Guidelines' for New Zealand, which call for an upfront commitment by the profession to promoting the well-being of the Maori peoples as *'tangata whenua'*, or people of the land, suggesting that practice-learning placements provide a pivotal learning experience for students to develop this disposition (ANZASW and CSWEANZ, 2016: 5); and the 'Global Standards for the Education and Training of the Social Work Profession' (IFSW and IASSW, 2004) and the Council on Social Work Education's (CSWE, 2015) 'Educational Policies and Accreditation Standards', which both suggest that the teaching of respect for diversity is best achieved by having a student cohort that is itself diverse, including on religion and belief, as well as 'Knowledge of how traditions, culture, beliefs, religions and customs influence human functioning and development at all levels, including how these might constitute resources and/or obstacles to growth and development' (IFSW and IASSW, 2004: 6). In addition, Irish social workers are expected to understand 'and take account of factors such as gender, marital status, family status, sexual orientation, religious belief, age, disability, race or membership of the Traveller community and socioeconomic status' SWRB, 2013: 24).

Thus, religion and belief appear widely, though briefly and incoherently, across the policy framings of health and social care nationally and internationally, and are often not prioritised, appearing late in lists of identities to be addressed. Moreover, placing religion alongside characteristics such as sexual orientation, age or cultural affiliations may have a diluting effect on all the forms of identity listed in this way. Nevertheless, there are some common themes that emerge. First, religion and belief are prioritised where they are problematic, particularly in relation to Northern Ireland and indigenous Australians (though, inexplicably, not for indigenous peoples in other countries such as Canada and the US). This appears to reify them as risky and difficult. Perhaps this misses the opportunities for thinking about religion and belief more positively, that is, as sources of relationship, wisdom and well-being, as is increasingly envisaged in some theoretical work (Arat, 2016; Stacey, 2018). Second, there is a common elision of religion, belief and spirituality, often expressed in the designation 'religion/spirituality'. Yet, these are themselves highly differentiated categories in the literature, as well as in the lived experiences of individuals and communities. Insensitivity to the differences is likely to be felt by service users, many of whom might object to the minimisation of their religion as spirituality, or vice versa. Third, references to religion and belief, and their inclusion and removal, are recognisably subject to debates between the policymakers who frame the guidelines. There are issues of agency that might themselves benefit from analysis. Put more simply, how much religion and belief literacy do policymakers have themselves?

It is also critical to recognise that guidelines do not necessarily reflect either what is taught to or learnt by students (Harden, 2001). Furthermore, when guidelines concerning religion and beliefs are characterised by a lack of clarity and specificity (Leka et al, 2011), they are open to interpretation by individual programme providers and educators, who might provide much less – or even more – input on topics than had been the intention of those drafting the guidelines.

It would appear that professional training and regulatory standards, at least in the examples of health and social care examined here, are beginning to recognise that some degree of religion and belief literacy is required for a diverse range of workplaces and roles. However, they remain too vague and inconsistent to have real traction in practice. They are silent on the question of what counts as religion or belief, or how to think about them. Likewise, there is very little requirement to develop a reflective, self-critical awareness of one's own stance towards them, though there are a number of requirements to avoid imposing one's own religion or belief on service users. The knowledge and skills required are implicit, not specific. Patel and Shikongo (2006) highlight the shortfall in their study of Muslim health care students' understanding and handling of spirituality in secular training programmes. They detect bias in the system, especially apprehensions about demonstrating religious commitment. This is also reflected in Kristellar et al's (1999) study of spiritual distress in cancer patients. One of their key findings is that while physicians identify themselves as primarily responsible for addressing matters of spiritual distress, only a minority feel comfortable in dealing with it.

A central problem appears to be the separating of spirituality from religion (Sanzenbach, 1989), or, more commonly, subsuming it within more palatable notions of 'values' (Constable, 1983). For example, the British Association of Counselling and Psychotherapy's *Ethical Framework for the Counselling Professions* (BACP, 2018) does not contain a single reference to religion, but does make one single reference to spirituality, in relation to 'spiritual abuse', which it does not define or specify practice towards. Likewise, the *Code of Ethics for Social Work* (BASW, 2012) covers issues of human rights, social justice and professional integrity in the conduct of social work, and again makes not a single mention of 'religion', though it does include two very brief mentions of spirituality. Another BASW report in the same year, titled *Race, Religion and Equalities: Report on the 2009–10 Citizenship Survey*,[3] is effectively a study of the wider population and says nothing of religion and belief in social work workplaces. Another example is a Royal College of Nurses' *Pocket Guide*, which states that spiritual care 'is *not* the sole responsibility of the chaplain', and provides guidelines in relation to 'religion/spirituality' that state:

> The practice of spiritual care is about meeting people at the point of deepest need. It is about not just 'doing to' but 'being with' them. It is about our attitudes, behaviours and our personal qualities i.e. how we are with people. It is about treating spiritual needs with the same level of attention as physical needs. (RCN, 2012)

It defines spiritual care very loosely and, in doing so, raises more questions than it answers, especially about 'the human spirit' and how to recognise it, defining it as:

> That care which recognises and responds to the needs of the human spirit when faced with trauma, ill health or

sadness and can include the need for meaning, for self worth, to express oneself, for faith support, perhaps for rites or prayer or sacrament, or simply for a sensitive listener. (RCN, 2012: 3)

It goes on to try to flesh this out, saying that spirituality is about 'hope and strength, trust, meaning and purpose, forgiveness, belief and faith in self, others, and for some this includes a belief in a deity/higher power, peoples' values, love and relationships, morality, creativity and self expression' (RCN, 2012: 4).

The guide advises that if nurses feel out of their depth, they should go to the chaplain, their own faith group or to the psychosocial team (defined as social work, counselling and psychology) (RCN, 2012: 6). This provides some significant starting ground but it is not further operationalised in the materials as they stand.

Conclusions

Treatments of religion and belief in workplaces are widespread but brief, inconsistent and undefined. Many policy documents make only a single reference to religion and belief. A handful of terms are used interchangeably and without definition, so that 'religion', 'belief', 'spirituality', 'well-being', 'values' and 'world views' frequently substitute for one another, pretty much randomly. No rationale is given for why religion and belief should be taken seriously in the first place. The relationship between different policies and guidelines is unclear and often inconsistent. The result is a lack of joined-up thinking about how ethics, practice, values, knowledge and skills are communicated, taught and learned. There emerges a vague sense that religion and belief ought to be taken into account in working life, accompanied by an almost complete absence of knowing why, how, where, what and when.

The question of why religion and belief are thought to be important at all can be split into two areas, each of which adds to the muddle. First, equality law has opened up a space in workplaces for religion and belief that constructs them largely as a risk to be mitigated and managed. More recently, framings have emerged that see this as having potentially positive effects, not just for individuals, but also for organisations more generally, who may find themselves experiencing happier, more stable workforces, service users and customers as they become more skilled at engaging with religion and belief diversity. Nevertheless, the goal in the equality arena is to avoid litigation, as well as to promote that diversity. At the same time, legal cases turn on their own facts and rarely point neatly to the solution or practice for next time.

The second key arena concerns the spirituality of customers, service users and staff, which is increasingly regarded as an aspect of health and well-being. This is true of the health and social care professions in particular but has been emerging in commercial and business settings too. This comes with the major problem that spirituality is largely undefined, as well as almost never operationalised. It is not easy – perhaps not even possible – to know what workplace spirituality is, what it enables or how to nurture it. It also suffers from the widespread implicit assumption that 'spirituality' is always a good thing. The word has a cosiness to it that is difficult to argue against. However, spirituality might sometimes pose difficulties, as suggested by the counselling professions' references to 'spiritual abuse'. Moreover, without understandings of what 'spiritual' really means, workplaces and trainees will struggle to recognise, remedy, prove or prevent benefits and problems. Within this is an important critique about separating out the concepts of spirituality and religion or belief (Sanzenbach, 1989) as there is a tendency to aggregate matters of religion within less sensitive notions, such as 'values' (Constable, 1983). Thus, religion tends to be bracketed off and other words like 'spiritual' and 'well-being' act instead as interchangeable and apologetic proxies. Closer inspection of the ways in which individuals use and apply such terms across the professions may well reveal important insights into how religion and belief are encountered and constructed within professional settings. In this light, as Stiffoss-Hanssen (2009) argues, 'spirituality' still needs to be better defined if it is to serve as a more useful and operative term.

The challenge, then, is for workplaces and professions to move from this emerging sense that they ought to take religion and belief seriously, to knowing why, with what purposes and how to do it. Not being sued and having happier staff and customers may be laudable goals of any organisation but they will not be consistently achieved without a strong awareness of what terms mean, as well as how to recognise them, act on them and demonstrate the impacts. This is a challenge for both professional training and workplace policies, which each have a major role to play in helping leaders, staff, customers and service users to be secure in their expectations of how religion, belief and spirituality will be perceived and handled.

8

Religion and belief in community education and learning

Introduction

There has been a long tradition of education and learning in community spaces, both formal and informal. Much of this emerges from a 20th-century movement that itself evolved from three main strands. The first was the school-based village and community college movement initiated by Henry Morris in Cambridgeshire during the 1920s. This led to the establishment of 'integrated adult education' in the 1930s to backfill the gaps left by inadequate childhood provision (Fairbairn, 1979). It is also closely connected to trades unions and mutual aid movements, such as the Fabian Society, Settlement House, the Cooperative Movement and places like Ruskin College, where working-class people could engage in education for activism, democracy and rights. The second strand concerned experiments arising out of the UK's Educational Priority Area Projects between 1969 and 1972, which attempted to provide 'compensatory education' in disadvantaged areas in inner cities and was also intended to equip adults who had been let down as children (Hawley and Svara, 1972: 26). The third strand was community education work undertaken by a number of the UK government's community development projects in the late 1960s and early 1970s. These were area-based regeneration initiatives designed to address the problem of so-called 'sink' housing estates. The community education approach often takes a radical stance, drawing on the Freireian concept of 'conscientisation' (Freire, 1985: 74), which sees education as the route to the discovery and surfacing of innate talents and abilities in everyone. It is regarded as the route to empowerment and liberation (Lovett, 1975).

These traditions of adult and community education have in common a concern to challenge the deficiencies of early education and to seek to fill gaps in children's and adults' education and skills that have arisen as a result of poverty and disadvantage. The liberation dimension has emerged and somewhat displaced the 'deficiency' focus with the idea of education for emancipation and empowerment. More recently, critics have observed ways in which the empowering radical dimension has given rise to a type of 'active citizenship' that instrumentalises people for specific policy purposes. As a result, new forms of community education have emerged that seek to underpin the production of 'useful citizens'. This has tended to produce a conservative, not radical, citizen, capable of plugging practical gaps in needs within communities but omitting the critique of poverty and government that goes with the empowerment strand. This has been joined to a vocational focus on literacy and numeracy, or on science, technology, engineering and maths (STEM). This is far removed from the challenge posed by Freire. Much of what is learnt about religion and belief in community spaces tends to reflect this instrumental turn, which is primarily expressed in preoccupations with community education for the promotion of cohesion, on the one hand, and the prevention of extremism, on the other. This has been criticised for constructing religion and belief as problematic and risky, as well as leaving out those aspects that emphasise less tangible dimensions, such as spirituality or 'wisdom'. This is despite a growing sense of the thinness of a public sphere without them (Stacey, 2018; Baker et al, 2018). These twin tensions between religion and belief as opportunity versus risk, and as spiritual versus instrumental, are an important part of the public muddle. This chapter examines the tensions across three strands of community education: cohesion education, which emphasises skills in multi-faith action; anti-extremism education, which trains community leaders to spot and prevent religion and belief extremism (including non-religious, political extremism) and increasingly addresses anti-Semitism; and citizenship education, which is something of a blend. It also looks at supplementary education in 'out-of-school settings', the majority of which are faith-based, the curricula of which are largely unknown and whose very existence has therefore been controversial. This all sits in a context of the widespread absence of forms of adult education focused on politics, power and inequality, much of which once took place in universities. However, many universities have lost such spaces in the period since around 1980.

Policy framings of community cohesion

Cohesion is an arena with a lot of baggage. The drivers of the community cohesion agenda in the UK were originally located in race and immigration (see Cantle, 2005: 3). A range of pressures have been identified that contribute to the breakdown of community cohesion in the context of immigration: the role of 'modern communications allowing trans-national identities to be much more easily supported' (Cantle, 2005: 5); the fact that as 'home' citizens' rights have expanded, so foreigners have taken note and asserted their own; and resentment by established residents of newcomers in a context of already-established disadvantage in housing, education and employment, which can lead to racism and conflict. Thus, it has been observed that following mass immigration, 'the pronouncements of far right-wing organizations such as Combat 18, the National Front and the British National Party did little to allay the unfounded fears of the white majority that public services, jobs and even the country as a whole were being taken over by undeserving foreigners' (Billings and Holden, 2008: 7). Cantle (2005: 6) argues in that context that this resulted in communities fracturing and that 'the immigration problem was now, more evidently than ever before, a matter of "race"'. However, in the evolution of the agenda for community cohesion, the swiftness with which the fracturing of local communities was transformed from a 'race' issue to a 'faith' issue is striking. The categories have much to connect them in the public imagination. Thus, Cantle (2005: 12) observed that 'ethnic and faith divisions have now begun to replace those based upon ideas about "race"'. However, following 9/11, this was already the case by the end of 2001, when community tensions were seen as being not between 'Asians and white people', but between 'Muslims and Christians'. Under the impetus of growing concerns about Islam following this, the angry young Asians of that summer were already popularly cast as 'Islamic militants' by the end of the year (see Amin, 2002: 964).

Policy responses to immigration and the perception of a breakdown of cohesive communities along lines of race were initially focused on anti-discrimination laws (see the UK's Race Relations Acts 1965 and 1968), on the one hand, and education characterised as 'limited attempts to "promote good race relations" by working with the white community to improve their understanding of the black and minority ethnic communities' (Cantle, 2005: 6), on the other. These were the first forms of instrumental community education in this arena. The links between race, poverty and disadvantage were not widely accepted until the Scarman Report in the UK in 1981, which associated racial tension with structural disadvantages holding back immigrants from the sorts of educational opportunities and employment seen as key to the success of others. Another significant moment in the UK was the MacPherson Report in 1999, which identified 'institutional racism' in the London Metropolitan Police Force – the sort of racism that is built into the structures and processes of policing, not only in the personal racisms of individual officers. Yet, as Cantle (2005: 8) notes, approaches to the anti-cohesive forces of division along racial lines continued to be based on a combination of 'controlling behaviour and making good the deficits'. This, in turn, has frequently led to counterclaims of the preferential treatment of black and minority ethnic people. At the same time, such approaches are also criticised for 'problematising' minorities, on the one hand, and for ignoring 'the white community who were experiencing as much, if not more, difficulty in coming to terms with the change' (Cantle, 2005: 9), on the other. Cantle argues that what 'prevention and promotion' strategies in relation to race seem most to have achieved is a sense of 'separateness'. It is feared that, in some cases, this separateness may result in the building of 'a common bond of disaffection, both within nation states and across national borders, embracing a transnational identity, rather than with their fellow citizens' (Cantle, 2005: 10). It is this that is primarily seen as the threat to cohesion – and that is often thought to be playing out in the ideas of the Caliphate and the Muslim ummah in Syria, Iraq and elsewhere.

This is crucial because, despite the critiques of them, these are the very approaches that have also been emerging in relation to religion and belief. The UK government's approach first emerged under two contrasting policy rhetorics. One is for multi-faith citizenship, which constructs people of faith as good at community, better volunteers and more strongly networked and connected than others. This is the aspect that 'promotes'. The other is under the banner of 'Prevent'. This strand of policy has evolved – and, indeed, was reviewed wholesale in 2010 – but started with the premise that governments must 'deal firmly with those prepared to engage in … extremism; and most particularly those who incite or proselytize it' (Home Office, 2005: 1). The overall aim was 'to build resilient communities able to challenge robustly the ideas of those violent extremists who seek to undermine our way of life' (Home Office, 2007).

Cohesion learning through interfaith and multi-faith work

Community policy on religion and belief first focused on interfaith and multi-faith cohesion in the document *Face to Face, Side by Side: A Framework for Partnership in Our Multifaith Society* (DCLG, 2008). This presented four 'building blocks' of learning: 'developing the confidence and skills to "bridge" and "link"; shared spaces for interaction and social action; structures and processes which support dialogue and social action; and opportunities for learning which build understanding'

(DCLG, 2008). The policy document promised to 'support a stronger dialogue between people of different faiths and beliefs in every community and encourage the kind of practical interfaith cooperation that can make pleasant and harmonious neighbourhoods for all' (Casey, 2016: 173).

In the same vein, in the UK, a 2012 government strategy paper, *Creating the Conditions for Integration*, announced that 'We will encourage links and dialogue between people from different faith and cultural backgrounds, defend the valuable role of faith in public life, and will tackle cultural isolation and segregation' (DCLG, 2012: 10). Both policies are striking in their commitment to the value of religion and belief as public categories. However, this itself is a patchy and uneven commitment across government. The 2012 document conflates religion and culture, which are not the same things. The goals of the document are therefore rather unclear, except to say in a general, undefined way that people should get on. The document also focuses on participation as creating a sense of belonging and, within this, the promotion of 'common ground'. This is identified as one of five key factors contributing to integration. Christianity is highlighted as part of this 'common ground' and measures are given to 'provide sufficient legal powers for all major local authorities in England to now include prayers as part of the formal business at council meetings, if they so wish' (DCLG, 2012: 11). Responding, Gidley (2012) asks: 'How can it be that – in a country where only two thirds of us are Christian (and only a third of Christians go to Church) – saying Christian prayers unites us more than not saying Christian prayers?'

A number of community education initiatives have been supported by the government to underpin this approach. One approach was to fund national bodies to create spaces for working together better: 'We are encouraging interfaith activity by supporting the Faith-based Regeneration Network to link and strengthen faith-based social action projects. We are also supporting the Inter Faith Network for the UK to encourage, resource and link up inter faith groups at the local, regional and national level' (DCLG, 2012: 15). These organisations embody the idea that encountering each other across difference will lead to cohesion. In the multi-faith work of the FbRN, the assumption is that by focusing on social action, faith differences will disappear. In the interfaith work of the IFN, the idea is that safe spaces can be curated in which difference can be addressed and commonality discovered. Both imply that the challenging interface is between people of different religions and beliefs. Neither addresses the question of how religion and belief meet the secular and non-religious.

Since 2011, the government has also funded the Near Neighbours initiative. This is a small initiative, delivered through the Church of England, which implies the idea of a Christian, specifically Anglican, country – itself questionable as a deeply nostalgic presupposition (Dinham, 2012a). A small number of its projects are defined as educational in focus (seven out of 311 between May 2016 and March 2017), most prominently, its Catalyst youth leadership programme. This works with young people of any faith and none, exploring the relationship between faith and identity. It is described as 'an interactive, leadership programme for young people between 16 and 30 years of age'.[1] The programme has been delivered 25 times (April 2011–March 2016) in a range of locations across England and a total of 313 young people have completed it. The course includes a focus on 'Faith and Identity – exploring the context of multi-faith, multi-cultural Britain; reflecting on the role of faith in a liberal democracy; exploring the relationship between faith and identity and analysing sources of information'.[2] This focus on interfaith work has been promoted at the highest levels of government. For example, the then Secretary of State for Communities, Sajid Javid, pronounced government support for interfaith activity but no method is given other than the heralding of Near Neighbours:

> Interfaith dialogue needs to happen at all levels of society. It needs the ordinary members of your synagogues, the congregation from the local church, the people who attend the mosques and temples and gurdwaras. All of us need to come together and see just how much common ground we share. As rabbis, I think you're in a great position to make that happen. You are teachers, counsellors, leaders who can share the importance of dialogue and help to bring it about. But don't worry. I'm not just going to stand here, and issue some kind of order, and expect you to get on with mobilising your flock. We all have a role to play. I want to make sure government is playing its part. Five years ago we started a programme called Near Neighbours.[3]

The commitment to interfaith work first makes the assumption that encounter leads to cohesion. Then, it constructs the problem as between different religions and beliefs, rather than between the sacred and the secular. Finally, it funds the Church of England to facilitate interfaith and multi-faith work for cohesion on behalf of everybody. These are muddled messages in themselves. A number of community bodies have reflected and reproduced these constructions. For example, the Faith and Belief Forum (formerly the Three Faiths Forum and then 3FF) has provided training in this space for schools, community groups, third sector organisations and local authorities. These focus on what they call 'faith awareness' and 'intercultural competence'. This training is based on the premise that bringing people together in meaningful activity is always good for relations (Shaw, 2014; Trethewey and Menzies, 2014), though this is not a well-evidenced claim and some have cautioned against the simple proposition that knowing each other results in loving each other. The creation of 'safe spaces' and the communication skills for dealing with controversial issues is seen as a key element. The focus is on meaningful dialogue and relating this to context-specific issues in communities. A school-linking programme particularly exemplifies this, drawing on the idea of sustained friendships as the foundation for positive intergroup relations (Davies et al, 2011).

There have also been many arts-based initiatives to promote learning across religion, belief and cultural differences. Some examples include the Faith and Beliefs Forum's 'Urban Dialogue' and 'What Women Believe', an oral history and art installation in an inclusive space designed to encourage dialogue. In 2012, the British Library held the exhibition 'Haj – Journey to the Heart of Islam', which included interviews with British Muslims about their experiences of Haj. 'Faith & Fashion' was an initiative at the London College of Fashion with participants from secular and religious communities. This was a fashion show that also provided an open forum for discussions about the opportunities and challenges associated with what religious people wear. The 'Belief & Beyond Festival' at London's Southbank Centre in 2016 was supported by Coexist House and the Cambridge Interfaith Programme to explore the music, art, culture, science, philosophy, ritual and traditions that have risen out of religion in its many guises: 'This included talks on a range of issues including abortion, same sex marriage, holy wars and martyrdom. The goal was to engage in some "difficult conversations".'[4] The Birmingham Museum and Art Gallery hosts 'Faith in Birmingham', which is designed to explore the faiths that make up the city and how they have influenced and shaped it.

More widely, the Council of Europe hosts the Intercultural Cities Programme, rooted in the report *How Can We Unlock the Potential of Cultural Diversity in Cities?* (Wood et al, 2006). This programme is based on the concept that cultural diversity is an advantage rather than a burden for cities if it is managed in the right way. It develops standards and guidance on the management of cultural diversity in cooperation with and based on the concrete experience of the city.[5]

The programme includes a whole series of 'educative spaces' with city leaders, policymakers, community organisations and schools to help reshape policy and services to be more effective in diverse contexts. Within this, religion is constructed as part of culture, though the religion dimension of intercultural education is given much attention and includes recognition of the relationship between religion and non-religion.

Prolific though such community learning may have become in recent years, the evidence for its effects is extremely limited, mostly appearing only in qualitative evaluations, many of which are carried out by their own providers. In any case, the multi-faith and interfaith space has been criticised for being more rhetoric than reality:

> It has no religious creed, buildings, explicit practices, or formal leaders. It struggles to deliver complex partnership and the broadest of participation. It finds it especially hard to engage with the marginalized, radicalized and extreme whom policy-makers most want to address. In these ways, multi-faith practices risk constituting a parallel world running alongside 'real' faith communities, seeming to respond to policy hopes but unable to bring constituencies of faith with them. (Dinham, 2012b)

Likewise, interfaith initiatives are criticised for being conversations of the willing, and for assuming that encounter results in cohesion, when, in fact, it might equally lead to the opposite. Finally, the language slips more or less interchangeably between 'interfaith', 'multi-faith' and 'intercultural', without really pinning down the meanings, methods or rationale. These are confusing contexts for learning.

Anti-extremism education

The confusion deepens in the context of anti-extremism education. This space is dominated by Prevent, the second big arena alongside cohesion for learning about religion and belief in communities. A 2011 review recognised this to the extent that it led to a separation of Prevent initiatives (associated with security and administered by the Home Office) and integration (associated with cohesion and administered by the Department of Communities, Housing and Local Government). It has been observed that this went so far as to end cohesion initiatives as a matter for the state, which has since focused only on security: 'Under Prevent 2 the coalition government officially ended any national support for, and interest in community cohesion ... saying this was purely a local matter. Britain now has an increasingly centralised and securitised Prevent strategy and no national cohesion strategy at all' (Thomas, 2012: 176). Thus, the focus shifted to public authorities identifying and reporting those at risk of radicalisation, and a 'Prevent duty' was imposed on schools (see Chapter 4) and public bodies to require professionals to report concerns (Thomas, 2012). Although Prevent 2 extended its focus to all types of extremism, including political extremism, Thomas notes that 'its recommendations are all about "oversight of religious supplementary schools" ... "extremist preachers" ... in universities and the need for "Muslim chaplains" in prisons' (Thomas, 2012: 175). He criticises the implicit essentialising and homogenising of Muslims, as demonstrated most starkly in the focus on Muslim-only youth projects, suggesting that lessons should have been learnt from previous ethnically targeted anti-racist education with white young people (Thomas, 2012: 176). Within this, he sees Muslims as constructed as both 'risky' and 'at risk', that is, vulnerable to radicalisation (Thomas, 2012). He concludes that 'In focusing on Muslims as an essentialized community, Prevent is clearly contradictory to community cohesion. By focusing on an entire Muslim community, Prevent inherently stigmatizes and risks hardening defensive identifications within Muslim youth, as clumsy anti-racism did with some white communities previously' (Thomas, 2012: 184). Thomas also criticises the weakness of pedagogy within Prevent and cites examples of cricket lessons for young Muslims (Kundnani, 2009, cited in Thomas, 2012) and youth work with no discussion or meaningful engagement with extremism itself (Thomas, 2012).

The Casey Review (Casey, 2016) makes similar observations. Based on conversations (and approximately 200 written submissions) with more than 800 members of the public (community groups, officials and academics, as well as teachers, pupils and faith leaders), this highlights a lack of integration in some religious communities, particularly Muslim, which it links to regressive religious and cultural practices. The report calls upon religious leaders to work harder to 'promote shared human values' and for Muslim leaders to 'respond to the demand in their communities for a clearer interpretation of Islam for modern life in Britain' (Casey, 2016: 136). Thus, it recognises diversity within Muslim communities but responds with a 'one-size-fits-all' solution. This attempt to define a version of Islam that is seen as compatible with British identity is criticised in Kundnani's analysis of the official narrative on extremism (Kundnani, 2015), which highlights an apparent return to cultural assimilation and its alienation of British Muslims.

Other suggestions for the creation of a 'compatible Islam' relate to mosques:

> During the review, Baroness Warsi called publicly for the development of mosque architectural designs that better contextualised Islam in 21st Century Britain. Such a step could be symbolic of a wider desire in the Muslim population to cultivate a British flavour of Islam, comfortable in its identity, discussed later in this chapter. (Casey, 2016: 127)

The review observes that 'Now more than ever, mosques and their leadership need to be open and transparent to the communities around them to help break down suspicion and build trust. A new approach to engagement between mosques, Government, local authorities and communities is needed urgently' (Casey, 2016: 127). The review also thinks that Muslim communities themselves have a responsibility to educate the wider community about their faith and to counter stereotypes and suspicion. It calls on 'liberal' religious leaders to make their voices heard:

> We hope those leaders will respond positively to this review and push this important work harder and faster, including through their education and school arms, to promote shared human values, confront the harms we have identified and enable anyone of any belief, or none, to feel respected, not condemned; protected by the laws and traditions of the United Kingdom. And we hope that Muslim leaders will respond to the demand in their communities for a clearer interpretation of Islam for modern life in Britain. (Casey, 2016: 136)

The focus on Muslims in this path-breaking review has been strongly criticised. Cantle commented in December 2016 that:

> just last week a new report, 'Unsettled Belonging' [Frampton et al, 2015], by Policy Exchange suggested that a strong focus on Muslim communities may no longer be justified. The largest opinion poll of British Muslims found an 'essentially secular character of most Muslim lifestyles'. In terms of their everyday concerns

and priorities, British Muslims answer no differently from their non-Muslim neighbours.[6]

At the same time, the review highlights the need for tackling difficult issues, suggesting that the focus on common ground needs to move beyond the comfortable to include challenging views and highly contested issues. There is an apparent paradox in that the review reports that 'some of the interfaith work not only avoided the difficult conversations that were needed but had also provided an unchallenged platform or legitimacy to those whose views and values actually undermined cohesion' (Casey, 2016).

Nevertheless, it plays out in grass-roots educational initiatives too. Online training for communities is provided by the government[7] and focuses on the grooming and radicalisation process through the use of two case studies: one related to Far Right political extremism and one to Islamist extremism. The case studies reflect a shift in the discourse, moving away from a causal relationship between ideology and radicalisation, and towards a focus on vulnerability arising from the social and personal circumstances of individuals. This shift away from Islam as 'risk' is also expressed in the work of the Islam–UK Centre at Cardiff University, which has introduced the Wales Muslim Young Leaders Awards with Citizens Cymru Wales. The goal is to 'send the message that young Muslim leaders in Wales are indeed committed to working for the common good of their communities'.[8] The 'Islamophobia 2017' project[9] aims to renew awareness of the causes, nature, facets and dangers of Islamophobia. It works to develop and strengthen counter-narratives relating to citizenship, secularism, pluralism and justice, and provides resources, lesson plans, activities and course outlines for schools, colleges, universities and communities. Launched in 2012, the 'Big Iftar' is another community-led initiative, with a focus on building relationships of learning with one another and building bridges between Muslim communities and wider populations. Muslim Action for Development and Environment (MADE) is partnering up with Ebrahim College to run 'An Introduction to Activism', which is a seven-week intensive programme that looks at the Islamic concept of serving society through active campaigning. The course covers the Islamic perspective on activism, why we need activism, campaigning skills, community organising skills, media skills and leadership skills.[10] The preponderance of Islam-focused education and learning reveals how the public conversation in communities continues to revolve around the problem of Islam. An attempt is made to tackle this Islam-as-problem focus in the Tony Blair Institute for Global Change's Generation Global programme (formerly known as Face to Faith). Promoting interfaith and intercultural dialogue as a means of preventing radicalisation and recruitment into violent extremism, the programme has run in over 2,500 schools around the world. A recent study at Exeter University (Doney and Wegerif, 2017) found that the programme had a positive impact in breaking down stereotypes and creating open-mindedness, and described it as 'inoculation against extremist violence'.[11] Its resources have also been included on the UK Department for Education's Educate against Hate website, and are highlighted in both the United Nations Educational, Scientific, and Cultural Organization's (UNESCO's) 'Guide for Policy-Makers Preventing Violent Extremism through Education' and the report on 'Measuring Global Citizenship Education' by the Brooking's Institution (a US policy research organisation). Such an approach shares much with that of the Council of Europe's intercultural education. It is based on a critical pedagogy that is 'founded on the principle of accepting multiple realities, feeling comfortable with ambiguity and searching for multiple truths, not one truth' (Davies, 2008: 192) These approaches explore the complexities of religion and identity. Increased awareness of and tolerance for complexity is seen as effective in preventing future radicalisation. As Kundnani (2015: 26) concludes: 'The debate on multiculturalism is securitised so that a series of distinct issues involving Muslims in public life are interpreted through the lens of clashes over identity that can only be remedied by demands for assimilation.'

Education for anti-Semitism

A related space that has been opening up in recent years across Europe is education to address the growing problem of anti-Semitism. It is noted that 'Despite the international efforts to stamp out anti-semitism … it has continued to threaten Jewish livelihoods, culture and security' (UNESCO, 2018: 12). In survey research in 2019, 85 per cent of respondents considered anti-Semitism and racism to be the most pressing problem facing EU states, with 89 per cent believing that anti-Semitism has increased in their country over the last five years (EUFRA, 2019: 3). The report concludes that 'anti-semitism pervades the public sphere' (EUFRA, 2019: 3). In 12 of the largest EU states, fewer than 5 per cent of respondents thought that anti-Semitism was not a problem in their country, and between 56 per cent and 95 per cent thought that it was a 'very big' or 'fairly big' problem (EUFRA,

2019: 4). In 2016, research by the World Jewish Congress (2016) found that 90 per cent of anti-Semitic posts on social media in the UK were made by white males under the age of 40 with affiliations to extreme right-wing groups. In the UK, in the period between 1997 and 2018, the total number of reported anti-Semitic incidents increased from 219 to 1,652, with the number doubling and then rapidly increasing, especially after 2014 (CST, 2018).

There may be important intersections between different religions and beliefs in this field too. According to Mehdi Hasan (2013), 'anti-Semitism isn't just tolerated in some sections of the British Muslim community; it's routine and commonplace'. So, education against anti-Semitism appears as an issue among younger white men and between Jewish people and other religions and beliefs. UNESCO has been developing education tools in this space for use across Europe, and the OSCE's Office for Democratic Institutions and Human Rights (ODIHR) has undertaken work to 'facilitate the exchange of good practices among participating States on educational initiatives and other measures to raise awareness of anti-Semitism and overcome challenges to Holocaust education' (UNESCO, 2018: 3). This is constructed primarily as an issue of security and human rights since 'anti-Semitism threatens the realization of all people's human rights and the overall security of states where it occurs' (UNESCO, 2018: 7). The call is for governments to ensure that they are 'providing education *about* anti-Semitism. At the same time, governments need to respond effectively to anti-Semitism *in* educational settings' (UNESCO, 2018: 8).

In the UK, this has resulted in the introduction of a Jewish Community Protective Security Grant for the security of synagogues and Jewish schools. At the same time, the Holocaust has become the only compulsory subject in the national curriculum for history at ages 11–16. Thus, anti-Semitism is primarily constructed in terms of security and hate crime. The community learning spaces that result are focused on these issues too. Jewish learning centres have been funded in London, Nottinghamshire and Huddersfield by the Heritage Lottery Fund to promote conversation and awareness of Jewish and anti-Semitic history, especially awareness of the Holocaust. The national Imperial War Museum has dedicated two floors to the Holocaust. A UK Holocaust memorial and learning centre has been approved to be built next door to the Houses of Parliament. The Centre for Holocaust Education at University College London provides training and resources for schools. It broadens the frame towards an existential question about self-knowing but remains rooted in these concerns about contemporary security, on the one hand, and historical and persistent anti-Semitism, culminating in the Holocaust, on the other: 'Not long ago, and not far from where we live, ordinary people across Europe became complicit in the murder of their neighbours. What will young people's education amount to if they do not confront this appalling truth?' (UCL, 2019). The broader implications of community learning about religion in this space are that it is problematic, divisive and connected to division and hate. The learning responses assume that engagement with the terrible history of anti-Semitism will lead to an enlightened rejection of it. This sidesteps the possibility that people who already hold anti-Semitic views may not be ignorant of these histories, and may not be convinced by encounter with them. An approach that actively acknowledges, engages with and challenges the tropes of anti-Semitism might be more effective in revealing their absurdity.

Supplementary schools education

Supplementary education is defined as all out-of-school-hours learning. It includes what are broadly described as 'cultural enrichment activities', including faith, arts and sports. Provision takes place within a range of contexts, such as tuition groups, after-school clubs, 'mother-tongue' classes, Saturday schools and faith-based tuition in temples, synagogues, mosques and churches. Some of it is home-based. Supplementary schools offer this range of educational support outside the school day and very often within the context of a specific ethnic or faith community. They are established and managed by community members, generally on a voluntary basis. There are estimated to be 3,000–5,000 supplementary schools in the UK. They are not classified as 'schools' by the government and cannot be registered as such or inspected.

In 2016, the UK government's Department for Education confirmed that the government does not have plans for the implementation of regulation for the provision of out-of-school education, though there was a consultation on the matter in 2015. In part, this was prompted by a commitment in the government's wider counter-extremism strategy to enable intervention in out-of-school settings, which attract suspicion because so little is known about what happens in them. This frames the debate in two key policy terms: as a safeguarding issue concerned with the protection of children against abuse and neglect; and as an issue of the prevention of extremism (DfE, 2018). The call for evidence received 3,082 responses online, of which 55 per cent were faith groups and a further 20 per cent were parents. The results appear to consolidate concerns: 74 per cent were against any requirement to register with the local authority and 58 per cent were against providing details of ownership, location, the education offer and the numbers of children (DfE, 2018: 8–9). Likewise, 75 per cent were against Ofsted having a power to investigate concerns (DfE, 2018: 11). When asked about prohibited activities in supplementary schools, 65 per cent disagreed that this should include 'teaching which undermines or is incompatible with fundamental British values, or which promotes extremist views' (DfE, 2018: 14). Nevertheless, the review concludes that 'It is clear from the responses … that there was broad support for [safeguarding]'; on extremism, it concludes that 'there are many legal powers already in place … and many out of school settings do a great job in providing enriching activities in many subjects … including religion' (DfE, 2018: 18). Therefore, it states that 'We want to ensure any future system of regulation … targets the small minority of settings which may be exposing children to harmful practices' (DfE, 2018: 18). The overall conclusion is that 'we have decided not to pursue the model proposed in our call for evidence' (DfE, 2018: 19) and to develop the evidence further instead. There was also a reference to a possible voluntary code of practice and work with local authorities to provide guidance for parents. This means that 3,000–5,000 out-of-school settings are providing community education of an unknown character to an unknown number, of which more than half are faith-based. It is difficult to avoid the sense that out-of-school education remains something of a black box, while what little is known about them suggests that there is a strong view among their supporters that they need not align themselves with the sorts of values and world views that mainstream schools are certainly expected to reflect. In effect, there is a two-tier system in which formal education is subject to high levels of scrutiny while informal settings are only engaged once they are seen to have broken the law. In practice, this stands capable of adding to an atmosphere of suspicion and 'otherness'.

The citizenship test

Since 2010, when a Conservative–Liberal Coalition government came to power in the UK, policy on cohesion and extremism has been recast once again, this time with a focus on security. What is even more striking is the relocation of the debate within the terms of a recast citizenship based not in the unfettered multiculturalism of the period prior to this, but in a more defined Britishness in which one's nationhood is invited to take precedence over one's faith, race or other dimensions of identity. This emphasis on citizenship reflects the idea that community has come to be seen as 'a realm of governance through which to counter the apparent crisis in social cohesion' that was shown up in the disturbances in the UK in 2001 (Robinson, 2005: 1412). The rhetoric of community has long provided an imagined space, convenient for policymakers to populate with all they find too difficult to solve with actual policy. It also casts 'cohesion' within the terms of a new kind of multicultural settlement, the parameters of which are not made clear, except to say that they are 'British'. This reflects Cantle's observation that we are in a 'moment of transition' (see Dinham et al, 2009). The 'Life in the United Kingdom Test' was introduced in 2005 and is one of three requirements for migrants applying for British citizenship, along with obtaining the required proficiency in the English language and swearing an oath of allegiance. This was extended to those seeking 'Indefinite Leave to Remain' in 2007. The current citizen test was amended in 2011 to have a stronger focus on British history and culture (Turner, 2014; Brooks, 2014). The introduction of the test is understood as a response to a growing sense of cultural fragmentation and is connected to a perception of risk to security (Turner, 2014). Analyses of citizenship tests in the UK, Europe and the US have examined the extent to which they are assimilatory and thus illiberal (see Michalowski, 2011). The actual questions for the UK test are unpublished (to avoid cheating), though sample questions are available on many websites. According to Michalowski (2011), the test's question relating to religion assumes a relationship between the church and state, a liberal disposition towards freedom of religion, and knowledge about the so-called 'main' Christian holidays.

The government handbook provided to help participants prepare for the test contains seven pages on religion (out of 180). It starts with the statement 'The UK is historically a Christian country' (Home Office, 2019: 76). Startlingly, on Northern Ireland, it says 'There is no established church in Wales or Northern Ireland' (Home Office, 2019: 77), a statement that might imply to a newcomer to the UK that there is no significant church presence there of any kind. This is followed by a section about patron saints (Home Office, 2019: 77–8), a large photograph of Westminster Abbey and then five pages on 'customs and traditions'. This section includes: Christmas Day, Boxing Day and Easter in a section called 'main festivals' (Home Office, 2019: 79); then Diwali, Hanukkah, Eid and Vaisakhi in a section called 'other religious festivals' (Home Office, 2019: 81–2); and, finally, New Year, Valentine's Day, April Fool's Day, Mothering Sunday, Father's Day, Halloween, Bonfire Night and Remembrance Day in a section called 'other festivals and traditions' (Home Office, 2019: 82–3). At the same time, Hogenboom has noted a shift in emphasis since 2013 from practical knowledge to a focus on identity, culture and history (Hogenboom, cited in Turner, 2014), and an especial focus on legal norms and factual knowledge. Thus, citizenship tests are constructed as 'acts which specifically focus on cultural homogeny – often in denial of the liberal stress on individual rights and equality' (Joppke, quoted in Turner, 2014: 334). Likewise, 'the examination of would-be citizens [is] based on a model of assimilation rather than tolerance where the principles of pluralism, individualism and equality are silenced' (Kim, quoted in Turner, 2014: 334). Thus, tests are seen as exclusionary by nature. Others raise the question of the right of minority values to be heard within this 'democratic' notion and note Kundnani's observation of a shift from multiculturalism to demands for cultural sameness (Kundnani, 2015).

This locates citizenship education, and the test, within a drive for cohesion and strengthening the bonds of mutual understanding. Immigration is seen as a risk to cohesion in this approach. An active role is required of the would-be citizens to participate in and purchase the materials for the test, and 'the practice of learning ... becomes a powerful totem of the "active" and "committed" subject who will become a citizen' (Hoing, quoted in Turner, 2014: 342). As Turner summarises:

> In asking the would-be citizen to perform certain functions (to pay, learn and provide evidence of achievements) before rights are distributed ... the subject of the test is acted upon as a 'risk' – but one that can be modified and made safer through certain techniques of 'inclusion' (self-improvement, education, understanding). (Turner, 2014: 343, 345)

Conclusions

Learning about religion and belief in communities reflects the wider muddle and follows many of the same lines of separation. Some aspects focus on good relations across difference in and between communities. Others are very much about managing risk, as in the prevention of extremism, and ensuring a sort of compliance with certain sets of values, as in citizenship. Here, there is a sense of incoherence as to what role religion and belief play in communities: are they a relational force or a sinister threat? Perhaps they are capable of being both, but in the absence of a conscious, overarching narrative, communities may struggle to make sense of the inconsistencies.

9

The future of religion and belief literacy: reconnecting a chain of learning

Introduction

Religion and belief continue in a public sphere that largely thinks of itself as post-Christian, post-religious and secular, while having limited understanding of either religion and belief *or* the secular. This makes it a particularly difficult subject for discussion and learning. As the previous chapters show, messages about religion and belief are messy and often contradictory within learning spaces, as well as between one learning space and another. While this might be said of all sorts of topics, this one has some particular features that single it out.

First, the woolly secular-mindedness at its root often stops the conversation before it begins. The UK is neither programmatically secular (ideologically committed to a public sphere that is neutral on religion or belief), nor procedurally so (bracketing religion or belief out in public practices and policy) (Williams, 2006). Yet, the public sphere widely acts on religion and belief as though both are the case. It also does so in starkly contradictory ways. On the one hand, religion and belief are, at best, irrelevant and, at worst, risky. On the other, they are repositories of resources for wisdom and social action, and the arbiters of an essentially Christian culture that cannot be escaped, even if it is forgotten. A constitutional monarchy, with the monarch as head of both church and state, is one part of this. The Equality Act 2010 is another, placing religion or belief at the heart of public life by making them a protected characteristic against which it is illegal to discriminate. Yet, as an idea, secularity proves to be one of sociology's greatest successes, at least in terms of how widely it is recognised and embedded, if not fully or widely understood. It results in a classically pragmatic space in which the relationship of religion and belief to the public sphere is left fuzzy at best. National rituals, like Remembrance Day, memorials and royal weddings – what Davie (2006) calls vicarious religion – will frequently take a Christian form, albeit with leaders from other world religions turning up, while the serious business of what is actually to be believed or done remains comfortably out of focus. In this, it is more British than religious. Arguably, this has been a successfully liberal approach, allowing for the quiet continuation of both religious and non-religious citizenship in a polis in which neither much mattered. However, the 21st century is stretching such pragmatism as old and new forms of religion and belief intrude very visibly, especially in terms of extremism, where they are noticed most. This has shifted the focus from indifference to anxiety and even hostility.

Second, what is being discovered in this space is a lack of ability to talk about religion and belief. The suppositions of secularity precisely produce this lack of ability since the more the public sphere is assumed to be secular, the less either religion or the secular are treated as legitimate topics for analysis. As this self-perpetuating pattern held through the second half of the 20th century, the capacity to be critical and reflective about religion or belief has been more and more obscured, despite the renewed visibility of religion and belief after 9/11, as well as the persistence of RE in schools, whose presence in the curriculum in many ways adds to the confusion.

Third, at their core, religion and belief engage with existential questions in which everybody has a stake, regardless of how they answer them. They therefore carry within them an inherently lived and often controversial dimension, especially where they touch on issues of life, death, sex and love. This is sometimes managed by avoiding the topic altogether. At other times, it gives rise to debate and argument, often producing more heat than light. At the same time, many people arrive at the topic with deeply felt experiences of religion and belief in their own lives, and others'. Stories abound in many people's lives of religious exclusion and inclusion, very often revolving around sex, death and illness, and frequently speaking of prejudice and pain. The opposite can also be true, where people experience their religion or belief in profound and positive ways, often feeling themselves to be in a critically important relationship with a transcendent being who cares for them and whose callings matter more than anyone else's. This is space in which things can be both deeply controversial and deeply important. The combination is sometimes combustible.

Fourth, religion and belief deal in both certainty and doubt. Religious certainty tends towards conflict while doubt can give rise to fear and defensiveness. Coupled with the capacity of religion and belief to be highly visible, in terms of what people wear, the buildings they go to and some touchpaper moral issues such as abortion, euthanasia and same-sex marriage, the lines of difference are often readily perceivable. They can easily transmute into dividing lines. Since religion and belief also have their roots in geographical locations, such lines are often conflated with lines of ethnicity and culture, so that, for example, Islam may be widely regarded as Middle Eastern and the Middle East as politically tyrannous. Before we know it, a chain of assumptions is established that reifies difference as 'the other' and homogenises that 'other'.

These characteristics of religion and belief both strain the chain of learning and make it more difficult to reconnect. They challenge spaces of learning to help publics make better sense – of religion and belief, *and* secularity, *and* how to think and talk about them. This emerges as an important expression of religion and belief literacy, for where teaching and learning about religion and belief is fragmented and contradictory, publics are left muddled. Often, it feels so messy and complicated that it seems easier not to think about it at all.

Religion and belief literacy

The religious literacy framework, re-imagined and evolved as religion and belief literacy, provides a lens on the issues. By exploring the questions it poses, it might be possible to find a greater coherence within each learning space explored in this book, and ultimately between them. To this extent, it can act as a method for clarifying what a connected chain of learning could entail. Thus, as 'category', what does each space count as religion and belief, and how does it propose to think about it? Does it take a narrow perspective confined to the five world religions, or possibly nine? Or, does it go wider to include new and revived forms, non-religious beliefs, non-religion, world views and values? Then, how does the learning space think about what it has chosen to count? Should religion and belief be treated as functional (from sociology), pathogenic (from psychology) or corresponding to some sort of transcendent (from theology)?

As 'disposition', does the learning setting know what deep feelings and attitudes it reflects and contains? What baggage is there, and how aware is the learning space of it? Are feelings and dispositions known, acknowledged, contested, shared and understood? Or, does a patchwork of muddled and varying standpoints underpin the space in a thicket of feeling, much of which is on or beyond the edge of awareness? This part of the conversation can be the most difficult and, because of its emotional aspects, might put people off trying in the first place. However, moving from accidental resistance to purposeful engagement seems a key part of the journey towards religion and belief literacy, and towards the reconnected chain of learning.

Having worked out what counts and how to feel about it, spaces of learning might then find themselves better able to discern what knowledge it makes sense for them to project. At one level, this is about the range of religions and beliefs that a learning space will choose to work with. It also engages with the critical lenses through which it approaches them. These might be focused somewhat narrowly on theological and ethical aspects, especially in schools, for example. They might engage more broadly with these but also sociological insights into the contemporary religion and belief landscape, which could help open up a more 'lived' understanding. At another level, this engages with questions of purpose. What is the problem that the learning is trying to address? Is it cohesion, extremism, equality, diversity, morality or citizenship? Perhaps it is a blend, or something else entirely. A key pragmatic question is: does the target problem actually exist in the setting in question? A religion and belief literacy that attempts to answer every problem, in every way and in relation to every identity is obviously impossible. However, clarity about content, feeling and purpose can, in turn, shed light on what skills should be learned, whether for interfaith dialogue, workplace relations, lifelong encounter with diversity or something else. This chapter now turns to these questions in each of the learning spaces in the book. The current and potential key messages in each learning space are summarised in Table 1.

RE

RE in schools is perhaps the most prominent public space for religion and belief because it is compulsory and universal; (almost) everybody studies it from age five to 16. This implies a centrality to public life that does not play out in practice. Its continuing presence is mandated under an Act of Parliament from 1944, and despite piecemeal modifications over the decades since, it is widely regarded as outdated and unfit for 21st-century purposes. The paradox is that at the same time as being compulsory, it is also marginalised in schools and policy, often being dropped as an examined subject at age 14 and seen as a result as strangely compulsory and optional at the same time. In schools, it receives relatively little time and funding. In policy, there are few incentives for reform: in being both controversial and uncared for, there are few (electoral) advantages to going there.

The future of religion and belief literacy

Table 1: Summary of current and potential key messages in learning spaces

Learning space	Key current messages	Religion and belief literacy messages
RE	• Society is Christian and post-Christian • The task is to learn its stories and values, and to develop awareness, toleration and respect for 'others'	• Society is Christian, secular, non-religious and plural all at once • Acceptance and understanding that religion and belief are pervasive, lived and ordinary • People should be equipped to encounter the fullest range of religion and belief well, regardless of their own religion, belief or none
Schools	• Schools are not religious, except the ones that are! • Religion is private but schools are nevertheless places of worship and spiritual development • All share in a Christian country connecting to shared British values • Religion and belief is a difficult topic, from which you have the right to withdraw	• RE compulsion removed from the 1944 Act and added to the national curriculum • Clarity about the purposes and content of RE as equipping young people for encounter with a diversity of religion and belief • Sociological as well as theological lenses are applied • No right to withdraw, no daily act of collective worship and no role for SACREs in curricula
University practices	• Religion and belief are risks to be managed in relation to equality law • Religion and belief are potentially dangerous in terms of extremism and radicalisation • Diversity requires that accommodations such as halal food and prayer rooms should be provided • Tradition requires that chaplaincy be provided but there is uncertainty about its purposes and roles	• Religion and belief diversity audited and responded to in similar ways to race, ethnicity and gender as a matter of social justice and good practice, not law • Chaplaincy inclusive of the broadest range of religion, belief and non-belief • Engagement with the potentially formational contributions of religion, belief and spirituality
University curricula	• Religion is private, not public • Religion is in terminal decline and there is no need to study it • Religion is irrational and not a proper subject of study	• Recognition of religion and belief identity as pervasive and engageable by all, regardless of one's own religion, belief or none • Teaching and learning about religion and belief incorporated as a matter of employability readiness (for encounter with diversity) and citizen and personal formation

(continued)

Table 1: (continued)

Learning space	Key current messages	Religion and belief literacy messages
Workplaces and professions	• Religion and belief diversity should be managed to avoid litigation • Religion and belief are tricky in workplaces so it is often easier to do nothing • Religion and belief are parts of identity that should be welcomed at work in pursuit of productivity and effectiveness • Workplace faith networks imply that encounter leads to love • The language of spirituality and mindfulness is preferred because it is thought to be safer than religion	• Professions are trained and equipped for encounter with religion and belief diversity • The professions engage with their secular and pre-secular roots to understand their stances better and adapt and evolve • Spirituality is defined and differentiated from religion and belief
Communities	• Religion and belief are risks in terms of extremism and radicalisation • Religion and belief play an important role in social action and community building • Communities should be vigilant and equipped to spot warning signs about religion and belief • A Christian ethos and values are part of citizenship • Communities should learn together about each other's diversity of religion and belief, which will help them love each other better • Minority religions and beliefs are secretive, teaching subversive ideas in private spaces	• The construction of religion and belief communities as both heroes and villains is acknowledged across community teaching and learning initiatives, and the villainous side set clearly in context as a minority dimension • Religion and belief are constructed in their lived, fluid complexity in the citizen test • Supplementary schools are subject to Ofsted inspection in order to normalise them and remove widespread suspicion

In terms of religion and belief literacy, the 1940s' legacy means that as a matter of 'category', RE retains a core connection to Christianity, despite the inclusion of other religions and beliefs. This belies dramatic changes in the religion and belief landscape, which continues to be Christian, though much less so, as well as secular, plural and non-religious. Yet, despite some excellent examples of innovative RE across Britain and Europe, provision is patchy and inconsistent, and religion and belief continue to be taught by large numbers of non-specialists, many of whom fall back on teaching schemes of which they have a limited understanding. The result is a tendency to teach religions more than beliefs, and as monolithic blocks of facts, rather than as the lived, fluid, heterogeneous identities that they really are.

In terms of disposition, the mixing of learning about religion with religiousness is also unhelpful because it fails to communicate or socialise the differences. The ongoing role of SACREs in RE curricula is easily seen as putting the vested interests of religious people at the centre, even though this may be largely unjustified. The daily act of collective worship in the Christian mode is required but often ignored, and parents can decide to withdraw their children from it. This gives religion and belief a special status that is nevertheless unexplained. It is a messy space in which to first encounter learning about religion and belief, implying that this is difficult ground without ever unpacking why. Yet, as research suggests, young people appear to have an appetite for it (Dinham and Shaw, 2017). Students report seeing RE as important preparation for encounters with diversity. They also see it as the single most important space in which to explore their spiritual development, as well as seeing it as the basis of readiness for the workplace. They want to learn about a wider range of religion and belief, including traditions, informal forms and non-religion, and to emphasise lived religion and religion as a contemporary social issue. However, they describe being confused by the introduction of themes such as disability and climate change, which they think properly belong elsewhere, especially to PSHE and citizenship education. Above all, they see RE as low in status, if not low in interest, given its absence from the national curriculum, despite its being compulsory.

From a religion and belief literacy perspective, RE is conservative in relation to category, remaining rooted in the Christianity of the Education Act 1944, even where it has attempted to go beyond into a post-Christian consciousness. While this stretches its origins, it nevertheless remains in the Christian orbit and other religions and beliefs are defined by their difference to it. In relation to disposition, these issues are consolidated in a marginalisation of RE that renders it unloved, often ending up as a dumping ground for issues that are otherwise difficult to place or discuss. In turn, this gives way to a construction of knowledge as a strange mix of facts and experiences. As facts, religion and belief are rendered unchanging blocks of knowledge that can be taught and learnt as though religion and belief are fixed, not fluid. As experience, they are untethered from theological and sociological insights that might help learners make sense of what they are seeing. Clarification of the content and purpose of RE would seem a very helpful step forward in re-forging this particular link in the chain of learning.

Schools

This muddle within RE ripples out into the wider life of schools, not only through the confusion of confessional spaces (such as collective worship) with educational ones, but also in the range of formational spaces that also overlap. SMSC, 'British values', the 'Prevent duty', citizenship education, PSHE and SRE all have important religion-and-belief-related messages within them but these are almost never connected to each other, or to RE. The overlaps are implied but the boundaries are not defined. The points of connection and disconnection are rarely spelt out. Thus, the 'spiritual' and 'moral' revolves around laudable but vague goals for 'exploring', 'respecting', 'enjoying', 'imagining' and 'reflecting', while entirely omitting any attempt at a definition of 'spiritual' or 'moral', apart from being able to tell the difference between right and wrong. There is also no acknowledgement of their relationships to religion and belief. These dimensions are required to be taught primarily in the PSHE space instead, where religion and belief are largely constructed in relation to extremism, forced marriage, honour-based killing and FGM, which, though cultural issues, carry an implied connection to religion that goes unchallenged. In religion and belief literacy terms, the wider life of schools construes 'category' in similarly Christian and post-Christian terms, emphasising respect and tolerance for difference and an oversimplified appeal to a handful of supposedly shared British values, imbued with normative ideas of 'right and wrong'. As disposition, this resonates with anxiety about how to manage the 'other'. The six spaces across schools in which religion and belief are taught and learned outside of RE both blur the boundaries of RE and send out a shower of competing messages: religion and belief are subjective, individual and fluid but also fixed and homogeneous across traditions; they are a humanities discipline like any other but also part of the spiritual formation of children, *unlike* any other; and they enjoin tolerance and respect but are also violent and risky. Of course, it is possible for all these messages to coexist, just as the world itself is messy and complex. However, RE takes place without a thoughtful articulation of the connections to the other spaces that overlap: SMSC, 'British values', the 'Prevent duty', citizenship education, PSHE and SRE. This is devastating to clarity because they all stake claims to the religion and belief space, and each with differing meanings and boundaries. Pupils in schools might well ask what RE is for when religion and belief are treated so variously in all these other spaces: what are the boundaries and purposes of the educational, formational and confessional dimensions of religion and belief in schools? The relationship between these various parts could be much more fully addressed in individual schools through an audit, however informal, of what religion and belief messages are being communicated, where and with what relationship to all the other messages around. Regular review of the relationships between policies and curricula for British values, PSHE, SMSC, SRE, citizenship education and RE could be an effective way forward.

Universities

The challenge in universities is to move from a secular self-perception to something post-secular, both in operational matters and in curricula. This is certainly a matter of leadership and it has been wryly noted elsewhere that many university vice chancellors are of an age which means that they were at universities themselves when secular assumptions were at their height, in the 1960s and 1970s (Dinham, 2015b). The question of how they choose to think about religion and belief as a category is a part of how it feels across the rest of their institutions. Assumptions of some sort of neutrality are likely to result in a bracketing off of religion and belief to a couple of specialist areas of the university, especially chaplaincy and equality teams. Conversely, constructing religion and belief across their fullest spectrum could make them an issue for everyone, regardless of individuals' religion, belief or none. There is a sense in which this can bring religion and belief in from the margins to being a mainstream consideration of every aspect of the institution. In turn, this determines the extent to which universities might make accommodations for religion and belief. They could do the bare minimum to be compliant with the law, possibly leading to a sense of being in a somewhat grudging environment. Conversely, it could translate into an atmosphere of proactive interest, welcome and engagement that is interested in the wisdoms and challenges posed by religion and belief identities, which might enrich the learning environment. Many institutions will land somewhere in between these poles. The challenge is to do so consciously, knowing why, how and where to engage.

The possibilities of a broad sense of ownership of religion and belief identity across universities also draw attention to the challenge to close the gap between the environment, on the one hand, and curricula themselves, on the other. This draws attention to the schism in universities, which recognises the value and challenges of religion and belief diversity in students while, at the same time, largely refusing it in teaching and learning. Much of this resides in a disposition that reflects a long intellectual inheritance that struggles with religion, and the submission of academic disciplines to the logic of the natural sciences. However, being equipped for engagement with the fullest diversity of religion and belief is demanded by the new emphasis on employment readiness, by equality law and by the sheer realities of internationalisation and diversity brought about by globalism. Universities are challenged by this to examine their own assumptions and actions, just as many are beginning to do so on race and gender through movements like #MeToo and 'decolonising the curriculum'.

Professions and workplaces

In the professions that have moved into the universities, this is even more pressing as emerging professionals go into practice with increasingly diverse service users. Universities will need to be clear what they want to say about religion and belief in these spaces, as will the regulatory bodies that validate their trainings.

At the same time, while there is evidence of a widespread opening up towards 'spirituality' in professions and workplaces, this is almost entirely undefined and there are very few indications of how to put 'spirituality' into practice. Work to develop clear understandings of what professions and workplaces mean by 'spirituality' is likely to help them to work meaningfully in these spaces, rather than stating a commitment that is incapable of going anywhere. It will also enable them to think through the distinctions between religion, belief and spirituality in ways that could lead them to conscious, active decisions about the categories they include and accommodate, and those that fall outside their scope. The transparency that results is one benefit; organisational resilience and readiness for dilemmas posed by issues such as time off, workplace dress and prayer rooms is another. This connects to questions of disposition about religion and belief more generally. Seeing them as problematic is likely to lead to risk-management approaches; seeing them as important aspects of staff and user identity is likely to lead to engagement. Either may be entirely valid but deliberateness about which path to take enables transparency and clarity, which might help with recruitment, retention and well-being at work.

Communities

In relation to disposition, community spaces have a negative starting point, constructing religion and belief in problematic terms as secretive and sinister, that is, as risks to security and cohesion. As 'category', they narrow the spectrum to focus on relations between a culturally Christian environment and Muslim 'others'. At the same time, they recognise a small number of other religious traditions, though without saying why they need our attention except in the most general of terms about good relations between a handful of different traditional religions. Other traditions, beliefs, spirituality and non-religion are largely absent in these spaces. In the end, religion and belief diversity is expected to be resolved into a broadly Christian ethos that is regarded as being at the root of British values. Everybody is expected to submit to these logics, whatever their religion, belief or none. Yet, lived communities are full of highly diverse engagement, encounter and shared social action between people of all religions, beliefs and none, as research repeatedly shows.[1] The learning that resides in those spaces has been captured in a large number of community evaluations and reports over the years (see Dinham et al, 2009) but is not reflected in the community learning initiatives that predominate. Their inclusion could help rebalance the space such that the risks and the benefits set each other in context. While Prevent education incorporates the promotion of cohesion, it could also do much more to communicate the benefits that religion and belief groups bring in terms of plugging welfare gaps, promoting community relations (what has often been referred to as social capital) and generating well-being, manifesting as prayer meditation, mindfulness and neighbourliness (Dinham et al, 2009; Dinham, 2012b).

Conclusions

Messy as they are, it is in some ways amazing that spaces of learning about religion and belief exist at all in the 21st century. The internal and cross-cutting muddle that they produce both reflects and confounds the idea that religion and belief are behind us. However, each link in the chain has its own weaknesses and gaps. Together, they make up a chain of learning in which each part exists in its own silo and is entirely disconnected from the others, even where they appear to overlap.

The fact that school RE is compulsory for all suggests that it is a national priority. Its omission from the national curriculum suggests that it is not. The requirement for a daily act of collective worship suggests that schools are there to socialise young people in Christianity. The right to withdraw and the widespread emphasis on religion and belief diversity suggests that they are there to foster plurality. The accommodations made in universities for a diversity of religion and belief, including the provision of multi-faith chaplaincies, suggests that religion and belief are embraced. The widespread neglect of religion and belief in university disciplines suggests that they are irrelevant. The commitment to the religion, belief and spirituality of employees, customers and service users in workplaces and the professions suggests that religion and belief are widely regarded as public matters. The almost total omission of them from professional and workplace training suggests that they are private. They are both required and ignored. The wealth of community and adult learning initiatives on religion and belief suggests a widespread public demand and interest. Their focus on extremism and cohesion suggests that this is more about what policy wants than what publics demand. The appearance of 'Prevent' in different guises in schools, universities and communities underlines a common emphasis on risk. As people pass through these spaces of learning, the messages they hear are internally muddled, as well as contradictory from one to another. In schools, we are Christian but also diverse. In universities, we are diverse but also secular. In workplaces, we must be equipped to encounter diversity but the professions are steeped in a sort of subconscious secularism, and religion and belief are private. In communities, religion and belief groups are both heroes and villains, and the task is to assimilate through grasping that the country has a Christian ethos and values. Hardly anyone is equipped to teach through the muddle.

Of course, in each of these spaces of learning, there are variations in practice and some exceptional examples of more nuanced teaching and learning. However, each link in the chain of learning has multiple weak spots and is poorly shaped to hold firm in itself. The chain as a whole is also full of tangles. It is very challenging for individuals to feel their way along that chain as they pass through their lives. This leads to the lack of a clear or coherent sense of religion and belief, how to think about them, and what to do in response. This chapter has set out some of the ways in which the links could be strengthened (see Figure 2).

Figure 2: A reconnected chain of learning about religion and belief

Schools
Academic, optional RE including theology and sociology, and extending to the fullest range of religions, belief and worldviews

Workplace
Religion and belief diversity and inclusion training for all, along with all other 'protected characteristics'

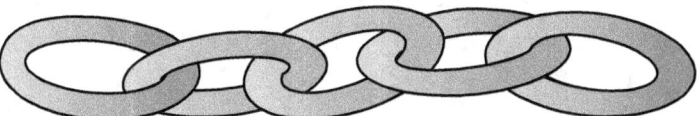

Religious Education
Society as Christian, secular, plural and non religious; religion and belief as fluid and heterogeneous, not a 'national' singularity

Universities
Post-secular in curricula; accommodating, proportionate, diverse and inclusive in operations, without claims to 'secularity' or 'neutrality'

Communities
Rebalancing risk and opportunity to emphasise the contributions as well as the threats of religions, beliefs and worldviews as community assets and sources of relationships of resilience

The application of a religion and belief literacy analysis to each space is a first stage in this so that each can bring into focus the category, disposition, knowledge and skills that they need and want to reflect. Connecting the whole chain of learning is an even bigger challenge. It will require serious work across sectors, combining pedagogical expertise at each level with serious knowledge from theology, sociology, law, professional studies, management studies and others. The goal should not be consensus, but a clarity about points of connection and disconnection, agreement and disagreement, such that teachers and learners can know what parts of the debate they are exploring as they learn, and how they relate to the others. In this, differences are entirely acceptable, just as they are inevitable. However, where learning spaces have done the work to make them conscious and articulated, publics will be better equipped for a deep religion and belief literacy capable of handling the diversity that is all around them.

Notes

Chapter 1
1. See: www.christian-research.org/
2. See: www.reonline.org.uk/wp-content/uploads/2019/05/Woodhead-copy.pdf

Chapter 3
1. See: www.gov.uk/government/statistics/schools-pupils-and-their-characteristics-january-2017
2. See: www.birmingham.gov.uk/downloads/file/1579/investigation_report_trojan_horse_letter_the_kershaw_report

Chapter 4
1. See: www.legislation.gov.uk/uksi/2014/3283/schedule/made
2. See: www.resilience.org.uk
3. See: www.familiesmatteruk.org/familiesmatter.org.uk/online-safeguarding/index.html
4. See: www.theguardian.com/commentisfree/belief/2015/oct/22/under-this-government-jesus-would-have-been-done-for-extremism
5. See: https://assets.publishing.service.gov.uk/government/uploads/system/uploads/attachment_data/file/402173/Programme_of_Study_KS1_and_2.pdf
6. See: https://assets.publishing.service.gov.uk/government/uploads/system/uploads/attachment_data/file/239060/SECONDARY_national_curriculum_-_Citizenship.pdf
7. See: https://webarchive.nationalarchives.gov.uk/20100607215838/http://www.standards.dfes.gov.uk/schemes2/citizenship/?view=get
8. See: www.gov.uk/government/publications/relationships-education-relationships-and-sex-education-rse-and-health-education
9. See: www.gov.uk/government/publications/relationships-education-relationships-and-sex-education-rse-and-health-education
10. See: www.gov.uk/government/publications/relationships-education-relationships-and-sex-education-rse-and-health-education
11. See: www.gov.uk/government/publications/relationships-education-relationships-and-sex-education-rse-and-health-education
12. See: https://www.gov.uk/government/publications/relationships-education-relationships-and-sex-education-rse-and-health-education
13. See: www.gov.uk/government/publications/relationships-education-relationships-and-sex-education-rse-and-health-education
14. See: www.gov.uk/government/publications/relationships-education-relationships-and-sex-education-rse-and-health-education
15. See: www.gov.uk/government/publications/relationships-education-relationships-and-sex-education-rse-and-health-education
16. See: https://schoolsweek.co.uk/sarah-hewitt-clarkson-headteacher-anderton-park-primary-school-birmingham/

17 See: www.gov.uk/government/publications/relationships-education-relationships-and-sex-education-rse-and-health-education
18 See: www.gov.uk/government/publications/relationships-education-relationships-and-sex-education-rse-and-health-education
19 See: www.gov.uk/government/publications/relationships-education-relationships-and-sex-education-rse-and-health-education
20 See: www.gov.uk/government/publications/relationships-education-relationships-and-sex-education-rse-and-health-education
21 See: www.gov.uk/government/publications/relationships-education-relationships-and-sex-education-rse-and-health-education
22 See: www.gov.uk/government/publications/relationships-education-relationships-and-sex-education-rse-and-health-education
23 See: www.gov.uk/government/publications/relationships-education-relationships-and-sex-education-rse-and-health-education
24 See: www.gov.uk/government/publications/relationships-education-relationships-and-sex-education-rse-and-health-education
25 See: https://assets.publishing.service.gov.uk/government/uploads/system/uploads/attachment_data/file/281929/Collective_worship_in_schools.pdf
26 See: https://assets.publishing.service.gov.uk/government/uploads/system/uploads/attachment_data/file/281929/Collective_worship_in_schools.pdf
27 See: https://assets.publishing.service.gov.uk/government/uploads/system/uploads/attachment_data/file/281929/Collective_worship_in_schools.pdf
28 See: https://assets.publishing.service.gov.uk/government/uploads/system/uploads/attachment_data/file/281929/Collective_worship_in_schools.pdf
29 See: https://assets.publishing.service.gov.uk/government/uploads/system/uploads/attachment_data/file/281929/Collective_worship_in_schools.pdf
30 See: https://assets.publishing.service.gov.uk/government/uploads/system/uploads/attachment_data/file/281929/Collective_worship_in_schools.pdf
31 See: https://humanism.org.uk/education/parents/collective-worship-and-school-assemblies-your-rights/
32 See: https://assets.publishing.service.gov.uk/government/uploads/system/uploads/attachment_data/file/281929/Collective_worship_in_schools.pdf
33 See: https://assets.publishing.service.gov.uk/government/uploads/system/uploads/attachment_data/file/281929/Collective_worship_in_schools.pdf
34 See: https://assets.publishing.service.gov.uk/government/uploads/system/uploads/attachment_data/file/281929/Collective_worship_in_schools.pdf
35 See: https://assets.publishing.service.gov.uk/government/uploads/system/uploads/attachment_data/file/281929/Collective_worship_in_schools.pdf
36 See: https://assets.publishing.service.gov.uk/government/uploads/system/uploads/attachment_data/file/281929/Collective_worship_in_schools.pdf

Chapter 5
1 See: www.gov.uk/government/publications/prevent-strategy-2011
2 See: www.gov.uk/government/publications/prevent-strategy-2011
3 See: www.gov.uk/government/publications/prevent-strategy-2011
4 See: www.gov.uk/government/publications/prevent-strategy-2011
5 See: www.gov.uk/government/publications/prevent-strategy-2011
6 See: www.gov.uk/government/publications/prevent-strategy-2011

Notes

Chapter 7
1. See: https://tanenbaum.org/religion-at-work-resource/
2. See: https://religiousfreedomandbusiness.org/changing-religion-and-changing-economies
3. See: http://tedcantle.co.uk/publications/067%20Citizen%20Survey%202011%20race%20religion%20equalities.pdf

Chapter 8
1. See: www.near-neighbours.org.uk/catalyst
2. See: www.cuf.org.uk/catalyst
3. See: www.gov.uk/government/speeches/understanding-our-differences-the-importance-of-inter-faith-dialogue
4. See: www.southbankcentre.co.uk/whats-on/festivals-series/belief-and-beyond-belief
5. See: www.coe.int/en/web/interculturalcities/results-and-impact
6. See: http://tedcantle.co.uk/2016/12/
7. See: www.elearning.prevent.homeoffice.gov.uk
8. See: http://sites.cardiff.ac.uk/islamukcentre/community-engagement/muslim-young-leaders-award/
9. See: www.facebook.com/Islamophobia2017
10. See: www.mcb.org.uk/an-introduction-to-activism-course/
11. See: https://institute.global/sites/default/files/inline-files/2019_challenges_in_counter_extremism.pdf

Chapter 9
1. See: https://civilsocietyfutures.org/

References

AASW (Australian Association of Social Workers) (2012) Australian Social Work Education and Accreditation Standards (ASWEAS) 2012 Guideline 1.1: Guidance on Essential Core Curriculum Content. Available at: www.aasw.asn.au/document/item/3552 (accessed 8 June 2018).

Amin A (2002) Ethnicity and the Multicultural City: Living with Diversity, *Environment and Planning A*, 34(6): 959–80.

ANZASW (Aotearoa New Zealand Association of Social Workers) and CSWEANZ (Council of Social Work Education Aotearoa New Zealand) (2016) Social Work Field Education Guidelines. Available at: https://anzasw.nz/wp-content/uploads/ANZASW-Social-Work-Field-Education-Guidelines.pdf (accessed 8 June 2018).

Arat A (2016) Practice Makes Perfect: Meditation and the Exchange of Spiritual Capital, *Journal of Contemporary Religion*, 31: 269–80.

Aune K, Guest M and Law J (2019) *Chaplains on Campus: Understanding Chaplaincy in UK Universities*, Coventry: CTPSR.

BACP (British Association of Counselling and Psychotherapy) (2018) *Ethical Framework for the Counselling Professions*, London: BACP.

Baker C and Dinham A (2017) New Interdisciplinary Spaces of Religions and Beliefs in Contemporary Thought and Practice: An Analysis, *Religions*, 8(2): 1–16.

Baker C, Crisp BR and Dinham A (eds) (2018) *Re-imagining Religion and Belief for 21st Century Policy and Practice*, Bristol and Chicago: Policy Press.

Barnes M and Smith JD (2016) Religious Literacy as Lokahi: Social Harmony Through Diversity, in Dinham A and Francis M (eds) *Religious Literacy in Policy and Practice*, Bristol: Policy Press.

Barnett C (1996) *The Audit of War: The Illusion and Reality of Britain as a Great Nation*, London: Faber and Faber.

Bartlett J and Birdwell J (2010) *From Suspects to Citizens: Preventing Violent Extremism in a Big Society*, London: Demos.

Bartram B (2009) Student Support in Higher Education: Understandings, Implications and Challenges, *Higher Education Quarterly*, 63(3): 308–14.

Beckford J (2012) Public Religions and the Post-Secular: Critical Reflections, *Journal for the Scientific Study of Religion*, 51(1): 1–19.

Berger PL (1999) *The Desecularization of the World: The Resurgence of Religion in World Politics*, Michigan: William B. Eerdmans Publishing Co.

Bessarab D and Ng'andu B (2010) Yarning About Yarning as a Legitimate Method in Indigenous Research, *International Journal of Critical Religious Studies*, 3(1): 37–50.

Beveridge W (1942) *Social Insurance and Allied Services*, London: HMSO.

Billings A and Holden A (2008) The Burnley Project: Interfaith Interventions and Cohesive Communities – the Effectiveness of Interfaith Activity in Towns Marked by Enclavisation and Parallel Lives, Department of Religious Studies, Lancaster University.

Blackmore J (2002) Globalization and the Restructuring of Higher Education for New Knowledge Economies: New Dangers or Old Habits Troubling Gender Equity Work in Universities?, *Higher Education Quarterly*, 56(4): 419–41.

Boisvert D (2015) Quebec's Ethics and Religious Culture School Curriculum: A Christianity, *Christian Higher Education*, 4: 99–108.

Bonino S (2016) The British State 'Security Syndrome' and Muslim Diversity: Challenges for Liberal Democracy in the Age of Terror, *Contemporary Islam*, 10(2): 223–47.

Borchgrevink K and Berg Karpviken K (2010) *Teaching Religion, Taming Rebellion: Religious Education Reform in Afghanistan*, PRIO Policy Briefing, Oslo: PRIO.

Bosetti L and Walker K (2009) Perspectives of UK Vice-Chancellors on Leading Universities in a Knowledge-Based Economy, *Higher Education Quarterly*, 61(4): 4–21.

Bradstock H (2015) Religion in New Zealand's State Primary Schools, *Journal of Intercultural Studies*, 36: 338–61.

Breakwell GM and Tytherleigh MY (2010) University Leaders and University Performance in the United Kingdom: Is it 'Who' Leads, or 'Where' They Lead that Matters Most?, *Higher Education*, online. Available at: http://springerlink.com/content/102901/?Content+Status=Accepted

Bretherton L (2006) *Hospitality as Holiness: Christian Witness Amid Moral Diversity*, Farnham: Ashgate.

British Social Attitudes Survey (2019) Available at: www.bsa.natcen.ac.uk/media/39293/1_bsa36_religion.pdf

Brown KW and Ryan RM (2003). The Benefits of Being Present: Mindfulness and Its Role in Psychological Well-Being, *Journal of Personality and Social Psychology*, 84: 822–48.

Browne J (2010) *Securing a Sustainable Future for Higher Education: An Independent Review of Higher Education Funding and Student Finance*, London: HM Government.

References

Busher J, Choudhury T, Thomas P and Harris G (2017) What the Prevent Duty Means for Schools and Colleges in England: An Analysis of Educationalists' Experiences, Centre for Trust, Peace and Social Relations, Coventry University. Available at: https://pure.coventry.ac.uk/ws/portalfiles/portal/11090509 (accessed 4 July 2017).

Cantle T (2005) *Community Cohesion: A New Framework for Race and Diversity*, Basingstoke and New York, NY: Palgrave Macmillan.

Casanova J (1994) *Public Religions in the Modern World*, Chicago, IL: Chicago University Press.

Casey L (2016) *The Casey Review: A Review into Opportunity and Integration*, London: Department for Communities and Local Government. Available at: https://assets.publishing.service.gov.uk/government/uploads/system/uploads/attachment_data/file/575973/The_Casey_Review_Report.pdf

CCfW (Care Council for Wales) (2013) The Framework for the Degree of Social Work in Wales. Available at: https://socialcare.wales/cms_assets/file-uploads/Social-Work-Degree-Rules-and-Requirements-1.pdf (accessed 8 June 2018).

Chater M and Erricker C (eds) (2013) *Does Religious Education Have a Future? Pedagogical and Policy Prospects*, Abingdon and New York, NY: Routledge.

CiCe (Children's Identity & Citizenship in Europe) (2008) *CiCe Guidelines on Citizenship Education in a Global Context: Religion and Citizenship Education in Europe*, London: CiCe. Available at: http://archive.londonmet.ac.uk/cice/MRSite/Research/cice/pubs/citizenship/citizenship-05.pdf (accessed 28 June 2017).

Clarke C and Woodhead L (2015) A New Settlement: Religion and Belief in Schools, unpublished paper.

Clarke J (2004) Dissolving the Public Realm? The Logics and Limits of Neo-Liberalism, *Journal of Social Policy*, 33(1): 27–48.

Coates J, Graham JR and Swartzentruber B (2007) *Spirituality and Social Work: Selected Canadian Readings*, Toronto: Canadian Scholars' Press.

Collini S (2010) Browne's Gamble, *London Review of Books*, 32(21): 23–5.

Commission on Religion and Belief in British Public Life: Community, Diversity and the Common Good (2015) CORAB, Woolf Institute.

ComRes (2017) Faith in the Workplace. Available at: www.comresglobal.com/faith/faith-in-the-workplace/ (accessed 31 May 2017).

Constable DSW (1983) Values, Religion, and Social Work Practice, *Social Thought*, 9: 29–41.

Council of Europe (2008) Recommendation CM/Rec(2008)12 of the Committee of Ministers to Member States on the Dimension of Religious and Non-Religious Convictions Within Intercultural Education.

Council of Europe (2015) *The Fight Against Violent Extremism and Radicalisation Leading to Terrorism: Action Plan*, CM(2015)74, 125th Session of the Committee of Ministers, Brussels, 19 May, Strasbourg: Council of Europe Publishing.

Cox E (1966) *Changing Aims in Religious Education*, London: Routledge.

Crisp B (ed) (2016) *Routledge International Handbook of Religion, Spirituality and Social Work*, Melbourne: Routledge.

Crisp B and Dinham A (2019) Do the Regulatory Standards Require Religious Literacy of UK Health and Social Care Professionals?, *Social Policy and Administration*, 53(7): 1–14.

CST (Community Security Trust) (2018) *Anti-Semitic Incidents Report*, London: CST.

CSWE (Council for Social Work Education) (2015) Educational Policies and Accreditation Standards. Available at: www.cswe.org/getattachment/Accreditation/Accreditation-Process/2015-EPAS/2015EPAS_Web_FINAL.pdf.aspx (accessed 8 June 2018).

Davie G (1994) *Religion in Britain since 1945: Believing Without Belonging*, Oxford and Cambridge, MA: Blackwell.

Davie G (2006) Vicarious Religion: A Methodological Challenge, in Ammerman NT (ed) *Everyday Religion: Observing Modern Religious Lives*, New York, NY: Oxford UP, pp 21–35.

Davie G (2015) *Religion in Britain: A Persistent Paradox*, Chichester: Wiley-Blackwell.

Davies K, Tropp LR, Aron A, Pettigrew TF and Wright SC (2011) Cross-Group Friendships and Intergroup Attitudes: A Meta-Analytic Review, *Personality and Social Psychology Review*, 15(4): 332–51.

Davies L (2008) *Educating Against Extremism*, London: Trentham Books.

Davies L (2014) *Unsafe Gods: Security, Secularism and Schooling*, London: IOE/Trentham.

Dawkins R (2010) *The God Delusion*, Oxford: Bantam Books.

DBIS (Department for Business, Innovation and Skills) (2009) *Higher Ambitions: The Future of Universities in a Knowledge Economy*, London: BIS.

DCLG (Department for Communities and Local Government) (2007) *Preventing Violent Extremism: Winning Hearts and Minds*, Wetherby: Communities and Local Government Publications.

DCLG (2008) *Face to Face, Side by Side: A Framework for Partnership in Our Multifaith Society*, London: HMSO.

References

DCLG (2012) Creating the Conditions for Integration, Crown Copyright. Available at: www.gov.uk/government/uploads/system/uploads/attachment_data/file/7504/2092103.pdf. (accessed 17 May 2017).

DCSF (Department for Children, Schools and Families) (2010) Religious Education in English Schools: NonStatutory Guidance 2010, Crown Copyright. Available at: www.re-handbook.org.uk/media/display/Religiouseducationguidancein-ennglish-schools2010.pdf (accessed 13 July 2017).

De Lissovoy V (1954) A Sociological Approach to Religious Literacy, *The Journal of Educational Sociology*, 27(9): 419–24.

Deloitte (2011) Only Skin Deep: Reexamining the Business Case for Diversity, Deloitte, Human Capital Australia.

Demaine J and Entwistle H (eds) (1996) *Beyond Communitarianism: Citizenship, Politics and Education*, Basingstoke: Macmillan.

DfE (Department for Education) (2013) *The National Curriculum*, London: GovUK.

DfE (2014) *Promoting Fundamental British Values as Part of SMSC in Schools: Departmental Advice for Maintained Schools*, London: GovUK.

DfE (2018) *Keeping Children Safe in Education*, London: GovUK.

DfEE (1998) *Education for Citizenship and the Teaching of Democracy in Schools*, London: QCA.

DfES (Department for Education and Skills) (2007) *Curriculum Review: Diversity and Citizenship*, London: DfES.

Diaz LDE (2018) A Comparative Analysis of Religious Education in Europe and Educational Guidelines in the Framework of Interreligious Dialogue and a Culture of Peace, *Mediterranean Journal of Social Sciences*, 9(1): 47–56.

Dinham A (2011) A Public Role for Religion: On Needing a Discourse of Religious Literacy, *International Journal of Religion and Society*, 2(4): 291–302.

Dinham A (2012a) The Multifaith Paradigm in Policy and Practice: Problems, Challenges, Directions, *Journal of Social Policy and Society*, 11(4): 577–87.

Dinham A (2012b) *Faith and Social Capital after the Debt Crisis*, Basingstoke and Chicago, IL: Palgrave Macmillan.

Dinham A (2013) Measurement as Reflection in Faith Based Social Action in Mayo M, Mendiwelson-Bendek Z and Packham C (2013) *Community Research for Community Development*, Basingstoke: Palgrave Macmillan.

Dinham A (2015a) Grace Davie and Religious Literacy: Undoing a Lamentable Quality of Conversation, in Day A and Lovheim M (eds) *Modernities, Memory and Mutations: Grace Davie and the Study of Religion*, Surrey and Burlington, VA: Ashgate.

Dinham A (2015b) Religious Literacy and Welfare, in Dinham A and Francis M (eds) *Religious Literacy in Policy and Practice*, Bristol: Policy Press.

Dinham A (2016) Religious Literacy in Public and Professional Settings in Crisp B (ed) *International Handbook of Religion, Spirituality and Social Work*, Melbourne: Routledge

Dinham A and Francis M (eds) (2015) *Religious Literacy in Policy and Practice*, Bristol and Chicago: Policy Press.

Dinham A and Jones SH (2010) *Religious Literacy Leadership in Higher Education: an Analysis of Key Issues and Challenges for University Leaders*, York: Religious Literacy Leadership in Higher Education Programme.

Dinham A and Jones S (2011) *Religious Literacy Leadership in Higher Education, Programme Evaluation, Phase 1: September 2010–February 2011*, York: RLLP.

Dinham A and Jones S (2012) Religious Literacy in Higher Education: Brokering Public Faith in a Context of Ambivalence, *Journal of Contemporary Religion*, 27(2): 185–201.

Dinham A and Lowndes V (2008) Religion, Resources and Representation: Three Narratives of Faith Engagement in Urban Governance, *Urban Affairs Review*, 43(6): 817–45.

Dinham A and Shaw M (2013) *Religious Literacy for Equality and Diversity*, London: EHRC.

Dinham A and Shaw M (2015) *REforREal: The Future of Teaching and Learning About Religion and Belief*, London: Goldsmiths and Culham St Gabriel's Trust.

Dinham A and Shaw M (2017) Religious Literacy through Religious Education: The Future of Teaching and Learning about Religion and Belief, *Religions*, 8(7): 119.

Dinham A, Furbey R and Lowndes V (2009) *Faith in the Public Realm*, Bristol: Policy Press.

Dinham A, Francis M and Shaw M (2017) Towards a Theory and Practice of Religious Literacy: A Case Study of Religion and Belief Engagement in a UK University, *Religions*, 8(12): 276.

DIUS (Department for Innovation, Universities and Skills) (2007) *Promoting Good Campus Relations, Fostering Shared Values and Preventing Violent Extremism in Universities and Higher Education Colleges*, London: Department for Business Innovation and Skills.

Doe N (2009) Towards a 'Common Law' on Religion in the European Union, *Religion, State and Society*, 37: 147–66.

Doney J and Wegerif R (2017) *Measuring Open-Mindedness: An Evaluation of the Impact of Our School Dialogue Programme on Students' Openmindedness and Attitudes to Others*, Tony Blair Institute for Global Change. Available at: http://institute.global/sites/default/files/field_article_attached_file/Tony%20Blair%20Institute%20for%20Global%20Change_Measuring%20Open-Mindedness.pdf (accessed 6 June 2017).

DTI (Department of Trade and Industry) (1998) *Our Competitive Future: Building the Knowledge Driven Economy*, London: Department of Trade and Industry. Available at: www.berr.gov.uk/files/file32392.pdf (accessed 31 January 2011).

Duffy RD (2006) Spirituality, Religion, and Career Development: Current Status and Future Directions, *The Career Development Quarterly*, 55: 52–63.

Eagleton T (2010) The death of universities, *The Guardian: Comment is Free*. Available at: www.guardian.co.uk/commentisfree/2010/dec/17/death-universities-malaise-tuition-fees (accessed 22 February 2011).

Eder K (2006) Post-Secularism: A Return to the Public Sphere. Available at: www.eurozine.com/pdf/2006-08-17-eder-en.pdf

Edwards MU (2006) *Religion on Our Campuses: A Professor's Guide to Communities, Conflicts and Promising Conversations*, New York, NY: Palgrave Macmillan.

Edwards MU (2008) Why Faculty Find it Difficult to Talk about Religion, in Jacobsen D and Jacobsen RH (eds) *The American University in a Postsecular Age*, Oxford: Oxford University Press, pp 81–98.

EHRC (Equality and Human Rights Commission) (2014) *Gender Segregation at Events and Meetings: Guidance for Universities and Students' Unions*, London: EHRC.

Erricker C (ed) (1987) *Teaching Christianity: A World Religions Approach*, Cambridge: Lutterworth Press.

EUFRA (European Agency for Fundamental Human Rights) (2019) *Experiences and Perceptions of Anti-Semitism: Second Survey on Discrimination and Hate Crime against Jews in the EU*, Brussels: EUFRA.

Ezzy D (2013) Minimising Religious Conflict and the Racial and Religious Tolerance Act in Victoria, Australia, *Journal for the Academic Study of Religion*, 26: 198–215.

Fair C (2008) *Madrassah Challenge: Militancy and Religious Education in Pakistan*, Washington, DC: United States Institute of Peace.

Fairbairn AN (1979) *The Leicestershire Community Colleges and Centres*, Nottingham: University of Nottingham Dept of Adult Education.

Fernando M and Jackson B (2006) The Influence of Religion-Based Workplace Spirituality on Business Leaders' Decision-Making: An Inter-Faith Study, *Journal of Management & Organization*, 12: 23–39.

Ford DF (2004) The Responsibilities of Universities in a Religious and Secular World, *Studies in Christian Ethics*, 17(1): 22–37.

Ford DF and Higton M (2016) Religious Literacy in the Context of Theology and Religious Studies, in Dinham A and Francis M (eds) *Religious Literacy in Policy and Practice*, Bristol: Policy Press.

Frampton M, Goodhart D and Mahmood K (2016) Unsettled Belonging: A Survey of Britain's Muslim Communities, Policy Exchange. Available at: https://policyexchange.org.uk/wpcontent/uploads/2016/12/PEXJ5037_Muslim_Communities_FINAL.pdf (accessed 4 July 2016).

Francis M and van Eck Duymaer A (2015) Religious Literacy, Radicalisation and Extremism, in Dinham A and Francis M (eds) *Religious Literacy in Policy and Practice*, Bristol: Policy Press.

Frank DJ and Gabler J (2006) *Reconstructing the University: Worldwide Shifts in Academia in the 20th Century*, Stanford, CA: Stanford University Press.

Freathy R, Doney J, Walshe K and Teece G (2017) Pedagogical Bricoleurs and Bricolage Researchers: The Case of Religious Education, *British Journal of Educational Studies*, 65(4): 425–43.

Freire P (1985) *Pedagogy of the Oppressed*, Harmondsworth: Penguin.

Frost S (2014) *The Inclusion Imperative: How Real Inclusion Creates Better Business and Builds Better Societies: Courage, Creativity and Talent*, London and Philadelphia: Kogan Page Limited.

Furman LD, Benson PW, Canda ER and Grimwood C (2005) A Comparative International Analysis of Religion and Spirituality in Social Work: A Survey of UK and US Social Workers, *Social Work Education*, 24: 813–39.

Furness S and Gilligan P (2010) *Religion, Belief and Social Work: Making a Difference*, Bristol: Policy Press.

Garcia-Zamor JC (2003) Workplace Spirituality and Organizational Performance, *Public Administration Review*, 63: 355–63.

GDC (General Dental Council) (2013) *Standards for the Dental Team*. Available at: www.gdc-uk.org/professionals/standards (accessed 27 June 2018).

Gearon L (2013) The Counter Terrorist Classroom: Religion, Education, and Security, *Religious Education*, 108(2): 129–47.

Germino D (2000) Plato and Aristotle, in Germino D (ed) *Order & History* (vol 3), Baton Rouge, LA: LSU Press.

References

Gidley B (2012) Blog: Creating the Conditions for Integration. Compas. Available at: www.compas.ox.ac.uk/2012/creating-the-conditions-for-integration (accessed 17 May 2017).

Gilliat-Ray S (2000) *Religion in Higher Education: The Politics of the Multi-Faith Campus*, Aldershot: Ashgate.

GMC (General Medical Council) (2015a) *Outcomes for Graduates (Tomorrow's Doctors)*. Available at: www.gmc-uk.org/-/media/documents/outcomes-for-graduates-jul-15-1216_pdf-61408029.pdf (accessed 12 June 2018).

GMC (2015b) *Outcomes for Provisionally Registered Doctors with a Licence to Practise (The Trainee Doctor)*. Available at: www.gmc-uk.org/-/media/documents/outcomes-for-provisionally-registered-doctors-jul15_pdf-61407158.pdf (accessed 12 June 2018).

GOC (General Optical Council) (2016) *Standards of Practice for Optometrists and Dispensing Opticians*. Available at: www.optical.org/en/Standards/Standards_for_optometrists_dispensing_opticians.cfm (accessed 27 June 2018).

Goldman R (1965) *Readiness for Religion*, London: Routledge and Kegan Paul.

GPC (General Pharmaceutical Council) (2017) *Standards for Pharmacy Professionals*. Available at: www.pharmacyregulation.org/sites/default/files/standards_for_pharmacy_professionals_may_2017_0.pdf (accessed 14 June 2018).

Graham G (2005) *The Institution of Intellectual Values: Realism and Idealism in Higher Education*, Exeter: Imprint Academic.

Greenbank P (2006) The Evolution of Government Policy on Widening Participation, *Higher Education Quarterly*, 60(2): 141–66.

Grimmit M (2010) *Religious Education and Social and Community Cohesion: An Exploration of Challenges and Opportunities*, London: McCrimmon.

Grossman P, Niemann L, Schmidt S and Walach H (2004) Mindfulness-Based Stress Reduction and Health Benefits, *Journal of Psychosomatic Research*, 57: 35–43.

Guest M, Aune K, Sharma S and Warner R (2013) *Christianity and the University Experience: Understanding Student Faith*, London: Bloomsbury.

Habermas J (2005) Equal Treatment of Cultures and the Limits of Postmodern Liberalism, *Journal of Political Philosophy*, 13(1): 1–28.

Habermas J (2007) Religion in the public sphere, unpublished lecture. Available at: www.sandiego.edu/pdf/pdf_library/habermaslecture031105_c939cceb2ab087bdfc6df291ec0fc3fa.pdf (accessed 4 June 2010).

Hart, D.G. 1999. *The university gets religion*. Baltimore: Johns Hopkins University Press.

Hasan M (2013) The Sorry Truth is that the Virus of Anti-Semitism Has Infected the British Muslim Community, *The New Statesman*, 21 March.

Hassner RE (ed) (2013) *Religion in the Military Worldwide*, New York: Cambridge University Press.

Hawley WD and Svara JH (1972) *The Study of Community Power: A Bibliographic Review*, Oxford: ABC-Clio.

HCPC (Health and Care Professions Council) (2013a) *Standards of Proficiency: Art Therapists*. Available at: www.hpc-uk.org/assets/ documents/100004FBStandards_of_Proficiency_Arts_Therapists.pdf (accessed 12 June 2018).

HCPC (2013b) *Standards of Proficiency: Chiropodists/Podiatrists*. Available at: www.hpc-uk.org/assets/documents/10000DBBStandards_of_Proficiency_Chiropodists.pdf (accessed 12 June 2018).

HCPC (2013c) *Standards of Proficiency: Dieticians*. Available at: www.hpc-uk.org/assets/documents/1000050CStandards_of_Proficiency_Dietitians.pdf (accessed 12 June 2018).

HCPC (2013d) *Standards of Proficiency: Occupational Therapists*. Available at: www.hpc-uk.org/assets/documents/10000512Standards_of_Proficiency_Occupational_Therapists.pdf (accessed 12 June 2018).

HCPC (2013e) *Standards of Proficiency: Orthoptists*. Available at: www.hpc-uk.org/assets/documents/10000516Standards_of_Proficiency_Orthoptists.pdf (accessed 12 June 2018).

HCPC (2013f) *Standards of Proficiency: Paramedics*. Available at: www.hpc-uk.org/assets/documents/1000051CStandards_of_Proficiency_Paramedics.pdf (accessed 12 June 2018).

HCPC (2013g) *Standards of Proficiency: Physiotherapists*. Available at: www.hpc-uk.org/assets/documents/10000DBCStandards_of_Proficiency_Physiotherapists.pdf (accessed 12 June 2018).

HCPC (2013h) *Standards of Proficiency: Prosthetists/Orthotists*. Available at: www.hpc-uk.org/assets/documents/10000522Standards_of_Proficiency_Prosthetists_and_Orthotists.pdf (accessed 12 June 2018).

HCPC (2013i) *Standards of Proficiency: Radiographers*. Available at: www.hpc-uk.org/assets/documents/10000DBDStandards_of_Proficiency_Radiographers.pdf available online at (accessed 12 June 2018).

HCPC (2014a) *Standards of Proficiency: Hearing Aid Dispensers*. Available at: www.hpc-uk.org/assets/documents/10002CBCStandardsofProficiency-Hearingaiddispensers.pdf (accessed 12 June 2018).

HCPC (2014b) *Standards of Proficiency: Speech and Language Therapists*. Available at: www.hpc-uk.org/assets/documents/10000529Standards_of_Proficiency_SLTs.pdf (accessed 12 June 2018).

References

HCPC (2015). *Standards of Proficiency: Practitioner Psychologists*. Available at: www.hpc-uk.org/assets/documents/10002963SOP_Practitioner_psychologists.pdf (accessed 12 June 2018).

HCPC (2017) *Standards of Proficiency: Social Workers in England*. Available at: www.hpc-uk.org/assets/documents/10003B08Standardsofproficiency-SocialworkersinEngland.pdf (accessed 8 June 2018).

Her Majesty's Government (2019) Prevent Duty Guidance for Higher Education Institutions in England and Wales. Available at: www.gov.uk/government/publications/prevent-duty-guidance/prevent-duty-guidance-for-higher-education-institutions-in-england-and-wales

Hervieu-Leger D (2000) Religion as a Chain of Memory, *Journal for the Scientific Study of Religion*, 51(1): 1–19.

Hewer C (2001) Schools for Muslims, *Oxford Review of Education*, 27(4): 515–27.

Hewlett SA, Marshall M and Sherbin L with Gonsalves T (2013) *Innovation, Diversity and Market Growth*, New York: Center for Talent Innovation.

Higher Education Funding Council for England (2008) *Islamic Studies: Trends and Profiles*, London: HEFCE.

Home Office (2005) *Improving Opportunity, Strengthening Society: The Government's Strategy to Increase Race Equality and Community Cohesion*, London: Home Office.

Home Office (2007) *Preventing Violent Extremism: Winning Hearts and Minds*, London: Stationery Office.

Home Office (2019) *Life in the UK Test: Handbook*, London: Stationery Office.

Horwath J and Lees J (2010) Assessing the Influence of Religious Beliefs and Practices on Parenting Capacity: The Challenges for Social Work Practitioners, *British Journal of Social Work*, 40: 82–99.

Hovdelien O (2015) Education and Common Values in a Multicultural Society: The Norwegian Case, *Journal of Intercultural Studies*, 36: 306–31.

Humphrey JC (2003) New Labour and the Regulatory Reform of Social Care, *Critical Social Policy*, 23: 5–24.

IFSW (International Federation of Social Workers) and IAASW (International Association of Schools of Social Work) (2004) Global Standards for the Education and Training of the Social Work Profession. Available at: http://cdn.ifsw.org/assets/ifsw_65044-3.pdf (accessed 8 June 2018).

Ipgrave J and McKenna U (2008) Diverse Experiences and Common Vision: English Students' Perspectives on Religion and Religious Education, in Knauth T, Dan-Paul J, Bertram-Troost G and Ipgrave J (eds) *Encountering Religious Pluralism in School and Society: A Qualitative Study of Teenage Perspectives in Europe*, Münster: Waxmann Verlag, pp 113–48.

Iversen HR (2013) Secularisation, Secularity, Secularism, in Runehov ALC and Oviedo L (eds) *Encyclopedia of Sciences and Religions*, Dordrecht: Springer.

Jackson R (2003) *International Perspectives on Citizenship, Education and Religious Diversity*, Abingdon: Routledge.

Jackson R (2014) *Signposts: Policy and Practice for Teaching about Religions and Non-religious Worldviews in Intercultural Education*, Strasbourg: Council of Europe Publishing.

Jackson R (2016) *Inclusive Study of Religions and World Views in Schools: Signposts from the Council of Europe*, Strasbourg: Council of Europe Publishing.

Jha V and Robinson A (2016) Religion and Medical Professionalism: Moving Beyond Social and Cultural Nuances, *Journal of Graduate Medical Education*, 8: 271–3. Available at: http://dx.doi.org/10.4300/JGME-D-16-00104.1

Joy M (2012) Revisiting Postcolonialism and Religion, *Journal for the Academic Study of Religion*, 25(2): 102–22.

Jurkiewicz CL and Giacalone RA (2004) A Values Framework for Measuring the Impact of Workplace Spirituality on Organizational Performance, *Journal of Business Ethics*, 49: 129–42.

Kanitz L (2005) Improving Christian Worldview Pedagogy: Going Beyond Mere Christianity, *Christian Higher Education*, 4(2): 99–108.

Kerr D (2003) *Citizenship Education in England: The Making of a New Subject*, OJSSE 2/2003.

King JE and Williamson IO (2005) Workplace Religious Expression, Religiosity and Job Satisfaction: Clarifying a Relationship, *Journal of Management, Spirituality & Religion*, 2: 173–98.

Kristeller JL, Sheedy-Zumbrun C and Schilling RF (1999) 'I Would if I Could': How Oncologists and Oncology Nurses Address Spiritual Distress in Cancer Patients, *Psycho-Oncology*, 8: 451–8.

Kundnani A (2009) *Spooked! How Not to Prevent Violent Extremism*, London: Institute of Race Relations.

Kundnani A (2015) *A Decade Lost: Rethinking Radicalisation & Extremism*, London: Claystone. Available at: www.claystone.org.uk/wp-content/uploads/2015/01/Claystone-rethinking-radicalisation.pdf (accessed 8 June 2017).

Landy J and Saler M (2009) *The Re-Enchantment of the World Secular Magic in a Rational World*, Stanford: Stanford University Press.

Lee L (2015) *Recognising the Non-Religious: Reimagining the Secular*, Oxford: Oxford University Press.

Leka S, Jain A, Widerszal-Bazyl M, Zołnierczyk-Zreda D and Zwetsloot G (2011) Developing a Standard for Psychosocial Risk Management: PAS 1010, *Safety Science*, 49: 1047–57.

Lovett TO (1975) *Adult Education, Community Development and the Working Class*, London: Ward Lock.

McKinsey & Company (2010) *Women Matter 2010: Women at the Top of Corporations: Making it Happen*, New York: McKinsey & Company.

Michalowski I (2011) Required to Assimilate? The Content of Citizenship Tests in Five Countries, *Citizenship Studies*, 15(6/7): 749–68.

Micklethwaite J and Wooldridge A (2009) *God is Back: How the Global Rise of Faith is Changing the World*, London: Allen Lane.

Milowski P and Plehwe D (eds) (2009) *The Road from Mont Pelerin: The Making of the Neoliberal Thought Collective*, Cambridge, MA: Harvard University Press.

Mindfulness Initiative (2016) *Building the Case for Mindfulness in the Workplace*, London: The Mindfulness Initiative. Available at: http://themindfulnessinitiative.org.uk/publications/building-the-case (accessed 29 July 2017).

Modood T (2006) Ethnicity, Muslims and Higher Education Entry in Britain, *Teaching in Higher Education*, 11(2): 247–50.

Moore DL (2006) Overcoming Religious Illiteracy: A Cultural Studies Approach, *Of Religion*, 78(4): 1112–38.

Moran M (2001) The Rise of the Regulatory State in Britain, *Parliamentary Affairs*, 54: 19–34.

Moss B (2003) *Research into Practice*, 23–29 October, Quadrant House, Sutton: Community Care.

NISCC (Northern Ireland Social Care Council) (2015) Northern Ireland Framework Specification for the Degree in Social Work. Available at: https://niscc.info/storage/resources/20151020_niframeworkspecificationfv_publishedsept2014_amendedoct2015_jh.pdf (accessed 8 June 2018).

NMC (Nursing and Midwifery Council) (2015) *Standards for Competence for Registered Midwives*. Available at: www.nmc.org.uk/globalassets/sitedocuments/standards/nmc-standards-for-competence-for-registered-midwives.pdf (accessed 12 June 2018).

NUS (National Union of Students) (2008) *Student Experience Report*, London: NUS/HSBC.

Oakley L and Kinmond K (2013) *Breaking the Silence on Spiritual Abuse*, Basingstoke: Palgrave Macmillan.

Ofsted (Office for Standards in Education) (2015) *School Inspection Handbook*, London: Gov.UK. Available at: www.gov.uk/government/publications/school-inspection-handbook- from-september-2015

Pantazis C and Pemberton S (2009) From the 'Old' to the 'New' Suspect Community: Examining the Impacts of Recent UK Counter-Terrorist Legislation, *British Journal of Criminology*, 49(5): 646–66.

Parekh B (2000) *Report of the Commission on the Future of Multi-Ethnic Britain*, London: Runnymede Trust/Profile Books.

Patel CJ and Shikongo AEE (2006) Handling Spirituality/Religion in Professional Training: Experiences of a Sample of Muslim Psychology Students, *Journal of Religion and Health*, 45: 93.

Pentaris P (2019) *Religious Literacy in Hospice Care: Challenges and Controversies*, London: Routledge.

Prochaska F (2006) *Christianity and Social Service in Modern Britain*, New York, NY: Oxford University Press.

Prothero S (2008) *Religious Literacy: What Every American Needs to Know – and Doesn't*, New York, NY: Harper.

PSHE (Personal, Social, Health and Economic) Association (2014) *Programme of Study Key Stages 1–4*, London: PSHE Association.

Putnam R (2000) *Bowling Alone: The Collapse and Revival of American Community*, New York, NY, and London: Simon and Schuster.

QCA (Qualifications and Curriculum Authority) (2004) *Religious Education: The Non-Statutory Curriculum Framework*. Available at: http://webarchive.nationalarchives.gov.uk/20090608220227/http://www.qca.org.uk/libraryAssets/media/9817_re_national_framework_04.pdf (accessed 13 July 2017).

RCN (Royal College of Nurses) (2012) *Spirituality in Nursing Care: A Pocket Guide*, London: RCN.

REC (RE Council) (2013) *Review of Religious Education in England*, London: REC.

Rees J (2017) SMSC, Wellbeing and School Improvement – The Links and Opportunities, *Education and Health Journal*, 35(3): 63–7.

Reuben JA (1996) *The Making of the Modern University: Intellectual Transformation and the Marginalization of Morality*, Chicago, IL: University of Chicago Press.

Roberts JH and Turner J (2000s) *The Sacred and the Secular University*, Princeton, NJ: Princeton University Press.

Robinson D (2005) The Search for Community Cohesion: Key Themes and Dominant Concepts of the Public Policy Agenda, *Urban Studies*, 42(7): 1411–27.

Royal Ministry of Church Affairs (1997) *The Transition from Initial Education to Working Life*, Oslo.

Rüegg W (2004) *A History of the University in Europe: Volume 3, Universities in the Nineteenth and Early Twentieth Centuries (1800–1945)*, Cambridge: Cambridge University Press.

Sabri D (2011) What's Wrong with the Student Experience?, *Discourse: Studies in the Cultural Politics of Education*, 32(5): 657–67.

Sanzenbach P (1989) Religion and Social Work: It's Not that Simple!, *Social Casework: The Journal of Contemporary Social Work*, 70: 571–4.

Schietle CP (2011) A Note Evaluating the Use of Search Engine Data in Social Research, *Social Science Quarterly*, 92: 285–95.

Schilbrack K (2010) Religions: Are There Any?, *Journal of the American Academy*, 78(4): 1112–38.

Schluter J, Winch S, Holzhauser K and Henderson A (2008) Nurses' Moral Sensitivity and Hospital Ethical Climate: A Literature Review, *Nursing Ethics*, 15: 304–21.

Schools Council (1971) *Religious Education in Secondary Schools*, London: Evans Bros, Methuen Educational.

Shirazi R (2017) When Schooling Becomes a Tactic of Security: Educating to Counter 'Extremism', *Diaspora, Indigenous, and Minority Education*, 11(1): 2–5.

Shortt J (2014) A Review of 'Christianity and the University Experience: Understanding Student Faith' by Guest M, Aune K, Sharma S and Warner R, *Journal of Christian Higher Education*, 13(5): 365–7.

Siddiqui A (2007) *Islam at Universities in England: Meeting the Needs and Investing in the Future*, Leicester: The Markfield Institute.

Skills Funding Agency (2012) *Religion and Belief in Adult Learning: Learner Views*, London: Babcock Research.

Smart N (1968) *Secular Education and the Logic of Religion*, London: Faber and Faber.

Social Care Wales (2018) *The Domiciliary Care Worker: Practice Guidance for Domiciliary Care Workers Registered with Social Care Wales*. Available at: https://socialcare.wales/cms_assets/file-uploads/Practice-Guidance-Version-1.pdf (accessed 12 June 2018).

Speed E and Gabe J (2013) The Health and Social Care Act for England 2012: The Extension of 'New Professionalism', *Critical Social Policy*, 33: 564–74.

SSSC (2016) Draft Revised Standards in Social Work Education in Scotland for Consultation Only November 2016. Available at: www.sssc.uk.com/about-the-sssc/multimedia-library/publications/70-education-and-training/2016-siswe-draft-for-consultation (accessed 2 June 2018).

Stacey T (2018) *Myth and Solidarity in the Modern World: Beyond Religious and Political Division*, Abingdon: Routledge.

Stiffoss-Hanssen H (2009) Religion and Spirituality: What a European Ear Hears, *The International Journal for the Psychology of Religion*, 9: 25–33.

SWRB (Social Workers Registration Board) (2013) *Guidelines on Code of Practice for Registered Social Workers*. Available at: www.swrb.org.hk/documents/Guidelines%20on%20Code%20of%20Practice_Eng.pdf (accessed 17 July 2018).

SWRB (2015) Principles, Criteria, and Standards for Recognizing Qualifications in Social Work for Registration of Registered Social Workers. Available at: www.swrb.org.hk/Documents/Principles,%20Criteria%20and%20Standards%20for%20Recognizing%20Qualifications%20in%20Social%20Work%20for%20Registration%20of%20RSWs_2015.pdf (accessed 8 June 2018).

Temple W (1928) *Christianity and the State*, London: Macmillan and Co.

Temple W (1941) *Citizen and Churchman*, London: Eyre and Spottiswoode.

Temple W (1942) *Christianity and the Social Order*, Harmondsworth: Penguin.

Thomas A (2012) *Towards a Critical Theory of Surveillance in Informational Capitalism*, e-book, Peter Lang.

Timmins N (2001) *The Five Giants: A Biography of the Welfare State*, New York, NY: HarperCollins.

Tisdell J (2008) Spirituality, Diversity and Learner-Centred Teaching: A Generative Paradox, in Jacobsen D and Jacobsen RH (eds) *The American University in a Postsecular Age*, Oxford: Oxford University Press, pp 151–66.

Toohey K and Sweigers G (2013) *Waiter, is that Inclusion in My Soup? A New Recipe to Improve Business Performance*, Sydney: Victorian Equal Opportunities and Human Rights Commission.

Trethewey A and Menzies L (2014) *Encountering Faiths & Beliefs – The Role of Intercultural Education in Schools and Communities*, London: 3FF.

Turner J (2014) Testing the Liberal Subject: (In)Security, Responsibility and 'Self-Improvement' in the UK Citizenship Test, *Citizenship Studies*, 18(3/4): 332–48.

UCL (University College London) (2019) Why Holocaust Education? An Educational Imperative. Available at: www.holocausteducation.org.uk/holocaust-education/educational-imperative/

UNESCO (United Nations Educational, Scientific, and Cultural Organization) (2008) *Guidelines for Intercultural Education*, Paris: UNESCO.

References

UNESCO (2018) *Addressing Anti-Semitism through Education: Guidelines for Policymakers*, Paris: UNESCO.

Vasquez M (2011) *More than Belief: A Materialist Theory of Religion*, Oxford: Oxford University Press.

Ward L (1953) The Right to Religious Literacy, *Religious Education*, 48: 380ff.

Weller P (2007) *Religions in the UK Directory 2007–10*, Derby: University of Derby.

West W (2010) *Exploring Therapy, Spirituality and Healing*, Basingstoke: Palgrave.

Williams L and Sewpaul V (2004) Modernism, Postmodernism and Global Standards Setting, *Social Work Education*, 23: 555–65.

Williams R (2006) Secularism, Faith and Freedom, presented at the Pontifical Academy of Social Sciences, Rome, 23 November 2006. Available at: http://rowanwilliams.archbishopofcanterbury.org/articles.php/1175/rome-lecture-secularism-faith-and-freedom

Wood P, Landry C and Bloomfield J (2006) *How Can We Unlock the Potential of Cultural Diversity in Cities?* York: JRF.

Woodhead L and Catto R (2012) *Religion and Change in Modern Britain*, London: Routledge.

World Jewish Congress (2016) *The Rise of Anti-Semitism on Social Media Summary Report of 2016*, New York: World Jewish Congress and Vigo Social Intelligence.

Wright A (1993) *Religious Education in the Secondary School: Prospects for Religious Literacy*, Abingdon: David Fulton Publishers.

Younghusband EL (1968) *Community Work and Social Change: Report of a Study Group on Training Set up by the Calouste Gulbenkian Foundation*, London and Harlow: Longmans.

Index

9/11 9, 10, 24, 28, 89, 137, 154
1994 Group 94

A

abortion 141, 154
abuse/neglect 25, 74, 75, 121, 148
academia 109
academy schools 45, 65
adult and further education 119–21
adult life, preparing for 56, 59, 60, 62
Afghanistan 67
agnosticism 55
alcohol 96
Anglican Church 23, 85, 88, 117, 140
anthropology 105
anti-extremist education 142–6
anti-Semitism 90, 136, 146–8
  see also Jewish people
anxiety 24, 27, 83, 89, 154
anxious re-visibility 21–3
Arendt, Hannah 105
armed forces 117
arts-based initiatives 141, 148
Asians 28, 137
assimilation 151
atheism 9, 55
atrocities 25
attendance, church 23
Attlee, Clement 17
Aune, K 88
Australia 14, 104, 128, 130

B

BACP *Ethical Framework for the Counselling Professions* 131
Baha'i 29
Bangladesh 97
Barnes, Michael 12
Bartram, B 93
BASW *Code of Ethics for Social Work* 131
BASW *Race, Religion and Equalities* 131
bed and breakfast case 40
Begum, Tamanna 36
'Belief and Beyond Festival' 141
believing/belonging 24, 46
Beveridge, William 15–17
Bible, The 38–9, 103
'Big Iftar' 145
Birmingham 22, 45, 78, 79, 141
birth ceremonies 43
black people 107, 114, 138
British Airways 35
British Association of Counselling and Psychotherapy 131
British Association of Social Workers 121, 131
British law 75, 77, 78, 99, 113, 137, 161
British Library 141
British Muslims *see* Muslims
British National Party 137
British Social Attitudes Survey 23, 24, 92
British values 43, 65–6, 89, 149, 160, 163
broken chain of learning *see* chain of learning
Brooking's Institute *Measuring Global Citizenship Education* 146
Browne Review 93
Buddhists 29, 40, 88, 119
buildings 144, 154
Building the Case for Mindfulness in the Workplace 118
Bull, Peter and Hazelmary 40
bullying 77, 118, 121
Bureau of Investigative Services (BIS) 91
business 114, 117, 118
Butler, Rab 20

C

Calcioli, Alessandro 40
Cambridge 85, 135
Canada 14, 104, 117, 128
Canary Wharf Chaplaincy, London 117
cancer patients 131
Cantle, T 28, 32, 137, 138, 144, 150
Cardiff, Wales 145
care workers 37, 123–4
Casey Review 143
Cathedrals Group 94
Catholics 21, 23, 45, 97, 117
Census 23, 24, 91–2
Center for Talent Innovation (CTI) 114
Centre for Holocaust Education 147
chain of learning 1–4, 9–26, 155, 164
Changing Aims in Religious Education 47
changing religion and belief landscape 91–2
chaplaincy 85, 88, 89, 96, 117, 120, 161
Chaplin, Shirley 35
Chater, M 50, 52

189

Children and Social Work Act 77
Children's Identity & Citizenship in Europe (CiCe) 73
child sexual exploitation 74
Chinese students 96
Christianity 9, 12, 82, 85, 88, 139
  ethos and social order 2, 15, 16, 163
  number of Christians 23, 91–2
  and schools 20–1, 44, 53
Christianity and the Social Order 17
Christianity and the State 15
Christianity and the University Experience 87
Christian Legal Centre (CLC) 36, 39, 40
church and state 18, 21
Churches Community Work Alliance (CCWA) 20, 30
Churchill, Winston 16
Church of England 21, 31, 44, 45, 86, 140
citizenship 5, 27, 136, 138, 159, 160
  in education 69–74
  tests 149–51
Citizenship and the Churchman 15
civil partnership 40
Civil Partnership Act 2004 38
civil service 117
climate change 159
Code of Ethics for Social Work 131
cognitive dissonance 87
cohesion 27–31, 138–42, 164
Cold War 67, 86, 87
collective worship 45, 81–3, 159, 164
colleges, village and community 135
Combat 18, 137
Commission on Religion and Belief in British Public Life 4
commodification of faith 31
common ground 49
communication and health professionals 124
communities 15, 18, 19, 20, 22, 30, 52, 163
  and cohesion 27, 136–8
  education and learning 135–42
'compartmentalisation model' 87
'compensatory education' 135
compulsory worship 20, 156
confessional literacy 11
conflict 32, 137
'conflict model' 87
Conservative government 69–70
Conservative-Liberal Coalition 149
constitutional monarchy 153
constructivism 50

'CONTEST' 89
cooperation 52, 117
Cooperative Movement 135
Coptic Christian 35
Cornwall 40
Council of Europe 73, 141–2
counselling 131
Counter-Terrorism and Security Act 90
counterterrorism strategy 67, 68, 89
Cox, Edwin *Changing Aims in Religious Education* 47
Crash 2008 106
Creating the Conditions for Integration 139
creedal, less 23
Crick Group 69, 71
criminal acts 76, 79
crisis 9–26
cross/crucifix, wearing a 35
cultural development 11, 63–5, 141, 161
'cultural enrichment activities' 148
'customs and traditions' 150

D

daily worship 20, 61
Davie, Grace 9, 24, 153
Dawkins, Richard 103
Day, Abby 24
DCLG *Face to Face, Side by Side* 29
death issues 14, 122, 154
de Lissovoy, Vladimir *A Sociological Approach to Religious Literacy* 10
Deloitte 114, 115
democracy 63, 109, 135
denominantional literacy 11, 20, 23
dentists 123
Department of Communities and Local Government : *Face to Face* 138
Dinham, A 117
disability 115, 124, 129, 159
Disability Discrimination Act 33
disadvantaged, the 19, 34, 135, 137
disciplines, university 110–11
discrimination 25, 33, 37, 38, 40, 77, 95, 118, 120
disposition 13, 155
diversity 2, 32–5, 51, 56
  employee 113–15
  of religion 1, 23, 27, 40
doctors 19
dogmatic religion 24

E

Educate against Hate website 146
education 9, 15, 66, 103, 137
  see also schools, universities

Index

Education Acts 20, 44, 45, 50, 61, 156, 159
Educational Priority Area project 135
education for anti-Semitism 146–8
Edwards, M.U. 86
emails 39
employees 113–16
employment 2, 16, 33, 137, 162
Employment Equality Regulations 2003 33
Employment Tribunals 35, 36, 37, 38, 39
enchantment 112
English language, proficiency in 150
English Literature courses 103
equalities 9, 27, 33, 91, 132
Equalities and Human Rights Commission 4
equality, diversity and inclusion 32–5, 113–18
Equality Act 2010 32, 33, 62, 78–9, 119, 153
Equality and Human Rights Commission (EHRC) 33
Equal Pay Act 1970 32
'erratic boulders' 12
Erricker, C 50, 52
established church 108
Ethical Framework for the Counselling Professions 131
ethnicity 10, 28, 63, 64, 161
 and education 65, 70, 76, 77, 148
 and universities 95, 99
 and workplaces 112, 113, 124, 128, 155
EU Employment Framework Directive on Religion or Belief 2000 33
Europe, racism in 146
European Court of Human Rights (ECtHR) 35, 36, 38
euthanasia 154
Evangelical Anglican Church 38
Eweida, Nadia 35
examinations 156
'excessive religiosity' 39–40
Exeter University 146
exhibitions 141
existentialism 5, 154
Exploring Therapy, Spirituality and Healing 127
extremism 5, 6, 7, 24, 27, 154, 160
 and education 51, 66, 67, 68, 69, 77
 prevention of 31–2, 111, 136, 138, 142–6
 and universities 86, 89, 91, 95, 108
 see also violent extremism
EY 117

F

Fabian society 135
Face to Face, Side by Side: A Framework for Partnership in Our Multifaith Society 29, 138
Faith and Belief Forum 141
Faith-Based Regeneration Network (FbRN) 29, 139
faith-based social action 2, 29
Faith Communities Capacity Building Fund (FCCBF) 29
Faith Communities Forum 30
faith schools 21, 45–6
Families Against Stress and Trauma 68
family, the 15, 76, 79
Far Right political extremism 28, 66, 137, 145, 147
fees/funding 93
female genital mutilation (FGM) 64, 75–6, 77, 79, 160
Ferguson, Rev. Sharon 39
Fernando 118
festivals and holy days 120
festivals/holy days/events 5, 9, 37, 43, 96, 150, 151, 153
'five great evils' 19
fixed identity 53
forced marriage 75, 76, 160
Ford, D.F. 12, 87
formal, less 23, 109
'formative-collegial' 95
'founding fathers' 48
frameworks of belief 24
Free Church of England 35
freedom of expression 35
freedom of expression/speech 38, 90
free-market 93
'free' schools 45
Freire, P 135
Frost, Stephen *Inclusion Imperative* 114
Fugler, Jake 37
funding 22, 29, 30, 31, 93
Furman, L.D 121
future/reconnecting 153–66
'fuzzy secularity' 24, 25

G

'gaycake' 53
Gearon, L 67, 72
gender diversity 113, 129
Gender Recognition Act 2004 33
gender segregation 91
General Dental Council 123
General Election 1945 17
General Medical Council 123
General Pharmaceutical Council 123
Generation Y 114

'genuine occupational reason' (GOR) 33
geography 105–6
Gidley, B 139
Gilliat-Ray, S 87, 92
Global Business and Interfaith Peace Awards 116
globalisation 1, 4, 27, 28, 92, 106, 122, 162
Global Standards for the Education and Training of the Social Work Profession 128, 129
Gove, Michael 51
Graham, G 87
Grimmit, M 49–50
grooming 145
Guest, M *Christianity and the University Experience* 87
Guide for Policy-Makers Preventing Violent Extremism through Education (UNESCO) 146
GuildHE 94
Gulbenkian Report, The 19

H

Habermas, J 1, 25
hairdressing salon 37
halal borrowing 96
Hall, Martyn 40
harassment 33, 118, 121
Hargreaves, D 71–2
harmony 12, 51
Haye (Ms) 39
headwear 10
health 15, 96, 109
Health and Care Professions Council 123
health and safety 36
health and social care 113, 121–32, 126, 133
heaven 23
Heritage Lottery Fund 147
Hervieu-Leger, D 1–2, 24
hetereosexuals 40
hierarchies 109
higher education, changes in 92–3
higher education and religion 86–8
Higton, M. 12
hijab/jilbab 36, 53, 108
Hinduism 29, 45, 57, 76, 88
Hodkin, Louisa 40
Hogenboom 151
holidays *see* festivals/holy days/events
Holocaust 28, 147, 148
homophobia 25, 38, 39, 62, 77
Hong Kong 128
honour-based killings 75, 77, 160

Horwitz and Horwitz 114
hospices 14
House of Lords 104
housing 22, 137
Huddersfield 147
humanism 9, 44, 47, 53, 55, 88, 120
Humanists UK 82
human rights 69, 74, 75, 131, 147
Human Rights Act 1998 33
Humbolt 92

I

immigration 28, 136
  see also migration
Imperial War Museum 147
implicit/explicit approaches 47–8
inclusion 2, 26, 32–5, 115, 154
Inclusion Imperative 114
'Indefinite Leave to Remain' 150
independent schools 65
India 117
indigenous communities 14, 128, 130
individual personality 1, 16, 48
indoctrinatory teaching 44
'institutional racism' 137
integration, lack of 143
Intercultural Cities Programme 141–2
interdisciplinary approach 110–11
inter-faith initiatives 28, 29, 139
international students 93, 95, 97–8
'interpretive' approach 48
intolerance 77
invisible presence 18–20
Ipgrave, J 48–9
Iran 117
Ireland 128
Islam 4, 24, 27, 28, 88, 89, 155
  Islamophobia 91, 145
  see also Muslims
Islam-UK Centre 145
Israel 90, 96, 117

J

Jackson, R 68–9, 72, 73–4, 118
Jainism 40
Japan 117
Javid, Sajid 140
jewellery 36, 37
Jewish people 88, 117, 146
  Holocaust 28, 29, 37
  schools 21, 45, 147
jilbab/hijab 36, 53, 108
job satisfaction 118
juries, diverse 114

K

kara bangle 37

Index

Keeping Children Safe in Education 74
Knowsley 23
KPMG 115
Kristellar, J.L 131
Kundnani, A 143, 146, 151

L

Labour government 69, 71
Ladele, Lillian 38
Lancaster Secondary RE Project 48
language skills 114
law, rule of 63, 65
leadership 31, 116, 119, 145
legal cases 35–41
lesbian, gay, bisexual and transgender (LGBT+) 22, 38, 62, 78–9, 114, 115
Lesbian and Gay Christian Movement (LGCM) 39
Lewisham Council 39
liberal approach 154
Liberty 37
liberty 16, 63, 65
'Life in the United Kingdom Test' 150
life issues 154
life skills 51
literacy, description of 9, 11
literature, distribution of 38–9
lived experiences 13, 14, 156
lived religion 12, 24, 55, 83, 117, 159
Liverpool 45
local authorities 20, 23, 38, 39, 61, 139, 149
local faith communities 78
London 16, 37, 45, 117, 147
London College of Fashion 141
London Metropolitan Police Force 137
London Olympics 115
London School of Economics and Political Science 16

M

MacPherson Report 137
Madrassah Challenge : Militancy and Religious Education in Pakistan 67
magical 110
Manchester 45
Maori peoples 129
marginalisation 106
marketisation of religion 108
marriage 27, 40, 76, 80–1
Marshall, T.H 70
McFarlane, Gary 38
McKenna, U 48–9
McKinsey 113
Measuring Global Citizenship Education 146

media 74, 109
mental health framework 125
Michalowski, I 150
Middle East 97, 155
midwives 123, 126, 127
migration 1, 4, 5, 27, 106, 122, 150
Million + Group 94
Milowski, P 21
minarets 53
mindfulness 109, 118–19, 163
Mindfulness Initiative *Building the Case for Mindfulness in the Workplace* 118
Ministry of Food 16
minorities 28, 40, 138
miracles 23
misconduct, gross 39–40
mixed economy 21, 25
mocking religious beliefs 39
modelling learning 5–6
Moore, Diane 11
moral issues 11, 62–3, 154, 160
Morris, Henry 135
mosques 144, 148
Moss, B 121
muddles 24, 46, 66, 83, 132, 136, 151, 160
 and legal cases 35–41
 in public policy 27–31
 and universities 99–101
multiculturalism 27, 108, 146, 149–50
multi-faith chaplaincies 164
multi-faith society 2
Muslim Action for Development and Environment (MADE) 145
Muslims 29, 36, 120, 131, 137, 138, 163
 and anti-Semitism 147
 number of 23, 92
 and schools 21, 22, 45, 46
 young 68, 96, 97, 143
mutual aid movements 135

N

naming ceremonies 43
National Association of Social Workers 121
national curriculum 45, 50–3, 62, 70, 147, 159
National Foundation for Educational Research (NFER) 72
National Front 137
National Health Service 17, 19, 35, 36
national insurance 17
nationalism 28
National Literacy Leadership programme 94
national rituals 153

Near Neighbours initiative 140
neighbourliness 139, 163
Newman 92
New Settlement on Religious Education, A 4
New Zealand 128, 129
non-believing 46
nondenominational Christians 23
non-religion 9, 109, 120
'no platforming' 90
no religion 24, 82, 88, 92
Northern Ireland 123, 130, 150
Norway 73, 104
Nottinghamshire 147
nurseries 43
nursery assistant 36
nurses 35, 123, 125, 127

O

oath of allegiance 150
occupational requirement 33
Office for Democratic Institutions and Human Rights (ODIHR) 147
Office for Standards in Education 51
online pornography 74
online training 74, 145
opticians 123, 124
opting out of work 38
ordination 86
Organisation for Security and Cooperation in Europe (OSCE) 67
'othering' 4, 27, 28, 91
out-of-school education 148, 149
Oxford 85

P

Paganism 53, 109
Pakistan 67, 97, 117
parents 78, 79, 148–9
parish welfare 18, 20
Parliament 104
pastoral care 88–9
Patel, C.J 131
paternalism 18
patron saints 150
peace-building 11, 116
pedagogical debates 47–50, 50
Pentecostal Church 38
people of colour 114
persecution and war 28
Personal, Social, Health and Economic Education (PSHE) 74–7, 159, 160
personal development 47, 50, 51, 93
'personal God' 23, 92
perspectives and religion 40
pharmacists 123, 124
phenomenonism, universal 48

places of worship 48
playgroups 43
Plehwe, D 21
plurality 10, 27
police 10, 65, 91, 137
policy *see* public policy
political philosophy 106–7
post-Christian society 153
'post-modern hermeneutics' 48
post-war period 10
poverty 106, 135, 136
practical religious issues 96
prayer, enforced 22
prayer and prayer facilities 91, 120, 139, 162
Preddy, Steven 40
preferential treatment 138
prejudice 62, 77, 115
Prevent 28, 31–2, 138, 142–6, 160, 164
  in schools 66–9
  in universities 89–91
Pride 43
priests 33, 86
prisons 117, 143
productivity 118
professional education 113–34
professions and workplaces 2, 162–3
Promoting Fundamental British Values as Part of SMSC in Schools 65
protected characteristic 33–4, 79, 113, 119, 165
Protestants 11
Prothero, Stephen 11
psychologists 126
psychosexual therapy 38
public life 4, 34
public policy 34, 104, 108
  community cohesion 136–8
  framings 27–34
public sector services 22, 25, 33, 137
public sphere 1, 25, 27, 153

Q

Qualifications and Curriculum Authority (QCA) 44

R

Race, Religion and Equalities 131
race and racism 28, 66, 124, 129, 136, 137, 146
Race Relations Act 1976 32
radicalisation 28, 68, 75, 107, 143, 145
RE *see* religious education
real world dilemmas 53
reception class 44
recruitment/retention 113, 117

Index

're-emergence' of religion in universities 87
Rees, J 61
ReEsilience Initiative 67
REforREal 53–60
registrar 38
regressive religious practices 143
regulatory bodies 113, 122, 123, 162
Rehabilitation of Offenders Act 32
Reimagining Religion and Belief for Policy and Practice 104
Relate 38
relationships 38, 76, 77
relationships and sex education (RSE) 77–81, 160
religion 34, 40
  and education 20–1, 46–7
  and universities 86–8, 99–101
religion and belief literacy 4–5, 10–14, 155
  future/reconnecting 155–6
  loss of 14–18
  and public anxiety 23–5
Religion at Work 116
Religion in the Military Worldwide 117
Religions of the Empire Conference 28
Religious Education 10
Religious Education (RE) 47–50
  national curriculum 50–3
  research 53–60
  in schools 44–6, 154–61
Religious Education Council 50
Religious Education in English Schools: Non-Statutory Guidance 51
Religious Education in Secondary Schools 47
religious festivals *see* festivals/holy days/events
religious harassment and victimisation 35, 39–40
Religious Literacy in Workplaces 117
religious literacy leadership in HE 93–9
religious spaces 24
religious studies 107
'repositories of resource' 95
Republic of Ireland 30
research 14, 53–60, 94–9, 104, 114, 118
  health and social care 123–4
Research Excellence Framework 110
respect 51, 63, 65, 66, 115, 116, 160
rights, assertion of 34, 135
Right to Religious Literacy 10
right/wrong, teaching 64, 160
ring, celibacy 36
risk, at 76, 143

Royal College of Nurses *Pocket Guide* 131
royal weddings 153
Rushdie, Salman *The Satanic Verses* 10
Ruskin College 135
Russell group 94

S

safeguarding, pupil 74
safe spaces 74, 79, 120, 121, 139, 141
same-sex couples and marriage 27, 38, 53, 75, 154
Saturdays 37, 96, 148
Scarman Report 137
Schleiermacher 92
School Curriculum and Assessment Authority (SCAA) 44
school governor bodies 22
schools 2, 11, 61–84, 160–1
school uniform 37
science, technology, engineering and mathematics (STEM) 136
Scientology 40
Scotland 123, 129
Second World War 15
Secular Education and the Logic of Reason 47
secularism 47, 53, 74, 85, 109, 153
security 2, 67, 68, 142, 149
segregation 139
sensitivity 51
separateness 32, 138
services 2, 22, 40
service users 131, 132, 133
Settlement House 135
Settlement Movement 16
Sex Discrimination Act 1975 32
sex education 5, 61, 77–81, 86
sexism 18, 25, 154
sexual images 74
sexual orientation 78, 124, 129
shame based violence 77
'sharedness' 5
sharia law 15
Shikongo, A.E.E 131
Siddiqui, A 89
Signposts 73–4
Sikhs 2, 10, 29, 37, 45, 88, 96
skills 14, 25
Skills Funding Agency 119
Smart, Ninian 48
  Secular Education and the Logic of Reason 47
Smith, Jonathan 12
social attitudes *see* British Social Attitudes Survey
social care 22, 123

social development 63
social enterprises 22
Social Insurance and Allied Services 16
socialisation 2, 5
social justice 131
social media 147
social policy 107–8
social skills 63
social work and social workers 19, 77, 103, 121–4, 126, 128–31
Sociological Approach to Religious Literacy 10
sociology and cultural studies 10, 91, 108–9
soft/hard neutral 94–5
South Africa 128
speakers, external 90, 96
spirit/life force 1, 23, 109
spiritual, moral social and cultural education (SMSC) 61–5, 160
spiritual abuse 127, 131
spiritual development 62, 159
spirituality 113, 119, 127, 132, 133, 162
sports 96, 148
Sri Lanka 118
Standing Advisory Councils for RE (SACREs) 44, 45, 159
state, rolling back the 21
stereotyping 77, 146
Stiffoss-Hanssen, H 133
strategic services 22
stress/need 24, 119
structures of meaning 109
students 88, 93, 95, 96, 99
Sundays 37
Sunday schools 43
supplementary schools education 148–9
'supreme deity' 40
surveillance 68, 90
Sussex 40
syllabuses 44
symbols 37
synagogues 37, 147, 148

T

talents and abilities 135
talking about religion and belief 9, 154
Tanenbaum Centre for Interreligious understanding 115
Taylor 112
teachers and teaching 19, 44, 50, 51, 68, 159
teamwork 117
Tebbit, Norman 37
Temple, William 15–17, 20
temples 148
tendering 22
terrorism 31, 55, 90
tests 85
Thatcher, Margaret 21
theology 12, 48, 86, 109–10
thinking critically 52, 77
Thomas, A 143
time off work 35, 37, 162
Toldeo Guiding Principles on Teaching about Religions and Beliefs in Public Schools 67
tolerance 63, 65, 66
Tony Blair Institute for Global Change's Generation Global 146
Tower Hamlets 23
Toynbee Hall 16
trades union 135
traditions 1, 10, 11, 117, 150, 159
transcendent reality 110
Travellers 129
'Trojan Horse' 22
Tufts University 114
Turkey 117
Turner, J 151

U

UK government 35, 69, 75, 89, 117, 135, 148, 149
unfair dismissal 37, 38
UN Global Compact Business for Peace 116
uniform policy 10, 35, 36
United States 114, 115, 121
universal benefits 17
universities 2, 4, 85–9, 161–2
 changes and leadership in 91–8, 99–110
 teaching and learning 103–12
University Alliance 94
University College, Oxford 16
University College London 85
University of Warwick 48
unmarried couples 40

V

'vicarious religion' 24, 153
victimisation 33
violence 25, 95
violent extremism 24, 28
 prevention of 31, 111, 146
 and universities 91, 108
visible religion 25–6, 35, 107, 108, 154
Voas, David 24
voluntary aided/controlled schools 20
volunteering 2, 22, 24, 89
vulnerable individuals 145

Index

W

Ward, L *The Right to Religious Literacy* 10
wear, what people 154
welfare and care 2, 9, 14–18, 105
welfare state 9, 15, 16, 21
wellbeing 62, 74, 81, 96, 109, 113, 119, 132, 163
Weller, P 28
West, W *Exploring Therapy, Spirituality and Healing* 127
Westminster Abbey 150
white people 137
Wicca 53, 109
Widdecombe, Ann 37
Willetts, David 37
Williams, Archbishop Rowan 15
'willing transfer of care' *see* welfare and care
Wired Working policy 39
wisdoms 12, 26, 136
withdrawal 45, 61, 79
women 114, 115
Woodhead, L 24
working class 135
workplaces 34–40, 56, 159, 162–3, 164
  and equality and diversity 113–17
  health and social care 121–8
  and mindfulness 118–19
World Congress of Faiths 28
World Jewish Congress 147
World Parliament of Religions 28
world religions 5, 9, 44, 155
worldviews 52, 74
Wright, A 48
  Religious Education in the Secondary School 11

Y

Younghusband, E.L. 19
young people 68, 143, 145

Z

Zionism 96

www.ingramcontent.com/pod-product-compliance
Lightning Source LLC
Chambersburg PA
CBHW071200070526
44584CB00019B/2869